Computers and the Law

Computers and the Law

David I. Bainbridge BSc, LLB, PhD, CEng, MBCS, MICE

Lecturer in Law, Aston University
Visiting Lecturer in Law, Staffordshire Polytechnic

Pitman Publishing
128 Long Acre, London WC2E 9AN

A Division of Longman Group UK Limited

First published in 1990
© Longman Group UK Limited

British Library Cataloguing in Publication Data
Bainbridge, David I.
    Computers and the law.
    1. Great Britain. Computer systems. Legal aspects
    I. Title
    344.103999

ISBN 0 273 03170 8

Typeset, printed and bound in Great Britain

To my wife, Sylvia

Contents

Contents

viii

Contents

Preface

A feature of computer technology is the speed at which it has developed and will continue to develop. The pace of change and improvement in the design of computer hardware and the scope and sophistication of computer software has been little short of phenomenal. It is hard enough for computer scientists and professionals to keep abreast of the changes and it is not surprising that the law's response to a continually evolving technology seems to lag far behind. Often, law develops in a reactive manner, responding to some new mischief long after it has become clear that it is a serious problem. Statute law may be the result of a lengthy campaign mounted by pressure groups to arouse sufficient interest in Parliament. Case law depends on the incidence of suitable disputes for the courts' consideration, and even if such cases conveniently present themselves for deliberation, case law development tends to be piecemeal in nature. Given these factors and the nature of the legislative process, much of the criticism that the law has been slow to come to terms with computer technology appears to be justified. Incredibly, the copyright protection of computer software was not confirmed until 1985 and, even then, only by way of amending legislation resulting from a private member's Bill. However, there are encouraging signs and the Copyright, Designs and Patents Act 1988 boldly, yet imperfectly, attempts to deal with the implications of new technology and possible future developments.

This book addresses the infusion of law and computer technology in two ways; first, by describing relevant areas of law in the context of computers and, secondly, by proposing practical suggestions as how to use the law, or allow for its deficiencies, so that the law can be used constructively and the many pitfalls can be avoided. It is hoped that this book will prove useful to those actively engaged in the research, development and commercial exploitation of computer systems and software; computer professionals and others responsible for, or involved in, the day to day operation of computer systems, such as data processing and information technology managers and personnel. This book should also prove useful to law students taking one of the increasing number of computer technology and law courses and to practising lawyers specializing in computer law.

During the research and preparation of this book, a number of people have given generously of their time and support and I thank them all. In particular, I wish to thank my colleagues and students and Richard Painter, whose encouragement has been very valuable.

David I. Bainbridge
February 1990

Table of Cases

Table of Statutes

Glossary of computer terms

Chip Sometimes referred to as 'silicon chip' or, more correctly, integrated circuit. A small piece of semiconducting material, quite often silicon, which, with layers of conducting and insulating materials, makes up a micro-electronic circuit incorporating numerous semiconductor devices (such as transistors, resistors and diodes). The contents of some chips are permanently fixed (called ROM chips − Read Only Memory) whilst the contents of others are volatile and can be changed (called RAM chips − Random Access Memory). The central processing unit (CPU) of a computer is contained on an integrated circuit; this chip is the 'brains' of the computer and carries out the machine language instructions derived from computer programs.

Computer program A series of instructions which control or condition the operation of a computer. Programs may be contained permanently in the computer on integrated circuits, or stored on magnetic disks or tapes, or punched cards, etc. which are loaded into the computer's memory as and when required.

Data and database Data comprises information which is stored on a computer or on computer storage media such as magnetic disks. A database is a collection of computer data, for example, a list of clients' names and addresses, or a list of employees and their details, stored in a computer file. A database is usually operated on by using a computer program to access and manipulate the data contained in it.

Firmware Computer programs which are permanently 'wired' into the computer are often referred to as firmware or as being 'hard-wired'. These programs are permanently stored on integrated circuits ('silicon chips').

Hacker A computer hacker now means a person who gains access to a computer system without permission, usually by guessing or otherwise finding out which passwords will allow him access. A hacker may simply inspect the contents of the system he has 'broken into' or may go on to alter or erase information stored on the system. 'Computer hacker' used to mean a person who was very enthusiastic about computers and who would spend most of his waking hours at a computer terminal.

Hardware The physical pieces of equipment in a computer system; for example, a computer, printer, monitor and disk drive.

High-level language A programming language which is relatively remote from the computer's machine language. A high-level language statement is equivalent to several machine language instructions. High-level languages often resemble English and are easier to use for writing and developing computer programs than low-level languages or machine language. A program in a high-level language is often referred to as a source code program. Examples of high-level languages are BASIC, COBOL, FORTRAN and PASCAL.

Low-level language   A programming language which is very close to the computer's machine language. Each instruction in a low-level language has a direct equivalent in machine language.

Machine language   The set of instructions and statements which control the computer directly. Most computer programs are written in high-level languages and have to be converted into machine language code by use of an interpreter or compiler program. An interpreter produces a temporary translation whilst a compiler produces a permanent translation into machine language which can be used on its own without the presence of the original program.

Object code and source code   A program which must be converted into a different form, such as machine language, before it will operate a computer is known as a source code program. Source code is the version of the program as it is written by the programmer and must be converted, temporarily or permanently, into object code before it can be executed by a computer. Most commercial computer programs are distributed in object code form only.

Software   Software includes computer programs and also associated documentation such as user guides and manuals. Software may be obtained 'off-the-shelf', as in the case of popular word processing and spreadsheet packages, or it may be specially written or adapted for a client ('bespoke' software).

Chapter 1
Introduction

Over the last forty years, computer technology has had an ever growing impact upon society and the way that society conducts its affairs. Computers have permeated almost every professional, commercial and industrial activity and many organizations would find it difficult, if not impossible, to function without relying heavily on computers. As far as the law is concerned, computers have been a mixed blessing. They have become useful tools allowing the use of massive legal information retrieval systems and are of increasing benefit to lawyers in the context of the preparation of documents, administration, accounting and conveyancing and, more lately, in terms of decision support. On the other hand, computer technology, by virtue of its special and volatile nature, has posed novel and complex legal problems. Frequently, the law has been found wanting when dealing with the issues raised by computers and the efforts of the legislators and the courts to come to terms with the technology have sometimes appeared clumsy.

An understanding of the legal issues involved remains of key importance to persons and organizations concerned with computing, and it is only armed with that understanding that the legal problems raised by the development and use of computers and computer software can be satisfactorily addressed and catered for. For example, when drawing up a contract for the acquisition of computer hardware or software, the technological implications are vital and the effect of them on the legal aspects requires careful consideration by lawyers and computer professionals alike. One of the purposes of this book is to bridge the gap between law and computers so that effective legal arrangements can be made for the use and exploitation of computer technology, providing an equitable framework within which the various persons and organizations involved can operate fairly and efficiently. This book can help by indicating various ways of avoiding expensive and lengthy litigation by suggesting suitable legal measures, using the law constructively, as a tool. A practical approach is adopted, giving advice of a preventative nature. If litigation is inevitable, however such as when the copyright subsisting in a computer program has been blatantly infringed, a knowledge of the legal implications should point the way to the most appropriate legal remedies and improve the likelihood of a successful outcome.

Four areas of law of special importance to computer professionals are concentrated on in this book, namely: intellectual property (which includes copyright and patent law); contract; criminal law and data protection law. Intellectual property law is important because it is the key to protecting innovation in computer hardware and software. Intellectual property rights, which include copyright, the law of confidence, design rights, trade marks, patents and regulations to protect integrated circuits, are first described in general terms in Chapter 2. These rights provide a basic framework of protection from piracy and plagiarism for computer programs and works created using a computer. The enormous scale of computer software piracy resulted in a general recognition of the desirability of effective laws in this area. Attempts have been made to adapt and improve intellectual property law to provide the necessary protection but there remain some difficulties which are discussed in detail in Part I, together with suggestions as to how their effects may be mitigated.

Part II concerns computers and contract. In terms of the acquisition or modification of computer hardware and software, satisfactory contractual provisions are important to deal with problems which may arise during the performance of the contract and subsequently. A well thought out contract can provide effective machinery for determining responsibilities and resolving disputes without recourse to the courts. The special nature of contracts for the writing of computer software or the purchase of 'off- the-shelf' software is discussed together with a description of the implications of licensing agreements and the scope and effectiveness of statutory controls on such agreements. Licence agreements between software authors and publishers and contracts for the acquisition of computer hardware are also discussed.

Computer crime is dealt with in Part III. It is a major concern to computer professionals, especially when the high incidence of computer-related crime is considered and related to the apparently poor security record of computer systems. Apart from problems of detection, the criminal law is perceived to lack teeth and recent publicity given to the activity known as 'hacking' (that is, gaining access to a computer system without permission) highlights this. The fact that it is a relatively easy matter for hackers and others to gain access to computer systems and commit further acts such as destroying computer data or leaving 'viruses' which will, in time, wreak havoc with a computer system, is a problem which surpasses the mere creation of new offences. A greater awareness of the need for secure computer systems must be impressed upon the computer industry and computer users alike. Improvements to criminal law legislation to deal with computer crime have so far failed to materialize, in spite of a detailed investigation by the Law Commission and its recommendations for the creation of new offences. The wider implications of enacting new criminal laws to combat computer crime are proving difficult to resolve and changes in the Government's support for new criminal measures are not helping to speed up this process. However, the present criminal law is better equipped to deal with computer crime than is generally realized and the ways in which established criminal offences can be used to combat computer crime are discussed in Part III.

Part IV deals with the Data Protection Act 1984 and contains an outline of the main provisions in the Act. Compliance with the Act is very important for computer users and computer bureaux who store and process information about living individuals and failure to comply can result in criminal penalties. Individuals ought to know about their right of access to information about themselves which is stored on computer and what they can do to have incorrect information corrected or deleted. Again, good computer security is important and is required of computer users and computer bureaux in respect of information about individual persons. Indeed, a common thread running throughout this book is the need for good security and good housekeeping systems, the application of which will prevent or minimize many of the legal problems which can result from the use of computers.

Although attempts have been made to develop and adapt the law to keep abreast of computer technology, these efforts have been imperfect and, consequently, the onus is on computer professionals and lawyers alike to be aware of the practicalities of the legal issues involved and to provide for the inevitable legal deficiencies by taking practical measures. For example, in Chapter 4, the difficulties relating to the ownership of copyright in a computer program written by a freelance programmer are discussed. An awareness of these problems permits care to be taken to make suitable arrangements to determine the ownership of copyright before the freelance programmer carries out any work. Similarly, many of the other problems associated with intellectual property rights in the context of computer technology can be overcome by making satisfactory contractual provisions.

Although the four main areas covered in this book appear to be quite separate, it should be noted that there is considerable overlap. Contractual provisions can affect copyright issues and vice versa. Computer hackers can interfere with information which is confidential and which may be subject to copyright protection; additionally, hackers can cause difficulties for the owners and managers of computer systems with respect to their responsibilities and duties under the Data Protection Act. Employees, working under a contract of employment may commit computer crime, affect rights and duties under the Data Protection Act and make pirate copies of computer programs, and so on.

Checklists, flowcharts and tables are included in this book at appropriate places to help with the identification and summarization of the legal position and to give practical suggestions as to how the effects of the law's shortcomings may be overcome or reduced.

In line with standard legislative practice, as confirmed by the Interpretation Act 1978, s.6, the masculine form, used throughout this book, should be taken to include the feminine form unless the contrary is stated.

Part I
Computers and intellectual property

This part deals with the branch of law known as intellectual property; which includes copyright law, patent law, trade marks, designs and related areas. The rights associated with these areas are of immense importance to those involved in the development, exploitation and use of computer hardware and software. Legal remedies are available against those who unfairly seek to take advantage of the efforts and investment of someone else.

From the point of view of the computer industry, copyright law had appeared weak and ineffectual until recently but it has now been substantially strengthened by the Copyright, Designs and Patents Act 1988. Prior to this an amending Act was passed in 1985 to confirm copyright protection in computer programs and other works produced using a computer. The courts had been unable or unwilling to put the matter beyond doubt.

The law of confidence is a very useful supplement to other areas of intellectual property law and is particularly important in the context of research and development and in matters relating to employees.

Computer programs are specifically excluded from the ambit of patent law but it appears that they can still be included in a patent application if, for example, the program is part of some new process. As a patent is generally considered to be a more desirable form of intellectual property than copyright, there have been several attempts to protect computer programs by patent law, with varying degrees of success.

Trade marks, the law of passing-off and design law are very important in terms of the commercial exploitation of products, including computer hardware and software. Integrated circuits have their own unique form of protection by virtue of regulations passed in 1989.

Chapter 2
Overview of intellectual property rights

'Intellectual property' is the collective name given to legal rights which protect the product of the human intellect. Basically, these rights are designed to provide remedies against those who steal the fruits of another person's ideas. For example, if a person writes a novel, a piece of music or a computer program, he will be able to take legal action to obtain an injunction and/or damages against anyone who copies the novel, music or program without his permission. In view of the large investment required to finance research, design and development of computer hardware and software, these intellectual property rights are of crucial importance to the computer world. Without such protection, there would be little incentive to invest in the development of new products.

What are these intellectual property rights? Some will be familiar, such as *copyright, patents* and *trade marks*; others will be less familiar such as the law of *confidence, design rights* and *passing-off*. The scope of these rights differs but sometimes they overlap. Different rights may be appropriate at different times during the lifespan of a product from inception through development to marketing and subsequent modification and updating. Sometimes, infringement of intellectual property rights gives rise to criminal penalties (described in Part III) but, primarily, this area of law falls within the bounds of civil law and it is the civil law with which this part of the book is concerned. At this stage, it will be useful to describe briefly the various intellectual property rights, by way of introduction.

COPYRIGHT LAW

As its name suggests, copyright protects works from being copied without permission. However, copyright goes beyond mere copying and extends to other activities such as making an adaptation of the work in question, performing or showing the work in public, broadcasting the work and dealing with copies of the work. The types of works protected by copyright are literary works (including computer programs), dramatic, musical and artistic works, sound recordings, films, broadcasts, cable programmes and typographical arrangements of published editions. Copyright protection has a long duration, the general yardstick being 50 years, although the starting point differs depending on the type of work in question. Major attractions of copyright as a form of protection are that it is free and that no formalities are required;

it is automatic upon the creation of the work in question. Additionally, copyright law is practical in nature and has developed to take account of technological changes and advances. In short, most things, if they have been recorded in some tangible form (for example, by writing or printing or by storing the work on a magnetic disk), are protected by copyright, subject to some basic requirements being satisfied. Copyright law is of vital importance to the computer software industry and to people who prepare all sorts of works (for example, literary works such as books, reports, letters, tables and compilations or musical works) using computer technology. Copyright law is governed by the Copyright, Designs and Patents Act 1988, the main provisions of which came into force on 1 August 1989.

PATENT LAW

Patent law is concerned with inventions such as a new design for computer hardware, a new type of pen or a new process for use in the manufacture of integrated circuits. For an invention to be protected by patent, an application must be made to the Patent Office, an expensive and lengthy process and, if granted, the patent can be renewed for a total period of up to 20 years. The relevant statute dealing with patent law is the Patents Act 1977. Most things which are protected directly by copyright law such as a literary work are excluded from patentability; therefore, a new computer program cannot normally be protected by patent although some indirect protection may be available. Many inventions which are patentable will also have some indirect protection through copyright law. For example, a new manufacturing process will be patentable and the specification and drawings for the process will be independently protected by copyright as literary and artistic works in their own right. However, as we shall see, the degree of protection offered by copyright law is not usually as strong as that of patent law.

THE LAW OF CONFIDENCE

The law of confidence protects information. Unlike copyright and patent law, the law of confidence is not defined by statute and derives almost entirely from case law. The scope of this branch of intellectual property is considerable and it protects trade secrets, business know-how and information such as lists of clients and contacts, information of a personal nature and even ideas which have not yet been expressed in a tangible form; for example, an idea for a new dramatic play or an idea for a new computer program. However, the major limitation is that the information concerned must be of a strictly confidential nature and the effectiveness of the law of confidence is largely or completely destroyed if the information concerned falls into the public domain; that is, if it becomes available to the public at large or becomes common knowledge to a particular group of the 'public' such as computer software companies. However, the law of confidence can be a useful supplement to copyright and patent law as it can protect ideas before they are sufficiently developed to warrant copyright protection or to enable an application for a patent to be made. Being rooted in the common law and equity, confidence is very flexible and has proved capable of taking new technological developments in its stride.

THE LAW OF DESIGNS

The statutory provisions covering design rights are complicated. Essentially, there are two types of right, **registered designs** which have to be registered and a brand-new **design right** which is not registerable. The former is available for features of articles which appeal to the eye whilst the latter is intended to protect any aspect of the shape or configuration of articles without any requirement for visual appeal. The complexity of this area of law is compounded by the fact that the distinction between the rights is not easy to draw as there appears to be some overlap between the rights *inter se* and with respect to copyright law. The duration of the rights is different, being a maximum of 25 years for registered designs and a maximum of 15 years for the design right. These rights in designs might be appropriate for items such as a new design for a functional computer 'mouse' or an aesthetically pleasing monitor case or a printer stand. These rights also have implications for the manufacturers of spare parts, where the design is dictated by the shape of the article with which the spare part must fit or match, as we shall see. The appropriate statutes are the Registered Designs Act 1949 (as amended) and the Copyright, Designs and Patents Act 1988.

TRADE MARKS AND PASSING-OFF

Everyone is familiar with trade marks; they are very common and there are many examples within the computer industry; for example the Apple logo, the words Microsoft and WordStar and the IBM monogram. Trade marks are often in the form of a name or a badge and registration is provided for by the Trade Marks Act 1938, for goods, or the Trade Marks (Amendment) Act 1984, for services. To be registerable, the mark must be distinctive. Trade marks are very important as they become associated with successful products and purchasers will often buy or order goods or services by reference to the trade mark. Marks such as 'Hoover' and 'Hovis' are examples of marks which have become very closely associated with the products concerned. The main purpose of trade mark law is to protect business goodwill and reputation but this has a secondary effect of protecting the buying public from being deceived.

A related area of law is passing-off. This is a tort, a civil wrong independent of contract which is not based on statute but derives from the common law and gives a right of action against anyone who 'passes off' his goods or services as being those of someone else. If a trader uses a particular name or mark or has a particularly unusual method of doing business, he can obtain legal remedies against others who use similar names or marks or business methods, especially if there is a serious possibility that the public will be deceived. The law of passing-off is independent of trade mark law and will often be useful where a mark has not been registered as a trade mark. However, for the law of passing-off to be effective, the trader concerned must have built up a reputation associated with the name or mark or business method. An example is afforded by the agreeable alcoholic drink known as champagne. The French producers of champagne were able to prevent a product called 'Spanish Champagne' from being marketed under that name. In some respects, the law of passing-off is wider than trade mark law where, to be registerable, the mark must conform to the definition of a 'mark' within the Trade Marks Act 1938. There is no such restriction with passing-off which can apply to marks which fall outside the scope of trade marks law and can also apply to other aspects of business and marketing. The rationale underlying passing-off is similar to that for trade marks, except perhaps, the emphasis lies more on the protection of the public from deceptive business practices.

SEMICONDUCTOR REGULATIONS

Integrated circuits, commonly called 'chips' or 'silicon chips' are protected by the Design Right (Semiconductor Regulations) 1989. They are given 15 years protection (15 years from creation or 10 years from commercial exploitation) similar in nature to an amended version of the new unregistered design right. As with the design right generally, there is no requirement for registration in the United Kingdom. It is the 'topography' of the chip which is protected, i.e. the patterns fixed on the layers of the semiconductor or the arrangement of the layers of semiconductor. The drawings and 'masks' used in the design and production of 'chips' may also have copyright protection as artistic works.

Before looking at each of the intellectual property rights in more detail in the following chapters, Table 1 summarizes the scope, duration and formalities associated with intellectual property rights.

Table 1 Intellectual property rights – summary

Right	Type of works protected	Examples with respect to computers	Duration	Formalities
Copyright	a) original literary, dramatic, musical or artistic works; b) sound recordings, films, broadcasts or cable programmes; c) typographical arrangement of published editions. (Computer programs are protected as literary works)	Computer programs, other types of work made using a computer or generated by a computer; e.g. a weather forecast automatically made by a computer linked to weather satellites or a computer-aided design or music made using a computer	Generally, 50 years after the death of the 'author' or when the work was made depending on the type and nature of the work	None. Copyright is automatic upon the work being created
Patent	New inventions including industrial processes	New type of printer, new design of computer, new method of making computer 'chips'	Renewable up to a maximum of 20 years	Application to Patent Office to be placed on the register of patents
Confidence	Almost anything of a confidential nature (whether or not stored on computer)	Idea for new computer program or for a new invention (prior to patent), lists of customers, business methods	Until subject matter falls into 'public domain'	None
Designs a) Registered design	New designs, being features of shape, configuration, pattern or ornament applied to an article and having 'eye-appeal'	Aesthetically pleasing designs for computer hardware including surface decoration, e.g. computer furniture	Initially 5 years renewable by 5 year periods up to a maximum of 25 years	Registration by application to the Patent Office
b) Design right	Original designs, being any aspect of shape or configuration (external or internal) of the whole or part of an article. Applies to functional and aesthetic designs. Spare parts and surface decoration excluded	Diskette case (partly) template for drawing computer symbols, acoustic hood for printer if not commonplace	15 years from 'creation' or 10 years from 'marketing'	None – automatic as with copyright
Trade Marks	A mark (e.g. device, brand, label, name, signature, etc.) used to indicate a connection in the course of trade between the goods (or service) and the rightful user of the mark	'IBM', 'Microsoft', 'Amstrad', the Apple logo	Initially for 7 years but renewable in 14 year periods indefinitely	Application to the Trade Marks Registry
Passing-off	Trade names, product 'get-up' or style	Software names which have not been registered as trade marks but around which a reputation has been built	Indefinite as long as the name, get-up or style still associated with reputation, e.g. by continued use	None
Semiconductor Regulations	Typography (patterns or arrangements of layers in 'chips')	New design of integrated circuit	15 years from creation or 10 years from commercial exploitation	None

Note: as far as periods for protection are concerned, for copyright, the design right and the semiconductor regulations, these periods are measured from the end of the calendar year during which the relevant event occurred, e.g. the creation of the work or the death of the author.

Chapter 3
Copyright basics

Note: in this and the following two chapters, unless otherwise stated, section numbers quoted refer to the Copyright, Designs and Patents Act 1988.

FUNDAMENTALS

Copyright protects a wide range of works and has developed enormously since its early beginnings as a form of controlling printing in the early sixteenth century. Copyright has a pragmatic approach and its coverage extends to all manner of works regardless of quality, subject to some basic requirements, which are usually easily satisfied. Since the end of the nineteenth century, tables, compilations and even code-books have been the subject matter of copyright law. During the twentieth century, copyright has flourished and now includes under its umbrella: photographs, films, broadcasts, sound recordings, cable programmes as well as computer programs and works stored in or produced by or with the aid of a computer. The practical development of copyright has been supported by the judges who have usually been sympathetic to the principle of protecting the results of a person's labour, skill and effort. As Peterson J. said in *University of London Press Ltd.* v *University Tutorial Press Ltd.* [1916]:

. . . what is worth copying is prima facie worth protecting.

Copyright is declared to subsist (that is, 'exist') in the following works by virtue of section 1 of the Copyright, Designs and Patents Act 1988:

a) original literary, dramatic, musical or artistic works,
b) sound recordings, films, broadcasts or cable programmes, and
c) the typographical arrangement of published editions.

providing that the requirements for qualification are met; for example, that the author of an original literary work is a British citizen or has certain other nationality or residential qualifications, or that the work was first published in the United Kingdom.

The owner of the copyright in a work is then given the exclusive right to do certain specified *restricted acts* in relation to the work, described below. The 'owner' of a copyright is usually the author of the work (the person creating it), except when the work is made by an employee in the course of his employment, in which case his employer will be the owner, unless otherwise agreed (section 11). The Copyright, Designs and Patents Act 1988 usually talks in terms of the creator of a work being the 'author' of the work, thus a person writing a piece of music is the author of the music and a photographer is the author of his photographs. For films, sound recordings and computer-generated works, the author is the person who makes the arrangements necessary for the making or creation of the work (section 9), so the author of a report produced automatically by a computer will normally be the person who manages the computer facilities. In many cases, ownership, as distinct from authorship, will reside with the manager's employer.

The acts restricted by copyright, and which only the owner of the copyright has the right to do, are set out in section 16. They are:

a) to copy the work;
b) to issue copies of the work to the public;
c) to perform, show or play the work in public;
d) to broadcast the work or include it in a cable programme service;
e) to make an adaptation of the work or do any of the above in relation to an adaptation.

A person infringes the copyright in a work if he does one of these restricted acts or authorizes another to do one of the acts without the permission of the copyright owner and such a person may be sued by the copyright owner for the infringement. There are certain exceptions contained in sections 28–50. Copyright is not infringed by 'fair-dealing' with a work for the purposes of research or private study or for criticism, review or news reporting or any of the other limited exceptions concerning, inter alia, educational and library use. There are additional ways of infringing copyright, most of which also carry criminal penalties, known as *secondary infringements*. In broad terms, these apply where the infringer has been dealing commercially with copies, such as by importing or selling them, etc. and, unlike the infringing acts described above, some form of knowledge is required; that is, that the person involved knew or had reason to believe that he was dealing with infringing copies. The equivalent criminal offences under copyright law are dealt with separately in Part III.

REMEDIES FOR INFRINGEMENT OF COPYRIGHT

If the owner of a copyright successfully sues a person for infringement of that copyright, there are several remedies available. In particular, damages, injunctions and accounts of profits might be appropriate and these are provided for by section 96. Copyright damages are usually assessed as the estimated loss resulting from the infringement; for example, the licence fee or royalties that the copyright owner would have been paid had he given permission for the acts complained of. For example, if a computer software pirate makes and sells 100 copies of a computer program valued at £500, the copyright owner might expect damages equivalent to a ten per cent royalty;

that is, $10\% \times 100 \times £500 = £5,000$. Damages are not available if the defendant did not know or had no reason to believe that the work was protected by copyright. However, an account of profits is available regardless of the defendant's knowledge and may be awarded where the person infringing copyright has done so innocently.

Injunctions are very important because they prevent continued or anticipated infringement of copyright. An injunction is a court order requiring the defendant to refrain from doing something. For example, an injunction would be appropriate to stop a computer software pirate continuing to sell unauthorized copies of computer programs. A particularly useful type of injunction is an 'interlocutory' injunction. If a pirate is sued for infringing copyright, it may be a considerable time before the case comes to trial and, in the meantime, considerable damage can be done to the copyright owner's business. This is very relevant in the context of a fast-moving technology, like computers and to deal with this problem, the court may be willing to accede to a request for an interlocutory injunction (that is, an interim injunction) pending the full trial. However, an interlocutory injunction will be granted to a plaintiff only if it appears that he has a reasonable prospect of winning at a full trial; that is, he has a prima facie case. Additionally, the 'balance of convenience' must be satisfied, meaning that the damage likely to be done to the plaintiff if the alleged infringement continues is greater than the harm that will be done to the defendant if the injunction is granted; see NWL Ltd v Woods [1979]. This balance of convenience is of particular importance if the granting or refusal of an interlocutory injunction would have very serious consequences for either party. An interlocutory injunction will not be granted if the payment of damages by the defendant at the full trial would be an adequate remedy.

The courts also have a discretion to award 'additional damages' under section 97(2), having regard to the flagrancy of the infringement and the benefit accruing to the defendant. Additional damages are suitable in cases where normal damages would not be appropriate; for example, where the plaintiff has not suffered purely economic loss as where the reputation or feelings of the copyright owner have been affected. This might be the case if the infringement concerned some material which the plaintiff did not want to publish such as the contents of his diary. In Williams v Settle [1960], additional damages were considered suitable when a professional photographer, without permission, supplied the press with a wedding photograph of a man who had been murdered. As far as computer programs are concerned, there is unlikely to be much call for additional damages, although they might be relevant if a computer program which has been written for private, and perhaps sensitive, use has been passed on to a third party.

In addition to the remedies mentioned above, the plaintiff may apply to the court for an order for the infringing copies to be delivered up to him or for those copies to be destroyed.

MORAL RIGHTS

Moral rights are a new concept in the United Kingdom, and are introduced by sections 77–89 of the Copyright, Designs and Patents Act 1988. (There were some minor forms of similar rights under the Copyright Act 1956.) These rights, which have long been recognized in some European countries, are independent and distinct from ownership of copyright and give the author of a literary, dramatic, musical or artistic work and the director of a film the right to:

a) be identified as the author (or director) of the work,
b) object to derogatory treatment of the work; for example, if someone rewrites a serious play in the form of a farce without the author's permission, and
c) refuse to have a work falsely attributed to him.

There is also a right to privacy with respect to photographs and films made for private and domestic purposes.

These moral rights last as long as the copyright in the work, with the exception of the false attribution right which lasts for 20 years after the death of the person involved. The rights are designed to give the creator of the work, who may no longer be the owner of the copyright itself, a degree of control and recognition in respect of the work. By section 103, infringements of moral rights are treated as a breach of statutory duty, injunctions and damages being appropriate remedies. Strangely, there is no provision for additional damages and, presumably, damages will be based on economic loss only.

As computer programs are considered to be literary works, it is surprising that the first two of the moral rights, mentioned above, are stated not to apply to computer programs. Less surprisingly, they also do not apply to computer-generated works. These exceptions may be justified on the basis of the commercial nature of most computer programs and computer output, and of preventing ex-employees of computer departments attempting to interfere with any future changes to the software they have developed. Problems could arise if computer programmers and systems analysts demanded to be recognized as authors, as many computer programs are the result of teamwork, involving many individuals, both in the development of the original program and in subsequent alterations and upgrades.

DEALING WITH COPYRIGHT

We have already seen that authorship and ownership of copyright are two distinct concepts and that, normally, an employee writing a computer program will be the author of that program but his employer will own the copyright. However, employers and employees are free to agree to any other arrangement if they wish.

Frequently, the owner of a copyright will want to use a third party to exploit that copyright for him. It might be more attractive financially to use a publisher to market and sell copies of the work, because he will have the marketing expertise and distributorships required to sell the work in large volumes. The usual way is for the owner to grant a publisher a licence. In terms of copyright, a licence is a permission to do one or more of the acts restricted by copyright and licences are usually contractual in nature, that is, the publisher will pay a licence fee or royalties in return for the permission. Often, the licence will be exclusive, which means that permission will be granted to one publisher only. In the case of marketing computer programs, the owner will usually grant an exclusive licence to a software publisher who will then grant non-exclusive user licences to 'purchasers' of the program. By section 92(1), an exclusive licence must be in writing and signed by or on behalf of the owner of the copyright.

The owner of a copyright may, however, *assign* (that is, transfer) that copyright to another person and an assignment must be distinguished from a licence. In an assignment, the copyright owner transfers all or part of his rights to another person, whereas a licence is a permission given to another person authorizing him to do certain specified things in relation to the copyright work. Furthermore, ownership in copyright can pass under a will or by way of intestacy or as a result of the bankruptcy of the copyright owner. Moral rights cannot be assigned (section 94) but may pass under a will or intestacy (section 95).

Chapter 4
Computers and copyright

Now that the basic principles of copyright law have been described in the previous two chapters, the relevance of copyright to computer technology can be examined. There are two main areas: the first concerns the protection of computer software, and in particular, computer programs from piracy or unauthorized copying; the second area concerns works of various types which have been created *by* or *with the aid of* a computer. The first area will be considered in this chapter and the second area will be considered in Chapter 5.

Computer technology has revolutionized our lives, directly and indirectly, over the last quarter of a century, but copyright law has only recently come to terms with the technology. The Copyright Act 1956, the former major source of copyright law, was silent on the question of computers as it was still early days for computers when the Act was brought into force. However, growing disquiet in the computer industry, and the perceived reluctance of the courts to come to grips with the question of copyright protection of computer programs, caused an amending piece of legislation to be passed, known as the Copyright (Computer Software) Amendment Act 1985. This Act confirmed that computer programs and works created using a computer or stored in a computer were protected by copyright. The Copyright, Designs and Patents Act 1988 consolidates the legal protection of computer programs and works created using computers or generated by computer, by and large satisfactorily. There are, however, some areas of doubt which will have to be resolved by the courts.

COMPUTER PROGRAMS

'Computer software' includes computer programs, computer files and associated printed documentation such as manuals for users. There has never been any difficulty with regard to printed materials as these have been and continue to be protected by copyright as literary works in the case of written or printed instructions, or, in the case of diagrams or flowcharts, as artistic works. The protection of the computer programs themselves has been less certain and before 1985, it was unclear whether computer programs were protected by copyright. One view was that listings of source code programs were protected as literary works by analogy with codebooks or because they resembled written English to some extent. On the whole, the courts appeared to be sympathetic towards the notion that computer programs were protected. For example, in *Sega Enterprises Ltd* v *Richards* [1983], which concerned alleged copies of the computer game 'FROGGER' (the object of which was to get a frog across a busy road without it being squashed by a lorry), the trial judge was of the opinion that the source code program was protected by copyright and the object code program was protected indirectly as an adaptation of the source code version. However, this was an interlocutory hearing only and the case did not go to a full trial, so the point was not finally decided. Indeed, cases involving copying of computer programs did not seem to get beyond the interim stage, probably because the relief granted by the court at that stage was sufficient to satisfy the plaintiff.

Following considerable pressure from the computer industry, notably from their lobby group FAST (the Federation Against Software Theft), the Copyright (Computer Software) Amendment Act 1985 was passed which made it clear that computer programs were protected as literary works. The Copyright, Designs and Patents Act 1988 follows this approach and places computer programs firmly within the literary work category for the purposes of copyright (section 3). Neither the word 'computer' nor the phrase 'computer program' are defined in the Act. This is sensible in view of the rapid rate of change in the computer industry as attempts to offer precise definitions would probably prove to be unduly restrictive in the light of future changes in technology. It is better to allow the judges to use their discretion sensibly, permitting a degree of flexibility in this respect. There should be no difficulty in a court deciding that copyright subsists in a program written in assembler language or in a computer program in object code form.

ORIGINALITY AND STORAGE

By section 3 of the Copyright, Designs and Patents Act 1988, for copyright to subsist in a computer program it must be 'original' and it must be 'recorded'. For the meaning of 'original', we must turn to case law prior to the Act and section 172(3) of the Act confirms that this practice is permissible (this is standard procedure unless it is clear that previous cases no longer represent the law). The requirement of originality is not an onerous one and does not mean that the computer program must be novel or unique in some respect. It merely means that the program has been the result of a modest amount of skill, labour or effort and that it 'originates from the author' (Peterson J. in *University of London Press Ltd.* v *University Tutorial Press Ltd.* [1916]. Compilations of existing information as in a street directory have been afforded copyright protection. In *Macmillan & Co Ltd* v *K & J Cooper* (1923), it was held that, although many compilations have nothing original in their parts, the sum total of the compilation may be original for the purposes of copyright. However, the courts will draw a line somewhere and in *Cramp* v *Smythson* [1944], a diary which contained the usual information contained in diaries, such as a calendar, tables of weights and measures, postal information and the like, failed to attract copyright protection. The reason given was that the commonplace nature of the information left no room for taste or judgment in the selection and organization of the material. In the light of these cases, virtually all computer programs will meet the requirement of originality, even if the program comprises little more than an arrangement of commonly used sub-routines, because the selection and structuring of those routines requires a reasonable amount of skill and expertise.

Another requirement for computer programs, and other literary, dramatic and musical works, is that they must be recorded *in writing or otherwise* (section 3(2)). This has a very wide meaning and 'writing' is defined by section 178 as including:

> any form of notation or code, whether by hand or otherwise and regardless of the method by which, or medium in or on which, it is recorded.

Storage of a computer program in a computer memory or on computer storage media such as magnetic disks should present no problems as the definition in s.178 is sufficiently wide to cover any existing form of storage and any new forms which might be invented in the future. Also, given the spirit of the Act, it is unlikely that the courts will attempt to narrow the concept of 'recording'. However, it must be noted that the House of Lords has decided that a password held transiently in a computer system was not recorded for the purposes of the Forgery and Counterfeiting Act 1981 (*see* the discussion of *R* v *Gold* in Chapter 21). If the only form of existence of a computer program is in a computer's volatile memory, there may be a possibility that, following the *Gold* case, the program will not be considered to be 'recorded'. But, because it is highly likely that the program will be saved onto a disk or tape before very long, this is unlikely to cause problems in practice. Of course, the program may have been written down by the programmer before entry into the computer or a print-out of the program listing taken, in which case the program will be protected anyway. As a matter of interest the scope of the Copyright (Computer Software) Amendment Act 1985 (now repealed) was possibly wider in that it specifically covered storage in a computer memory.

ANCILLARY MATERIALS

Copyright protection extends beyond the computer program itself and will cover written or printed listings of programs, flowcharts, specifications and notes. These will generally be protected as literary works although flowcharts and diagrams will be protected as artistic works. The artistic work category of copyright includes paintings, drawings, diagrams, maps, charts and plans which are all protected irrespective of artistic quality. All these ancillary materials must be original in the sense already discussed.

RESTRICTED ACTS FOR COMPUTER PROGRAMS

Of the acts restricted by copyright, three are worthy of special mention as far as computer programs are concerned. These are:

- copying,
- issuing copies to the public, and
- making an adaptation.

Copying in relation to a literary, dramatic, musical or artistic work means, by section 17(2), reproducing the work in any material form which includes storage in any medium by electronic means; for example, making a copy of a computer program on a magnetic disk. Additionally, in relation to all forms of copyright work, copying includes making copies which are transient or incidental to some other use of the work (section 17(6)). This implies that the act of loading a computer program into a computer only for the purpose of running the program will be considered to be making a copy of the program, even though this 'copy' will be lost as soon as the computer is switched off. In this way, any unauthorized use of a computer program will infringe the copyright in that program.

Issuing copies of a work to the public is a restricted act and will infringe copyright if done without the permission of the owner of the copyright. As regards computer programs, sound recordings and films, section 18 widens this restricted act to include rental of copies to the public. However, this restricted act is only relevant in the context of a particular work if copies of that work have not previously been put into circulation. The restricted act would apply to a situation where a person acquires a computer program which is not available to the public and then sells or rents copies of the program to the public. Usually, there would also be an infringement of copyright by making copies of the program.

Making an adaptation of a literary, dramatic or musical work is a restricted act. In terms of a musical work, a new arrangement of a song is an adaptation of the original. Changing a cartoon strip into a story told by words only is also an adaptation, as is a translation of a literary or dramatic work. For computer programs, by section 21(4), a 'translation' has a special meaning and includes:

> . . . a version of the program in which it is converted into or out of a computer language or code or into a different computer language or code, otherwise than incidentally in the course of running the program.

If a high-level, source code computer program is compiled (converted) into an object code program, this will be an adaptation of the source code program and, therefore, a restricted act. At first sight, it would appear that the object code program, because it is a 'computer program', should be protected as a literary work in its own right. However, the elements of skill, labour and effort will be missing from the object code version which will have been created simply by using an appropriate compiler program. These elements will, of course, be present as regards the source code program. Therefore, it is desirable that object code programs are protected as adaptations of literary works.

It could be argued that the meaning of 'translation' is too wide as it seems to catch a version of a source code program written in a different high-level language from that used for the original program. If a computer program is written using BASIC and someone then re-writes the program in COBOL, the latter will be an adaptation of the BASIC program because it has been *converted into a different computer language.* But, to produce a program in a different high-level language is not merely a question of translating the program instructions from one language to another as with spoken languages; the programmer would have to reduce the original program to its underlying concepts and ideas and from those concepts and ideas (not from the computer program itself) develop a new version of the program in another high-level language, as shown in Figure 1.

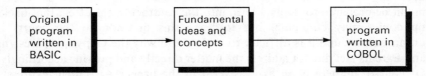

Figure 1   Conversion of computer program

The differences between the two programs could be as wide as those between 'Romeo and Juliet' and 'West Side Story', and, as a basic principle, copyright should not protect ideas as such, only the expression or recording of those ideas. However, it seems that the new version of a program in a different high-level language will be an adaptation, regardless of the quite considerable amount of skill and effort required to 'translate' the program.

Restricted acts apply to a work as a whole or to any substantial part of it (section 16(3)). What is substantial is a matter of fact and the courts will look to quality as well as quantity; *see Hawkes & Sons (London) Ltd* v *Paramount Film Service Ltd* [1934]. Therefore, a computer program which includes parts (such as sub-routines) copied from another program will infringe the copyright in that other program if the copied parts represent a substantial part of the original program and they may be substantial if they go to the root of the other program or capture its essence, even though they are small in terms of quantity.

BACK-UP COPIES OF COMPUTER PROGRAMS

It is essential that back-up copies of computer programs are made. A back-up copy will be needed if the original copy of the computer program becomes damaged or corrupted in any way. The original may be physically damaged if a cup of coffee is spilt over it or the magnetic impulses on the disk representing the program may be destroyed or altered by exposure to a strong magnetic field. The original may become contaminated with a computer 'virus'. If a computer program has been obtained for use in a commercial environment, whether it be a word processing package, accounts system or spreadsheet, the chances are that the original will fail at the worst possible moment. If a back-up copy is available a potential disaster can be averted and the urgent report or whatever can still be completed on time.

Australian Copyright law, by virtue of the Australian Copyright Amendment Act 1984, contains a presumption that back-up copies of computer programs can be made without infringing copyright. However, United Kingdom law contains no such provision and, in the absence of agreement otherwise, making a back-up copy of a computer program will infringe the copyright in that program. Fortunately, most organizations producing computer software are aware of the practicalities of the situation and specifically grant permission in their licence agreements for at least one back-up copy to be made. If the licence is silent on the matter, the courts might be prepared to imply a term into the contract to the effect that back-up copies may be made, but to leave this question to the courts is unsatisfactory and it is difficult to understand why the Copyright, Designs and Patents Act did not address the matter directly and provide accordingly. Of course, if there is an express term in the licence agreement expressly forbidding the making of any copies, including back-up copies then there will be an infringement of copyright as well as a breach of the licence agreement should any copies be made. Any person considering obtaining software should treat licence agreements containing an express term forbidding the making of back-up copies with apprehension and consider looking for an alternative package.

Although the Copyright, Designs and Patents Act 1988 does not deal directly with back-up copies, it does recognize the possibility that such copies may have been made. Section 56 deals with transfers of works in electronic form and the position with respect to copies which are not transferred along with the original software. This is best described by way of an example. A business, Acme Ltd. obtains a word processing package (WORDY); the licence agreement allows the making of one back-up copy. Acme use WORDY and makes two copies of it, one for back-up and one for use on another computer. Two years later, Acme decides to obtain some new computers and a more powerful word processing program. It looks at the WORDY licence and sees that the licence does not prevent it from transferring the package to someone else. Acme assigns its licence to use WORDY to the Zenith Co. and transfers the original copy of the program plus the single back-up copy.

By section 56, Acme was permitted to transfer the software because there were no express terms in the licence agreement prohibiting this, but it should have transferred all copies of WORDY. By section 56(2), the copy it has retained is treated as an infringing copy and could leave Acme liable to the owner of the copyright in the word processing programs. Additionally, because Acme made two copies instead of the one permitted under the licence agreement, it was in breach of that agreement and, depending on the terms

22

in the licence dealing with breach, may find that the licence was brought to an end and that the purported transfer to Zenith is void. The flowchart in Figure 2 illustrates the position regarding copies of programs when software is transferred and takes the practical approach in recognizing that more copies of programs may have been made than permitted under the licence.

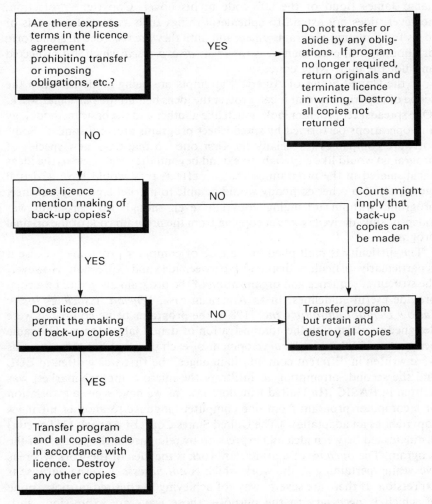

Figure 2   Transfer of computer programs and copies

'LOOK AND FEEL' AND THE LIMITS OF COPYRIGHT PROTECTION

Copyright does not give a monopoly in ideas; what it does is to prevent a person from copying or otherwise capitalizing on tangible expressions of ideas made by others. Copyright protects expression not idea. Therefore, in principle, it is quite acceptable to write a novel about a secret agent in the style of Ian Fleming as long as it does not contain copies of parts of James Bond novels. The late Ian Fleming did not have a monopoly of tongue-in-cheek, humorous adventures about secret agents, but a novelist might commit the tort of passing-off if he changes his name to Ian Fleming or uses the name James Bond or the 007 code in his novel. Copyright protection, however, does not extend to ephemeral things such as plots for novels or ideas for computer programs unless and until they are recorded in some form or another and, even then, it is the ideas *as expressed* which are protected and not the underlying concepts.

In the United States of America, attempts are being made to widen the scope of copyright so that it can protect the ideas behind the particular work. One spreadsheet program looks much like another and the basic methodology and operations performed by spreadsheet programs are very similar. Some software companies (especially the first ones to market a new species of programs) would like copyright to extend beyond the expression to the ideas encapsulated in the program so that, in effect, they would have a virtual monopoly. No other company would be able to market e.g., a spreadsheet program, without infringing copyright even though that program was independently derived, without copying from the program code of the original program.

The difficulty is multiplied in the case of computer programs because it is particularly difficult to distinguish between idea and expression. However, the structure, sequence and organization of the program alleged to be a copy provide useful guidelines. In an American case, *Whelan Associates Inc.* v *Jaslow Dental Laboratory Inc.* [1987], the programs being compared were designed to assist with the administration of dental laboratories. The same person was involved in the development of each program but the programs were written in different computer languages, the first was written in EDL and the second, attempting to infiltrate the micro-computer market, was written in BASIC. (In United Kingdom law, as we have seen, a translation of a computer program from one computer language to another infringes copyright as an adaptation.) The United States Court of Appeals (3rd circuit) distinguished between idea and expression by reference to the purpose of the program. The *purpose* of a utilitarian work is the idea of the work whereas everything pertaining to the work which is *not necessary to* the purpose is expression. If there are several ways of achieving the desired purpose, none of which is necessary to the purpose, those ways are expressions and, consequently, protected by copyright.

The purpose of the original program in *Whelan Associates Inc.* v *Jaslow Dental Laboratory Inc.* was to assist in the running of dental laboratories. Because there are several different methods which could be employed to achieve that same purpose, the structure of that original program was not essential to the purpose and, hence, the structure was expression and not idea. The purpose itself, being the idea, was not protected by copyright; it is quite acceptable for others to write programs to help with the running of dental laboratories. In this case the structures of the two programs were similar, the programs had a similar *look and feel* even though written in different computer programming languages and this, coupled with the fact that the same person had been involved in the two programs, raised a strong presumption that there had been copying and, hence, an infringement of copyright.

What is the possibility that copyright will be developed by the courts to prevent the marketing of 'lookalike' computer programs? Obviously, if a company makes a new type of computer program which proves to be very successful, other companies will want to bring out their own versions of that type of program to gain a share in the market created or stimulated by the first program. Essentially, copyright law does not prevent this as long as the original program is not copied or adapted. Even if copying, following the Whelan case, extends to the structure of a program this should not prevent competitors bringing out similar programs. A line must be drawn somewhere and the following hypothetical examples, involving two software companies, Acme and Zenith, indicate where it might be drawn. Acme developed a program to record and monitor drug dosages to hospital patients and Zenith, shortly afterwards, brought out a similar program.

1. Zenith did not know of the existence of Acme's program – no infringement of copyright.
2. Zenith knew of the existence of Acme's program but had not seen it in use – no infringement of copyright.
3. Zenith had seen Acme's program in use and decided to write a program to fulfil the same purpose, that is, to monitor drug dosages. Zenith did not refer to Acme's program further than this and Zenith developed its own methods of performing the purpose. The structures of the two programs are different in many respects and where they are similar this is the result of coincidence only – no infringement of copyright.
4. Zenith buys a copy of Acme's program. Zenith cannot see the source code because the copy is compiled (in object code), but by using the program extensively, Zenith gets a good insight into the workings and structure of Acme's program and based on this insight, Zenith writes its program (obviously without using a source code listing of Acme's program). Zenith's knowledge of Acme's program is no more than a competent user would achieve – possible infringement of copyright because the structure of Zenith's program is determined by Zenith's familiarity with the structure of Acme's program which Zenith copies indirectly.
5. Zenith disassembles Acme's program and re-writes parts of it to make its program, perhaps using a different computer language – definite infringement of copyright (the act of disassembly itself will probably constitute an infringement of copyright).
6. Zenith employs an ex-programmer of Acme who is familiar with the program; this person writes a program for Zenith using copies of listings and flowcharts that he retained – definite infringement of copyright.
7. As 6 above but the ex-programmer of Acme has not retained any materials

from his previous employment; he simply uses what he can remember — possible infringement of copyright.

The last example lies in a difficult area and is tied up with questions relating to the law of confidence and restraint of trade. Ex-employees always cause problems because of the difficulty in reconciling their continuing duty to their ex-employer with the need to be able to obtain other employment. If the ex-employee is not allowed to make use of anything at all from his past experience, he may well be virtually unemployable because what he has done previously is an integral part of his skill and expertise. This question will be considered further in Chapter 6 on the law of confidence; at this stage it needs to be noted that an ex-employee will be able to make use of his skills and what he remembers as long as these are not genuine trade secrets. In terms of writing computer software, a program to automate an existing manual process will probably not be considered a trade secret.

If company B writes a program independently and, by chance, it turns out to very similar to a program written by company A, there is no infringement of copyright because there has been neither copying nor adaptation of A's program and both A and B will have a copyright in their respective programs. A substantial similarity between programs, however, can suggest that one has been copied from the other and this can shift the burden of proof to the defendant, especially if there is something else to suggest that copying may have taken place, such as access to the original program by the defendant; *see L.B. Plastics Ltd.* v *Swish Products Ltd.* [1979]. This means that instead of requiring the plaintiff to show that copying had taken place, the defendant will have to show that he did not, in fact, copy the plaintiff's work and such a shift in the burden of proof can be exceedingly onerous to the defendant.

One approach to the question of copying (the restricted act under the Copyright Act 1956, equivalent to copying, is actually 'reproduction in a material form') was suggested by the Court of Appeal in *Francis, Day & Hunter Ltd.* v *Bron* [1963], a case concerning an alleged infringement of an old song entitled 'In a Little Spanish Town'. For copying to be proved, the test is:

a) there must be a sufficient objective similarity between the two works (an objective issue — that is, would the 'reasonable man' consider the two works sufficiently similar), and

b) there must also be some causal connection between the two works (a subjective question but not to be presumed as a matter of law merely upon proof of access).

It is possible to infringe copyright by subconsciously copying a work, although this is probably more relevant to the music industry than the computer industry. Thus George Harrison's song, 'My Sweet Lord', was alleged to have infringed an earlier song, 'He's so Fine', but it is thought that the evidence required to support this proposition would have to be quite strong.

Even if copyright protection of computer programs is developed by the courts and becomes stronger, the Copyright, Designs and Patents Act does contain safeguards. By section 144(1), as a result of a report of the Monopolies and Mergers Commission, the Secretary of State may grant a licence as of right if the public interest would be prejudiced; for example, if the copyright owner refuses to grant licences on reasonable terms. So, if a company has a virtual monopoly in a particular type of computer system and charges an exorbitant price for it and the Commission prepares a report to the effect that this situation is against the public interest, anyone will be able to apply for a compulsory licence to use the software. The licence fee and other terms of the licence will be decided by the Copyright Tribunal, a body set up to administer licensing schemes. By section 66 of the Act, the Secretary of State may also order that rentals of computer programs are to be treated as being licensed by the copyright owner subject to payment of a reasonable royalty. It is unlikely that this or the above provision will be needed but the fact that these provisions are there may help to prevent undesirable practices developing with respect to computer software.

EMPLOYEES AND FREELANCE PROGRAMMERS

The author of a work is the first owner of the copyright in the work. An exception which applies to literary, dramatic, musical or artistic works, is where the work is made by an 'employee in the course of his employment', in which case the employer becomes the first owner of the copyright in the work (section 11(2)). This raises the following questions:

- who is an employee?
- what is the position regarding freelance computer programmers and consultants?
- and what is the meaning of 'in the course of employment'?

The Copyright, Designs and Patents Act 1988 does not specifically define these terms but states that 'employed', 'employee' and 'employer' and 'employment' refer to employment under a contract of service or apprenticeship (section 178). The question of ownership of computer programs written by freelance staff will be considered first.

Freelance staff

It is not always easy to identify when a person is an employee and when he is not; various tests have evolved and some concern questions of 'control'. These tests include whether the 'employer' can tell the person what to do, when to do it and how to do it; does the 'employer' provide the person with time for holidays, sick pay or a pension? Does the person have to correct unsatisfactory work in his own time and at his own expense? Who pays income tax? In many cases the question will be answered by looking at the terms of the contract between the parties although a description of the parties as 'employer' and 'employee' is not conclusive. In many cases, freelance staff, hired to perform a particular task such as writing or modifying a specific computer program, will be deemed to be self-employed. The consequence of this is that the copyright in any program they write will, prima facie and in the absence of any agreement otherwise, belong to the freelance programmer.

It is essential, therefore, when employing freelance staff or anyone else who is not employed on a permanent contract of employment, to make contractual provision for determining ownership of copyright. The organization hiring the programmer or consultant may want to own the copyright so that it can exploit the resultant program itself, or it may simply want to prevent its competitors from obtaining a copy of it. In either of these situations the contract should specifically state that the first ownership of the copyright belongs to the organization and not to the programmer, and furthermore, there should be a written assignment of copyright, signed by the freelance programmer. Of course, the fee charged will probably be greater as a result because the freelance programmer might have envisaged making use of the program elsewhere; he may know of other businesses which would be interested in what he produces. On the other hand, if the hiring organization does not itself contemplate commercially exploiting the software or preventing others from using it, then it is important that a term is included in the contract granting a licence for the continued use of the program.

If the contract is silent on such matters, the freelance programmer may later decide to test his ownership of the program by offering it to others, or worse still, claim that, as owner, he will permit the continued use of the program only on payment of a licence fee. These difficulties may arise especially when the program in question turns out to be more useful and successful than the parties originally envisaged. There is a danger that a freelance programmer will try to hold his client to ransom if he later realizes that the value of the software he has produced is out of all proportion to the payment he received for writing it.

The employee and the course of employment

As regards persons who can safely be classified as employees, their employers cannot safely assume that they will own the copyright in everything produced by those employees. For example, if an employee writes a computer program to help with his work but he is not employed as a computer programmer, his job is not to write computer programs and an employer cannot necessarily assume that he owns the copyright of that particular program. A lecturer normally owns the copyright in any book or article he writes because he is primarily employed as a teacher and not as a writer of books and articles, even though his employer may encourage such writing. A person employed as an accountant who writes a computer program to help with the production of financial accounts will own the copyright in that program if he wrote it in his own time, using his own equipment. Initially, this may create no problems because the accountant may have been motivated by interest and a desire to improve his own efficiency at work, but problems could arise later, if the accountant moves to another firm or discovers that his program is commercially viable. If an employer is faced with the situation where an employee has, in his own time and using his own equipment, developed a useful computer program, then the employer should immediately try to reach agreement on questions of ownership and use of the programs with the employee concerned, rather than allowing the program to be used without such agreement.

If an employee has produced a computer program outside the normal course of his duties, but has used his employer's equipment or done it during the hours of his employment, the ownership of copyright is more difficult to predict, although it is more likely that the employer will be treated as owner. But, even here, it is wiser to seek agreement at the outset rather than leave matters until there is some disagreement about the continued use or the exploitation of the program. Employers should consider the introduction of, or extension of a 'suggestions' scheme to include computer programs or systems written by staff who are not employed to do this, with effective rewards and suitable provisions as regards ownership.

DEVICES TO OVERCOME COPY-PROTECTION

Some computer programs are marketed in a form that makes them difficult to copy. Almost inevitably, devices and software designed to overcome these attempts at copy-protection appeared on the market, to the intense irritation of the software industry. A distinction must be made at this stage between things which can be used to make unauthorized copies of programs, but which also have legitimate uses (for example, computers with two disk drives and cassette players with twin tape decks) and things specifically designed to overcome copy-protection such as software to be used to copy other software which has been copy-protected. Where a device or software has lawful uses, it would obviously be unsatisfactory to ban its sale. The music industry tried to interfere with the sale of twin cassette music centres in *CBS Songs Ltd.* v *Amstrad Consumer Electronics plc* [1988], on the basis that, by the sale and advertising of these machines, Amstrad was inciting the public to infringe copyright. The fact that the machines made by Amstrad had other legitimate uses, such as making copies of the purchasers' own music or of works not protected by copyright, was important, even though it was obvious that the largest use would involve copyright infringement.

However, there can be little sympathy for firms who make devices or software deliberately designed to permit the copying of works which are copy-protected. The whole raison d'être of these devices and software is to enable copy-protection to be overcome. By section 296 of the Copyright, Designs and Patents Act, devices or means specifically designed or adapted to circumvent copy-protection of works issued to the public in electronic form are controlled by treating the making, importation, sale or hire, etc. of the devices or software as an infringement of copyright. Furthermore, publishing information to enable or assist the circumvention of copy-protection is similarly treated. The use of the phrase 'device or means' should be wide enough to cover both hardware devices and software methods designed to overcome copy-protection.

Computers with dual disk drives and twin tape cassette machines are not caught by these provisions because they are not 'specifically designed or adapted to circumvent copy-protection'. Similarly, normal copying programs which come with a computer operating system are within the law because they are designed to be used legitimately, to take back-up copies of programs and data files. Indeed, such programs will usually fail to copy computer programs which are copy-protected. Section 296 should bring to an end the open marketing and distribution of these devices and means, but there are probably sufficient numbers in circulation to enable their continued use to be a thorn in the side of the software industry. A difficulty with this provision is that it is enforceable only by the person issuing copies of the copy-protected work in question to the public and the person making, importing, selling or hiring, etc. the device, means or information knows or has reason to believe that it will be used to make infringing copies. It is arguable that the opportunity should have been taken to deal with this matter by way of criminal penalties. However, there appears to be a move away from copy-protection because it is troublesome to customers who, understandably, wish to take back-up copies of important programs and increasingly, software companies are seeking to rely on the terms of their licence agreements to control unauthorized copying of their products.

Chapter 5
Computer-generated works

The Copyright, Designs and Patents Act 1988 expressly recognizes, for the first time in the United Kingdom, that works produced by or with the aid of a computer are worthy of copyright protection. Works produced by or with the aid of a computer were protected before the new Act but there were difficulties in determining the identity of the author of the work for copyright purposes. For example, random numbers selected by computer for a newspaper competition called 'Millionaire of the Month' were held to be protected by copyright in *Express Newspapers plc* v *Liverpool Daily Post & Echo plc* [1985]. Arguments that there was no human author and, consequently, the lists of numbers drawn by the computer were not protected by copyright were rejected by Whitford J., who said that such a claim was as silly as saying that a pen could be the author of a literary work. The human expertise in computer-derived works could be found to reside in the programs which produced the lists of random numbers.

In works produced by or with the aid of a computer, human skill can be found either in the person who enters information into the computer to produce the output or in the work involved in writing the program used or a combination of both. The Copyright, Designs and Patents Act 1988 specifically mentions computer-generated works and by section 9(3) states that, in the case of a literary, dramatic, musical or artistic work which is computer-generated, the author is the person by whom the arrangements necessary for the creation of the work are undertaken. This will generally mean that the person who has control of the computer will be the author of any computer-generated work. Section 178 further defines a work as 'computer-generated' when it is generated by a computer in circumstances such that there is no human author of the work. However, this approach can lead to difficulties because, in many cases of works produced *with the aid of a computer*, it will not be possible to say with any certainty whether the work has a human author.

At one end of the spectrum a work will be produced using a computer as a tool, just as a writer uses a pen or a typewriter, whilst at the other end of the spectrum, the computer will produce its works with little or no direct human input. Neither of these situations should cause any great difficulty; but in between these two extremes lie a great many types of work which are the result of a modest amount of human input and classifying such works will not be easy. In order to consider this question further, works which involve computers in their production will be categorized as follows:

a) works created *using* a computer,
b) works created *by* a computer, and
c) intermediate works.
In these cases, 'computer' means a *programmed computer*.

WORKS CREATED USING A COMPUTER

Examples of works which fall into this category are: documents produced using a word processing system; CAD (computer aided designs) such as plans for a house or a new car body panel; music written using a program designed to assist with the composition of the music (as opposed to a program designed to write music) and an accounts report produced using a spreadsheet program. In all these cases, the person operating the system is using the computer to achieve the results that he wishes to obtain. The programmed computer is merely a tool which allows the operator to use his creativity and imagination to the fullest extent and efficiency. Such works are not computer-generated, the skill and expertise (or at least the greatest part of these) derives from the user of the system. Word processed documents, drawings and music, etc., produced using packages which facilitate the making of these works are protected by copyright as literary, dramatic, musical or artistic works in their own right. The person using the system provides the expertise necessary for the making of the work and is, for copyright purposes, the author of the work. That expertise may be applied directly or indirectly; for example, a person writing a report may draft it out on paper and then hand it to a word processor operator who enters it into the computer. In these circumstances, the author is not the operator but the person writing the report. It is similar to the process of amanuensis in which a person dictating a letter will be the author of that letter, the person who writes the dictation down is merely his agent.

The person who wrote the computer program which was used to assist in the creation of the types of works described above has no rights in the work because, although the programmer may control or influence the *format* of the finished work, he has no control or influence on the *content*. The fact that many works of this category may be produced directly on a computer before any other tangible form exists, presents no serious problems because these works will exist, in terms of copyright protection, the instant they are recorded; that is, as soon as they are stored on a computer disk or printed out on paper.

WORKS CREATED BY A COMPUTER

These works, which may be literary, dramatic, musical or artistic are those in which there is 'no human author' (section 178). This implies that the direct degree of human intervention in the making of the work is minimal. Examples include:

a) the automatic generation of weather forecasts by a computer communicating with satellites;
b) the selection of lists of random numbers for a competition or for the Premium Bond draw;
c) programs which produce artistic designs or music automatically, being based upon a set of rules built into the program;
d) a program designed to simulate some particular environment, such as climate, monetary systems, battle scenarios, etc.

Many of these systems operate with no human effort or skill apart from switching the equipment on and checking that there is sufficient paper in the computer printer or plotter and so on. The human operator has very little or no control over the *format* or *content* of the output produced by the computer. The author of such a work is the person who makes the arrangements for the work to be created. Therefore, if a business organization buys and installs computer equipment and software to produce such works, that business organization will be regarded as the author and, as a result, the first owner of the copyright in the work. The Act contemplates non-human authors as, by section 154, an author can be a qualifying person if, inter alia, it is a body incorporated in the United Kingdom. In the case of an unincorporated body, such as a partnership, the partners will be considered to be the joint authors of the work. Because a company can be an author of a computer-generated work, there has to be a special rule for determining the duration of copyright in such works and the copyright expires at the end of the period of 50 years from the end of the calendar year in which the work was made (section 12(3)).

Interestingly, and controversially, the Act appears to ignore the skill and expertise of the person or persons who wrote the computer program used to generate these works. It could be argued that the computer programmer whose skill lies behind the computer output should have some recognition of authorship. However, this could cause difficulties because a person obtaining a computer program would expect to own the copyright of anything produced using the program, and any provisions sharing the ownership of the copyright between the user and the programmer could result in an undesirable fetter on the subsequent use of information and reports generated by the computer. The owner of the copyright in the computer program, suddenly realizing that he has rights with respect to the output generated from using the program, might attempt to interfere with the subsequent use of that output in the hope that he will be able to negotiate a fee for his permission.

A concept yet to be tested in the courts is that there is no such thing as a computer-generated work; that is, a work without a human author. After all, the argument that a list of numbers drawn at random by a programmed computer had no human author was rejected, as we have seen, in the *Express Newspaper* case. The approach adopted by the Copyright, Designs and Patents Act is a utilitarian one but it does not reflect the reality of the situation by failing to recognize that all computer output is the result, albeit in many

33

cases the indirect result, of human skill and effort. It would have been better if the programmer's skill were recognized making him the author or joint author of 'computer-generated' works. The practical difficulties resulting from this could be assuaged by raising a presumption that ownership of copyright would lie with the licensee, the ultimate user, of the computer program, subject to any agreement to the contrary.

INTERMEDIATE WORKS

These works lie in the area between computer-generated works and works made using the programmed computer as a tool. The *content* of the output produced is the result of the skill and effort of the person using the computer *and* the skill and effort of the person who wrote the computer program. There are many examples of these intermediate works, such as a specialized accounting system for a particular type of business, or a music synthesizer designed to produce music from a basic framework of notes entered by the user and expert systems.

A great deal of specialized software falls into this category where the skill required to produce the finished results is contained partly within the program, the remainder being provided by the user of the computer system. In some systems, the skill may come from more than two sources. For example, consider a computer system designed to be used to estimate the cost of building work. The system itself will comprise a suite of computer programs, which include routines to provide analyses and breakdowns of the costs derived, and a database of standard prices, based on sets of resources and performances. The person using the system to work out the cost of a building uses a substantial degree of skill in deciding whether the standard prices are applicable, and if not, by building up new prices and entering them into the database. The resulting computer output has three sources of expertise, that of the programmer, that of the persons responsible for developing the database of standard prices and the person using the system. Who is the author of the finished work? Because the person using the system brings an amount of skill to the task, it would not be unreasonable to suggest that he is the author. However, it could be argued that the finished work is created in part by human author, and part computer-generated. Alternatively, all three persons, programmer, database developer and user might be considered to be joint authors. In the absence of any clear guidance in the Act and until we have judicial precedent which explains the meaning of 'computer-generated', it is important that contractual provisions are made to cover the ownership of rights in the output of such intermediate works. In some cases, because all the persons involved are employees of the company commissioning and using the software, there will be little difficulty, but if outsiders are involved at any stage, terms should be inserted in contractual agreements dealing with ownership and use of the computer output.

The same applies to expert systems. These computer systems which are intended to emulate the thought processes, analytical reasoning and advice of experts contain a great deal of skill and expertise within the systems themselves. An expert system, in basic terms, contains three main elements, a knowledge-base (rules and facts provided by experts), an inference engine (a computer program which manipulates the knowledge-base and applies it to a particular problem) and a user interface to make the system 'user-friendly' and to provide explanations of the reasoning adopted and advice given by the expert system. When an expert system is used to produce some advice or a report, the expertise underlying the output comes from the following sources:

1. The experts who provided the knowledge.
2. The persons (sometimes called 'knowledge engineers') who refined the knowledge and formalized it so that it could be installed in the knowledge-base.
3. The persons who wrote the inference engine and the user interface (or adapted existing ones).
4. The user of the system.

The user of the system provides expertise because he will have to understand and respond to the system, he will have to interpret the questions asked by the system and to know what the scope and limitations of the system are. At this stage, most if not all, expert systems cannot be used by naive users; a reasonable general knowledge of the area of expertise covered by the system (its knowledge domain) is essential if the output produced is to be taken seriously, just as the scope, limitations and difficulties presented by a new piece of legislation can only be predicted with any certainty by a lawyer and, even then, not always correctly.

What will the law make of the output of expert systems when it comes to deciding the authorship and ownership of that output? To argue that it is computer-generated and has no human author runs counter to common sense. To say that the user of this system is its sole author might be convenient but is unrealistic. To attribute authorship to the experts and knowledge engineers who developed the knowledge base is unsatisfactory because they cannot predict how the system will be used and what responses will be made by the user; they have no *control* over its use. In reality, all the persons listed above are the joint authors, in differing proportions, of the output resulting from the use of the system. However, it must be said that, if the courts follow this interpretation, it will lead to all manner of complications regarding the commercial use of expert systems and other 'intermediate' systems. Although the courts might be willing to imply terms, for example, that the licensee or 'purchaser' of such systems *owns* the copyright in any output, it is obviously more sensible to recognize the difficulties associated with this part of the Copyright, Designs and Patents Act and to make suitable contractual provision for ownership (as opposed to authorship) of computer output.

Chapter 6
The law of confidence

The law of confidence is concerned with the protection of secrets whether they be trade secrets, secrets of a personal nature or concerning the government of the country. The fundamental rationale underlying the law of confidence is that it can prevent a person divulging information which has been given to him in confidence, on an express or implicit understanding that the information should not be disclosed to others or otherwise used by the recipient of the information. Alternatively, if the information has already been disclosed or used, damages may be awarded against the person divulging or using the information. The roots of the law of confidence lie in equity and it is almost entirely case law. It is given statutory recognition in the Copyright, Designs and Patents Act 1988, section 171 of which states:

> nothing in this Part [the part dealing with copyright] affects . . . the operation of any rule of equity relating to breaches of trust or confidence.

The modern law of confidence developed in the nineteenth century and then lay relatively dormant until the middle of the twentieth century. It soon became clear that breach of confidence was actionable per se, apart from the presence of any contractual relationship between the parties. An important case, *Prince Albert* v *Strange* [1849], helped to establish this area of law and concerned etchings made by Queen Victoria and her consort, Prince Albert. The Queen and the Prince made etchings for their own amusement, intended only for their own private entertainment, although they sometimes had prints made to give to friends. Etchings were sent to a printer to make some impressions and someone surreptitiously made copies which he passed on to the defendant who intended to display them in an exhibition to which the public could go on payment of an admission charge. It was held that relief would be given against the defendant even though he was a third party. He had argued that the prints were not improperly taken but it was said that his possession must have originated in breach of trust, confidence or contract and, therefore, an injunction was granted preventing the exhibition.

The law of confidence can be a very useful adjunct to other intellectual property rights. Copyright protects the expression of an idea, but the law of confidence is wider and can protect the idea itself. It can supplement copyright and patent protection especially in the early stages when there is nothing tangible or substantial enough for copyright or patent to protect. Additionally, confidence can be useful for certain types of secrets for which other rights are inappropriate such as the recipe for Coca-Cola or a secret research technique or industrial process.

A good working formula for the application of the law of confidence was laid down in *Coco v A N Clark (Engineers) Ltd.* [1969], by Megarry J. This involved a moped engine designed by the plaintiff who entered into informal negotiations with the defendant; no contract was executed. Megarry J. held that the defendant owed the plaintiff an obligation of confidence and said that, apart from contract, an action for breach of confidence will require three elements:

1. The information must have the necessary quality of confidence about it.
2. The information must have been imparted in circumstances importing an obligation of confidence.
3. There must be an unauthorized use of that information to the detriment of the party communicating it.

The third of these elements is self-evident, but the first two require further discussion.

QUALITY OF CONFIDENCE

To be protected by the law of confidence, the information must have a quality of confidence about it. If the information is commonplace or is common knowledge to a group of persons (for example, it is well known to computer programmers) or to the public at large, it cannot be confidential; instead, it will be considered to be in the public domain. Often, it will be obvious if the information is or is not confidential. The concept of confidentiality was considered in the case of *Thomas Marshall (Exports) Ltd.* v *Guinle* [1976], in which the defendant, who was the managing director of the plaintiff company, resigned half-way through his 10 year service contract to set up a rival business. The information involved sources of supply and the names of officials and other contacts in Europe and the Far East. Megarry V.C. found for the plaintiff and he said that four elements were necessary in testing for confidential quality:

1. Release of the information would injure the owner of the information or benefit others.
2. The owner must believe the information to be secret and not already in the public domain.
3. The owner's belief in 1. and 2. above must be reasonable.
4. The information must be judged in the light of usages and practices of the particular trade or industry concerned.

To come within the scope of the law of confidence, the information does not have to be particularly special, and mundane information, as in the above case, can be the proper subject matter of confidence as long as it is private to the person who has compiled the information, even though others could gather similar information if they took the trouble to do so. In this way, the law of confidence prevents others from gaining benefit from the work

37

of the person who accumulated the information in the first place. As a result, a great deal of material related to the running of a business will fall within the ambit of the law of confidence. Examples of information relevant to computers which may be the subject matter of confidence include:

1. Ideas for a new or improved computer system, hardware and software.
2. Details of existing computer systems which would be known by computer analysts or programmers or even users of the system. In terms of users, the system would have to be uncommon in some respect.
3. Lists of customers or sub-contractors and associated information; for example, what services they perform, what their credit rating is. Much information stored in computer databases will be confidential.
4. A company's strategy for future research and development, production and marketing.

OBLIGATION OF CONFIDENCE

An obligation of confidence will not be imposed on everyone. A person who is given confidential information and is unaware of its confidential nature (or has no reason to be aware) will be able to use the information freely. This is a major weakness of the law of confidence as it is largely ineffective against innocent third party recipients of the information. For example, if A tells B something in confidence and B (without A's permission) passes the information on to C, who has not been told that it is confidential and the circumstances are such that an obligation of confidence cannot be imputed to C, then C will be able to use the information freely, although B himself can be prevented from using the information or divulging it further.

Obviously, an obligation of confidence can arise by express agreement; for example, where a freelance computer programmer is engaged to carry out some work under a contract that contains a term stating that the programmer will not use or divulge details of the client's business. An obligation of confidence may also be implied by the courts where there is a duty of good faith as in the relationship between a client and a solicitor or patent agent or bank manager. Another situation where the obligation will be imposed is where a person discusses his ideas with business organizations with a view to the commercial exploitation of those ideas, e.g. if a computer analyst has an idea for a new computer system and discusses that idea with software houses interested in developing and marketing the system.

The employee/employer relationship is a special case and may be governed by express terms, as incorporated in the contract of employment, or implied terms or both. Generally, the duty of confidence owed by ex-employees will be less than for current employees who should always act in their employer's best interests. Ex-employees have to make a living and much of the ex-employee's skill will involve what he learnt whilst in his previous employment, thus providing the courts with a dilemma. In many cases, to complicate matters, there may be an overlap with copyright law. However, the courts have developed rules for resolving the conflict which strike a reasonable balance between the interests of employee and employer alike.

When there are no express terms, the employer will not be protected to any great extent. If the ex-employee remembers details of some of the previous employer's customers, there is nothing to stop him using this information, although it would be different if he deliberately memorized the customers' names or made a copy of them. In the absence of an express confidentiality term in the contract of employment, it was said in *Printers and Finishers Ltd.* v *Holloway* [1965], that there would be nothing improper in the employee putting his memory of particular features of his previous employer's plant at the disposal of his new employer. Even if there is an express term the employer would have to show that the information was over and above the employee's normal skill in the job and amounted to a trade secret.

In *Northern Office Microcomputer (Pty) Ltd.* v *Rosenstein* [1982], a South African case, the problem of where to draw the line was considered. In this case, a computer programmer developed a computer program which was similar to one he had written for his previous employer. The case involved copyright matters in addition to the law of confidence and is notable in that the court recognized that computer programs were protected by South African copyright law as literary works. The trial judge agreed that computer programs were protected by confidence but said that the protection should be of a limited nature. Although the defendant programmer would not be allowed simply to copy the programs in question, he would not be required to 'wipe clean the slate of his memory' because to do so would unduly restrict his use of his own training, skill and experience. There would be nothing, in principle, to prevent an ex-employee computer programmer writing a similar program by the exercise of his own mental effort provided he did not plagiarize his employer's program. To some extent, an important factor is the computer program itself, whether it is a commonplace program, carrying out mundane operations, or whether it is designed to do something novel, whether the purpose of the program can be said to be in the nature of a trade secret. The overlap between confidence and copyright law can be seen by comparison with the *Whelan* case, discussed in Chapter 4, in which it was held that the purpose of a computer program designed to perform a commonplace or utilitarian task was idea and not expression and, therefore, not protected by copyright.

In many cases, the employer's 'trade secrets' may be no more than the result of the application by an employee of his own skill and judgment, but if the employee was engaged specifically to produce that information then it can still amount to a trade secret. If the material is commonplace, however, there would be nothing to stop an ex-employee deriving the same or similar material again as long as he did not simply copy his employer's material. In such circumstances, all that would be protected would be the employer's 'lead time'; the advantage of getting his product to the market place first.

An important case laying down principles which can be applied to the employer/employee relationship was *Faccenda Chicken Ltd.* v *Fowler* [1985]. The employer's business was supplying fresh chickens and it was alleged that the employee had made wrongful use of sales information such as customers' names and addresses. The employer's action failed, but the following guidelines were laid down:

1. If there is a contract of employment, the employee's obligations are to be determined from the contract.
2. If there were no express terms, the employee's obligations would be implied.
3. Whilst still in employment, there was an implied term imposing a duty of good faith. This duty might vary according to the nature of the contract of employment but would be broken if the employee copied or deliberately memorized a list of customers.
4. The implied term imposing an obligation on the employee after the termination of his employment was more restricted. It might cover secret processes and trade secrets.
5. Whether information fell within this implied term to prevent its use or disclosure by an ex-employee depended on the circumstances and attention should be given to the following:
   a) the nature of the employment;
   b) the nature of the information;
   c) whether the employer stressed the confidential nature of the material;
   d) whether the information could be easily isolated from other material which the employee was free to use.

An ex-employee is thus allowed to make use of his own memory of the work he has carried out in his previous employment unless it involves genuine secrets or is covered by an express term in the contract of employment. Computer programmers and analysts will be allowed to make use of programming techniques and skill which they have learnt and which have become part of their skill and experience, unless there is something very special about them or they have expressly agreed not to make further use of them. However, a very restrictive express term which tries to prevent an ex-employee making use of mundane skills will be likely to be struck down by the courts as being in restraint of trade. The same fate will await any terms which restrict the ex-employee's future employment prospects to any great extent; for example, a term which states that a computer programmer cannot work for computer software companies in the United Kingdom for five years following the termination of his employment. Such restrictive terms will be upheld by the courts only if they are reasonable, such as when a computer programmer working for a bank agrees not to work for another similar bank within a five mile radius for the first year following the termination of his employment.

A computer hacker is a person who gains access to a computer system without permission. Computer hackers pose a serious threat to the security of computer systems and some of the activities in which they engage are potentially criminal in nature. These activities are fully discussed in Chapter 21. However, computer hackers might also be liable under the law of confidence, depending on the circumstances. If a hacker gains access to confidential files stored on a computer, it is possible that the law of confidence might be used to prevent the hacker from making use of the information, assuming, of course, that the hacker can be identified. In many cases, information stored in computer systems is highly confidential. It might, for example, concern medical records, credit-worthiness or employment details. But, will an obligation of confidence attach to a computer hacker? The case of *Prince Albert* v *Strange*, discussed earlier, suggests that an action might lie in breach of confidence even if the information was obtained surreptitiously. The court in that case were quite happy to imply an air of confidence even though it was not possible to say how the confidential information (that is, the prints taken from the engravings) came into the defendant's hands. It could only be assumed that the prints were obtained in a clandestine manner. In principle, this is very similar to the position of a computer hacker. A hacker must know that there is a strong possibility that the information he accesses will be confidential and, therefore, he will be fixed with an obligation of confidence. If the information turns out to have a quality of confidence, then there is no reason why the hacker cannot be sued for breach of confidence if he uses or threatens to use that information.

The Law Commission recommended codifying the law of confidence and its report, *Breach of Confidence* (Cmnd 8388, 1980), contains a draft breach of confidence Bill. Clause 5 of the Bill imposes an obligation of confidence on a person who improperly acquires information including by using or interfering with any computer or data retrieval mechanism. However, there has been no resulting legislation along these lines and it is unlikely that such action will be taken in the foreseeable future.

REMEDIES FOR BREACH OF CONFIDENCE

The most important remedy for breach of confidence is an injunction preventing the use or disclosure of the information. However, an injunction cannot be used against a third party who has come by the information innocently in circumstances where there is no express or implied obligation of confidence. If the information has been divulged to sufficient people so that it can be said to be no longer confidential, an injunction will not be of any help; it would be like locking the stable door after the horse has bolted. But, if this has happened and the information has been used to the detriment of the person to whom it 'belongs', damages will be available against the person responsible.

As an alternative to damages, an account of profits may be available and this may be more advantageous to the plaintiff, especially if the defendant has made substantial profit from his use of the information. Being an equitable remedy it is discretionary and the plaintiff must have 'clean hands' and have acted promptly in enforcing his rights. An example of the use of this remedy is the case of *Peter Pan Manufacturing Corp.* v *Corsets Silhouette Ltd.* [1963], which involved the use of confidential information, after the expiry of a licence agreement, in the manufacture of brassières. The plaintiff asked for the whole of the profits on the brassières but the defendant said that the account of profits should only be based on the profit resulting from the wrongful use of the confidential information; that is, the profit relating to the parts of the brassières incorporating the confidential information. The difference between the two sums was substantial and the plaintiff was awarded the higher sum because the defendants would not have been able to make the brassières at all without using the confidential information.

It can be seen that the law of confidence is very useful at an early stage when ideas are being formulated and discussed. Although the law of copyright gives some protection at this stage by protecting plans, specifications and notes, the protection does not extend to the ideas behind them. Confidence is particularly important during the development of inventions before they are granted patents because a patent will be refused if details of the invention have fallen into the public domain, as we shall see. In the computer industry, as any with any other, ideas have to be discussed with various persons and organizations with a view to raising finance and granting licences to use or make the resulting invention or copyright work. In most circumstances, an air of confidence will be implied but it is sensible to stress confidentiality; for example, by mentioning that the information is confidential and must not be disclosed to anyone else without permission.

Chapter 7
Patent law

A patent is a very desirable form of intellectual property because it gives the owner a monopoly in an invention, enabling him to exploit the invention for a number of years to the exclusion of other people. Like copyright, patent law has a long history and has developed as a means of protecting innovation which has a benefit to innovator and public alike. Inventors are encouraged to invent and investors are more likely to provide finance if the invention is protected from plagiarism. Society reaps a benefit because the invention will eventually fall into the public domain and because, in the meantime, commercial enterprise is stimulated.

Fundamentally, the inventor (or more usually, the employer of the inventor) applies for a patent to the Patent Office in London, whether the inventor wants a United Kingdom patent or one which extends to other countries as well. If the application is successful, a patent will be granted for four years initially and may be renewed, annually, up to a maximum of twenty years from the date the application is filed (the priority date). The renewal fees become progressively steeper throughout the life of the patent and most patents do not run the full twenty years. Obtaining a patent is a complex, expensive and lengthy process and the services of a patent agent are desirable because the drafting of the application and the specification is extremely important as regards the future scope of the patent. Until the Copyright, Designs and Patents Act 1988, only a registered patent agent or a solicitor could act for gain as agents for persons seeking patents, but now anyone can do this as long as he does not describe himself as, or hold himself out to be, a 'patent agent' or 'patent attorney'. However, in view of the complicated nature of the process, the person applying for a patent would be well advised to satisfy himself as to the ability of his agent. In some circumstances, it may be preferable to keep the idea secret and rely on the law of confidence; this costs nothing and there is no requirement that the invention must eventually fall into the public domain. Examples of the effectiveness of this approach are the recipes and processes used in many familiar drinks and foodstuffs such as Coca-Cola and Kentucky Fried Chicken. However, in many cases, the invention cannot be kept secret, especially if articles made to the invention are to be marketed commercially or if a large number of employees knows of the invention, in which case a patent is the only realistic solution.

The ponderous patent application process seems to be unsuited to a fast moving technology as it can take several years from initial application before a patent is finally granted. However, the monopoly granted extends back to the filing date, which is the time from which damages can be assessed should the patent be infringed, although legal proceedings cannot be commenced until the patent has been granted. For example:

Filing date (first application)	1 August 1982
Infringement commenced	1 July 1983
Infringement ceased	1 January 1985
Patent formally granted	1 February 1986

The patent owner will be entitled to damages based on the period of infringement (1 July 1983 to 1 January 1985) but cannot bring a legal action for damages against the infringer until after 1 February 1986. An interlocutory injunction, preventing further infringement, may be available before that date.

Not all ideas are capable of supporting a patent. The Patents Act 1977 lays down several requirements which must be satisfied before a patent can be granted and, furthermore, certain things are specifically excluded from patentability. The basic requirements for the grant of a patent will now be explained with reference to computer technology, followed by a consideration of the exclusions and their impact, especially with respect to computer software.

BASIC REQUIREMENTS

The basic requirements which an invention must possess for the grant of a patent are stated in section 1(1) of the Patents Act 1977, as follows:

> A patent may be granted only for an invention in respect of which the following conditions are satisfied, that is to say –
> a) the invention is new;
> b) it involves an inventive step;
> c) it is capable of industrial application;
> d) the grant of a patent for it is not excluded by subsections (2) and (3) below . . .

The exclusions referred to in (d), which include computer programs, will be considered later but first, the interpretation of the first three conditions will be examined because, if any one of them is not satisfied, a patent cannot be granted.

NEW INVENTION

The word 'invention' is not defined in the Act but its meaning is really a matter of common sense and it can be used in a fairly wide sense. It is obvious that a patent should not be granted for anything which is not new, which is already in the public domain, otherwise the grant of the patent could make illegal an act which was previously legal. For example, if a business has been making integrated circuits by a special process for several years but has failed to apply for a patent, another business, wishing to do the same type of work, will be refused a patent on the grounds that the invention is not new. If a patent were to be granted to the second business, it could prevent the first from using what it has used for some time and the first business should not be penalized for failing to obtain a patent. Section 2 of the Act expands on the meaning of 'new' and says that an invention is new if it does not form part of the 'state of the art'; this expression comprises all matter which has been made available to the public anywhere in the world, by written or oral description, by use or in any other way. Matters contained in prior patent applications are also included. The inventor must resist any temptation he might have to publish details of his invention before the filing date (the date from which the invention is retrospectively protected), otherwise he could inadvertently add his invention to the state of the art. Similarly, the inventor must be careful when discussing his invention with potential manufacturers and the like and the law of confidence is very important at this stage. However, if details of the invention are disclosed by a person acting in breach of confidence or who has obtained details unlawfully, the disclosure will be disregarded in determining the state of the art.

As technology advances and the pool of knowledge in the public domain grows, it is increasingly difficult to devise something which is absolutely 'new'. Indeed, it is not an easy task to find out if the invention has been anticipated and is already part of the state of the art, given the massive world-wide volume of published work, and it is possible that a publication which anticipates the invention will not be discovered. If that material is subsequently found and shows that the invention was not new when the patent was applied for, the patent is in danger of being revoked. Many patents could be on shaky ground as far as novelty is concerned if sufficient time and effort were expended on trying to trace anticipatory materials.

INVENTIVE STEP

By section 3 of the Patents Act 1977 an invention involves an inventive step if it is not obvious to a person skilled in the art. This test, known as the 'notional skilled worker test' takes account of the complexity of technology hence the reference to a skilled person rather than the ubiquitous 'reasonable man', so often used as a benchmark by judges. The reason is that a great many 'inventions' would not be obvious to a layman but would be to someone who knew something of the technology involved. It has been accepted that the 'skilled person' may be a team of highly qualified research workers such as a team of analysts and computer programmers. When it comes to applying the test, the skilled person is not endowed with any inventive faculties himself, a somewhat artificial premise, but to hold otherwise would mean that virtually all inventions would be obvious and not patentable.

'Obvious' has no special meaning but is judged by looking at the invention as a whole and considering the entire state of the art. Whether the invention is obvious is a question of fact and commercial success is a factor which can be taken into account. In *Technograph Printed Circuits Ltd.* v *Mills & Rockley (Electronics) Ltd.* [1969], Harman J. said:

> It was objected that in fact it was not until ten years after the invention was published that it was commercially adopted . . . and it was argued from this that it was not a case of filling a long felt want. I do not accept this argument. In the years immediately following the war, manufacturers could sell all the machines they wanted using the old point-to-point wiring and had no need to trouble themselves with anything better.

However, in that case it was held that the adaptation of a technique in a United States patent for making electrostatic shields and aerials to the manufacture of printed circuit boards was an obvious step.

Computer technology spreads into all sorts of other technologies and this may lead to patentable inventions, even though the computer technology itself is not new, if the application of the technology is new. In principle there is nothing to prevent the application of well-known technology to a particular problem being the proper subject matter of a patent. This may not be obvious if there has been a major problem and a solution has evaded many attempts to reach it. Here the commercial success of the invention is a useful guide, so in *Parks-Cramer Co.* v *G. W. Thornton & Sons Ltd.* [1966], the invention was a method of cleaning floors between rows of textile machines. There had been many unsuccessful attempts to find a satisfactory solution but none of them, unlike the present invention, actually worked. All the invention consisted of was an overhead vacuum cleaner which moved up and down the rows between the machines, and attached to the cleaner was a long vertical tube, reaching almost to the floor. It was argued that this was obvious because every competent housewife knows that dust can be removed from a floor by the passage of a vacuum cleaner. The patent, however, was held to be valid as the many unsuccessful attempts by inventors to find a solution, and the immediate commercial success of the invention denied the possibility of a finding of obviousness.

The courts have to draw a line somewhere when it comes to obviousness although it is difficult to lay down hard and fast rules. It is clear, however, that there must be a sufficient inventive step and merely taking two older inventions and sticking them together will not necessarily be regarded as an inventive step.

INDUSTRIAL APPLICATION

Another requirement is that the invention must have an industrial application but this is widely defined by section 4 of the Patents Act 1977 which states that the invention must be capable of being made or used in any kind of industry, including agriculture. The need for industrial application shows the practical nature of patent law, which requires that the invention should be something which can be produced or that it relates to some sort of industrial process.

Examples of refusal on the grounds that the invention does not have an industrial application are rare, but one example is provided by *Hiller's Application* [1969]. This case concerned an improved plan for underground service distribution schemes for housing estates; that is, the layout of the gas, sewerage and water pipes and electricity cables. It was held that this could not constitute a 'manner of manufacture' (the phrase used instead of 'industrial application' prior to the 1977 Act). Therefore, if someone develops a new form of layout for the components in a computer or a new configuration for printed circuit boards, these are unlikely to be granted patents. However, the layout of components and the configuration of a printed circuit board may be protected by copyright through any drawings which have been made indicating the layout. The copyright in the drawings will give a remedy against anyone who copies a particular layout, but the protection will not extend to the concept behind the layout. A new form of layout cannot, without more, usually be said to be capable of industrial application.

EXCLUSIONS FROM PATENTABILITY

Several things are excluded from the scope of patent law. Section 1(2) of the Patents Act 1977 contains those which can generally be classified as coming within the scope of copyright law or the law of confidence and in that context, computer programs are of particular interest. (Section 1(3) concerns things which might encourage offensive, immoral or anti-social behaviour or involve plants and animals and is outside the scope of this book.) Section 1(2) of the Act states that the following are not inventions for the purposes of the Act:

a) a discovery, scientific theory or mathematical method;
b) a literary, dramatic, musical or artistic work or any other aesthetic creation whatsoever;
c) a scheme, rule or method for performing any mental act, playing a game or doing business, or a program for a computer;
d) the presentation of information.

The above exceptions only apply to the extent that *a patent relates to that thing as such*. This means that these particular things mentioned in the above list of exclusions can be protected by patent indirectly if they are *part* of a patent application which includes other elements which are patentable in their own right. For example, a computer program to control the temperature of a furnace cannot be patented (it will, of course, be protected by copyright).

But, if an application is made to patent a computer-controlled furnace it may well succeed and be granted a patent.

The exclusion from patent of computer programs reflects international trends. Copyright is seen as the proper vehicle for the protection of computer programs although, when the current Patents Act was passed in 1977, it was far from clear whether copyright did protect computer programs. Even before the 1977 Act, computer programs were not generally patentable per se, but there have been cases, both in the United Kingdom and in the United States where computer programs have been granted patents indirectly, usually as being part of a piece of machinery or an industrial process.

In *Gever's Application* [1970], data processing apparatus was arranged to work in a certain way associated with punched cards inserted into it. The purpose of the apparatus was to file world trade marks in such a way that they could easily be produced to check for similarity and prior registration. The patent, which concerned a piece of machinery which functioned in a certain way because of the punched cards, was allowed to proceed. The cards were described by the judge as a 'manner of manufacture' because he thought that a punched card was analogous to a cam for controlling the cutting path of a lathe. This was distinguished from a card which merely had written or printed material on it, intended to convey information to the human eye or mind and not meant to be ancillary to some machine by being specially shaped for that purpose. However, with the advent of technology, integrated circuits, magnetic disks and tapes and optical character readers are used to enter information into a computer or to store the programs which control the computer. The analogy with a mechanical process no longer rings true and it is unlikely that this case will be followed.

In another case, *Burrough's Corporation (Perkin's) Application* [1974], computer programs controlled the transmission of data to terminals from a central computer (a communications system). The system, including the computer programs, was held to be the proper subject matter of a patent because the programs were embodied in physical form; they were 'hard-wired', permanently embedded in the electronic circuits of the equipment. In many respects the significance of the physical form of a program, whether hard-wired on a silicon chip or stored on magnetic disks, is an irrelevance and the position now, after the 1977 Act appears to be more rational.

Two alternative approaches have been made to the question of the patent protection of inventions which include a computer program. The first is that the patent application should be considered without the contribution of the excepted thing. For example, if a machine includes a computer program it is then a question of whether the machine, without taking the computer program into account, adds anything to the state of the art. Does the machine, ignoring the computer program, meet the requirements for patentability? If the only novel and inventive step concerns the computer program itself, then the machine as a whole is not patentable. The case of *Re Merrill Lynch, Pierce Fenner & Smith Incorporated's Application* [1988] illustrates this approach. The invention related to an improved data processing system for implementing an automatic trading market for securities. The system received and stored the best current bids, qualified customer buy and sell orders, executed orders as well as monitoring stock inventory and profit. The Principal Examiner of the Patent Office rejected the application for a patent and the appeal against his decision was dismissed. On appeal, it was held that where an invention involves any of the excluded materials in section 1(2), then the proper construction of the qualification in that subsection requires that the Patent Office inquires into whether the inventive step resides in the contribution of the excluded matter alone. If the inventive step comes only from the excluded material, then the invention is not patentable because of section 1(2). Falconer J. said:

> If some practical (i.e. technical) effect is achieved by the computer or machine operating according to the instructions contained in the program, and such effect is novel and inventive (i.e. not obvious), a claim directed to that practical effect will be patentable, notwithstanding it is defined by that computer program.

The application failed because there was no practical or technical effect, the operation was entirely software based.

In *Vicom Systems Incorporated's Patent Application* [1987], a different approach was taken. This case concerned an application to the European Patent Office and the invention related to digital image processing, the process steps being expressed mathematically in the form of an algorithm. It was held that this claim was allowable. It was said that if a claim was directed to a technical process which is carried out under the control of a program (whether implemented in the hardware or the software), then the claim cannot be regarded as related to a computer program as such. It is an application of the program for determining the sequence of steps in the process and it is the process for which protection is sought. In other words, the subject matter of the invention was the practical application of a computer program, not the actual computer program itself. This latter approach has been followed in a later case which involved one of the other exceptions contained in section 1(2); that is, a discovery. In *Genentech Inc.'s Patent* [1989], it was held in the Court of Appeal that, inter alia, a patent which claimed the practical application of a discovery did not relate to the discovery *as such* and was not excluded by section 1(2) of the Patents Act 1977 even if the practical application might be obvious once the discovery had been made.

Therefore, it would appear that whilst a patent will be refused for a computer program per se (or any of the other exceptions in section 1(2) for that matter) it will be allowed if the purpose of the program is to bring about some practical effect and it is that effect which is the subject matter of the patent application. The subject matter should make a *technical contribution* to the state of the art. It remains to be seen whether the more liberal attitude to the exception in section 1(2) displayed in the *Genentech* case will encourage more patent applications involving computer programs.

It has been argued that a special, hybrid type of right should be introduced for computer programs; something between a patent and copyright. Such a right would give a monopoly of the program, thus protecting the underlying ideas more effectively than copyright, but the right would last for a shorter period than a patent, say 5 or 7 years maximum. However, given the developments both in the United Kingdom and elsewhere over the last few years, it is now unlikely that this course will be taken. The Copyright, Designs and Patents Act 1988 confirms this forcibly by its clear inclusion of computer programs in the literary work category of works protected by copyright.

INFRINGEMENT, DEFENCES AND REMEDIES

A patent is infringed if a person does one of certain things in relation to the invention in the United Kingdom without the permission of the proprietor (owner) of the patent. Section 60 of the Patents Act 1977 defines what does and what does not constitute infringement. The nature of the infringement depends on whether the invention is a product (for example, a new type of computer printer) or a process (for example, a new method of making integrated circuits). If the invention is a product, the patent is infringed by making, disposing of or offering to dispose of, using, importing or keeping the product. Similar provisions apply to a process; for example, using the process, but, additionally, the patent in the process may be infringed by using or disposing of, etc. any product obtained directly from that process. Another difference between products and processes relates to the knowledge of the infringer. For a process, knowledge that a patent is being infringed is required; however, 'knowledge' is used in a special way and a person can still be deemed to have the requisite knowledge if it would be obvious to a reasonable man that a patent was being infringed. There is no requirement for knowledge as regards a product and, therefore, in the absence of a defence, liability for infringement is strict.

A patent is also infringed if a person supplies or offers to supply some other person with any of the means, relating to an essential element of the invention, for putting the invention into effect. Knowledge is required in that the person supplying knows, or it is obvious to a reasonable man, that those means are suitable for putting the invention into effect and that person so intends. This 'supplying the means' infringement is useful as it applies to persons who supply products in kit form. For example, if a person supplies a computer in kit form which, when assembled, infringes a patent, then the supplier of the computer kit infringes the patent even if he is just a middle-man as long as he has the requisite knowledge. This prevents a possible loophole in patent law such as where a person imports components made in a foreign country to be sold as a kit. The person assembling the kit computer will not be liable under patent law, however, if he assembles and uses the computer privately and for non-commercial purposes.

To give a practical example of infringement, consider the following situation:

An inventor, A, has invented a new type of computer 'chip' and a new process which will be used for making those chips. A has taken out patents for the process and for the chips.

B finds out about the process and decides to build a similar process for making these computer chips.

B asks C to supply equipment which is essential to the process. B then makes some computer chips and sells them to D, a trade supplier.

The position is, so far as infringement is concerned:

B, if he knows, or it would be obvious to a reasonable man, that the process was patented, has infringed the patent in the process. Even if B had no actual knowledge it would be most likely that he would be fixed with knowledge on the basis of the reasonable man test.

B has infringed the patent in the computer chips even if he did not know or could not be expected to know of the patent.

C has infringed the patent in the process if he knows, or it would be obvious to a reasonable man, that the equipment he supplied was suitable for putting the process into effect and the equipment was intended to do so.

D infringes the patent in the computer chips, regardless of knowledge.

The fact that some infringements do not require any form of knowledge may seem unduly harsh, but knowledge is required for some of the remedies and the situation is not as inequitable as it might appear, bearing in mind the need to protect the patent.

There are certain defences or exceptions to infringement, for example, if the act is done privately and for non-commercial purposes or for experimental purposes (on the basis that the proprietor's interests are not harmed by such use). There are other, unusual defences, but these are outside the scope of the book. Of more importance is whether, if someone has 'copied' an invention but has introduced some minor changes, the patent has been infringed. What is the scope of the patent? To determine whether there has been an infringement, the specification for the patent must be looked at and interpreted to find the limits of the patent. There are several ways in which a legal document (or statute) can be interpreted; for example, by taking a strict literal interpretation or by looking at the purpose of the document or statute. The latter, called the purposive approach, is commonly used nowadays and in terms of a patent, what is important is the purpose of the invention. The test for infringement should be to see if that purpose has been incorporated in the product or process which is alleged to have infringed the patent. In *Catnic Components Ltd.* v *Hill & Smith Ltd.* [1982], the plaintiff obtained a patent for a load-bearing lintel, the main strength of which came from a vertical metal face. The defendant made a similar lintel which had a metal face inclined at 6 degrees from the vertical. The House of Lords, by interpreting the word 'vertical' to mean 'vertical or nearly vertical' held that the patent had been infringed. The important feature was the metal face, the purpose of which was to support the load. This approach is in line with common sense and prevents others from flouting patent law by changing details of an invention whilst retaining the underlying principles involved. It also shows the different scope of patent law compared with copyright law, because patent law can protect purpose whereas, generally, copyright law cannot.

A patent, once granted, can be revoked if it is subsequently shown to fail to meet the requirements for patentability; for example, that it is not novel or does not have an inventive step, or if it was not granted to the person entitled to it. The fact that a patent has been granted by the Patent Office is not conclusive proof that the invention has satisfied all the requirements and the discovery of a prior publication showing the invention can result in the patent being revoked. A person sued for infringement of patent will often question the validity of the patent. As far as the alleged infringer is concerned, this can be a useful ploy as the proceedings will be drawn out and the proprietor of the patent will be put to extra expense in defending his patent. However, although the validity of patents is frequently brought into issue by defendants, only a handful of patents are revoked each year.

The remedies available for infringement of patent are injunctions, delivery up or destruction of infringing articles, damages and an account of profits. Damages and accounts of profits are alternatives. If the defendant proves that he was not aware or had no reasonable grounds for supposing that the patent existed, then neither damages nor accounts of profits are available. If a product carries the word 'patent' or 'patented' or similar, this does not automatically mean that the defendant knows of the patent unless the number of the patent also appears on the product concerned.

MISCELLANEOUS

Certain other provisions contained in the Patents Act 1977 are worthy of brief mention. An invention may be potentially very beneficial but might also destroy or seriously undermine an existing business; for example, a car engine that does 200 miles to a gallon, or an everlasting light bulb. To prevent the proprietor sitting on his patent, deliberately failing to use it, section 48 of the Act allows any person to apply for a compulsory licence under the patent, after the expiry of three years if, for example, the patent is not being worked or some abuse is being made of the patent monopoly such as if the product is not being made available at reasonable terms.

An employee who, in the course of his employment, has made an invention which belongs to his employer may be awarded compensation to be paid by the employer if the patent is of outstanding benefit to the employer (1977 Act, section 40). This provision is seldom used perhaps because reasonable employers reward such employees sufficiently well so that they do not apply for compensation.

Chapter 8
Trade marks and passing-off

TRADE MARKS

Marks have been used to identify the makers of goods for thousands of years. Individual marks become associated with a particular product and with the quality of that product. As regards the value of a trade mark to a manufacturer, two factors are important; the buying public's familiarity with the mark and their experience of reasonable quality or value for money in the past associated with the mark. A trade mark which is used with a successful product is of tremendous value to the owner of the mark and he will want to prevent others from using the mark or a similar one to capture some of his trade. The Trade Marks Act 1938, following previous legislation, serves two main purposes; first, to protect the goodwill and reputation which a trader has built up around the mark involved and, secondly, to prevent the public from being deceived into buying inferior goods in the belief that they are made by another manufacturer.

A manufacturer, trader or person who makes goods or provides a service may register a trade mark for one or more classes of goods or services. This will give the owner of the mark a monopoly in the use of that mark in the classes under which the mark has been registered. There is a total of 32 classes of marks for goods (for example, chemicals, electrical goods and scientific apparatus, vehicles, clothing, fancy goods and smokers' articles) and 8 classes for services (for example, advertising and business, insurance and financial, communications and miscellaneous). If anyone else uses the mark, or one deceptively similar, in the course of trade without the owner's permission, that person can be sued for infringement of trade mark. There may also, depending on the circumstances, be a criminal offence committed, as mentioned in Chapter 25. The remedies available to the owner of the trade mark are the usual ones of injunctions, damages or an account of profits as an alternative to damages. The infringing articles may be ordered to be destroyed if the offending marks cannot be removed.

In the computer industry, the power of trade marks can readily be seen as, in a relatively short space of time, names such as Apple computer, IBM, WordStar, Lotus 1-2-3 and BBC computer have become household names. Trade marks are especially important in a fast moving industry and it is very comforting to buy goods with familiar names when so many products and businesses come and go in rapid succession, as happened with microcomputers in the early 1980s. A familiar name or mark is very influential as many who buy computer hardware and software will look for a product which is likely to be of reasonable quality and will be supported in years to come. There have been few examples of trade mark infringement in the world of computers as most counterfeiters and software pirates have used different names or marks; for example, copies of the Apple computer imported into Australia were called the 'Wombat'. Other Apple lookalikes have been called 'Pineapples' and 'Microprofessors'. Perhaps this is a testimony to the effectiveness and relative straightforwardness of trade marks law.

WHAT IS A TRADE MARK?

Section 68(1) of the Trade Marks Act 1938 (the interpretation section) defines a trade mark as:

> a mark . . . used or proposed to be used in relation to goods for the purpose of indicating, or so as to indicate, a connection in the course of trade between the goods and some person having the right either as proprietor or registered user to use the mark, whether with or without any indication of the identity of that person.

Thus, a trade mark shows a link between certain goods and the owner or user of the mark. Originally, trade marks could only be registered in respect of goods but the Trade Marks (Amendment) Act 1984 extended the registration of trade marks to services such as banking and laundries. Computer bureaux fall within the miscellaneous category of services. 'Mark' is defined by section 68 of the 1938 Act as including:

> a device, brand, heading, label, ticket, name, signature, word, letter, numeral or any combination thereof.

However, a brand, heading, label and ticket cannot be service marks. A 'brand' simply means a mark made by a hot instrument such as a branding iron applied to cattle. The definition of marks is very wide and everyone is familiar with many examples of different types of mark, e.g., the stylized Cadbury signature, the Apple logo and the JPS monogram. Registered trade marks are often printed with a tiny circle containing a letter 'R' to signify their status as registered trade marks and to warn would be imitators.

Even the shape and colour of an article have been held to be acceptable as trade marks. For example, in *Smith, Kline and French Laboratories Ltd. v Sterling Winthrop Group Ltd.* [1976], it was held that coloured capsules for drugs could be registered as trade marks. However, an application for the Coca-Cola bottle was refused registration in *Re Coca-Cola Co.'s Application* [1986].

THE REQUIREMENTS FOR REGISTERING A TRADE MARK

There is a distinction in the Act between Part A and Part B marks. More stringent rules apply to Part A marks which require that the trade mark must be 'adapted to distinguish' the goods of the owner of the mark from goods of other traders. Part B marks must be 'capable of distinguishing' the proprietor's goods from those of other traders. Registration in Part A is more desirable in that the protection offered is stronger. Application is normally made for Part A and Part B registration might be granted if there is some doubt about the mark.

Section 9 of the Trade Marks Act 1938 sets out five categories for Part A marks:
a) names, business or individual;
b) signatures of applicant or predecessor;
c) invented words;
d) a word having no direct reference to the character or quality of the goods and not being a geographical name or surname;
e) any other distinctive mark.

Additionally, these marks must be 'distinctive'; that is, they are:

adapted to distinguish goods with which the proprietor . . . is or may be connected in the course of trade from goods in the case of which no such connection subsists.

OBSTACLES AND OBJECTIONS TO REGISTRATION; HOW TO REGISTER

By section 12(1) of the Trade Marks Act 1938, a mark will be refused registration if it is deceptive, i.e. if it is identical to or so similar to another mark already registered that it is likely to lead to confusion. Another form of deception is if the mark creates a misleading impression in another way about the goods involved (section 11). The objections may be made either by the Registrar himself or an objector, such as the owner of a similar mark.

Similar to another mark

This is only a bar to registration if the first mark is registered in respect of 'the same goods or description of goods'. It is acceptable to use the same name as someone else if it is used for a different class of goods or services to the ones for which the first mark is registered. However, there may be an action in passing-off if this is likely to cause confusion in the eyes of the buying public. For example, it may be permissible to use the Apple logo for brandy (providing it has not been registered against the wines and spirits class) and there would be little danger of the public thinking it had anything to do with the computer company. However, if the logo were used by a computer bureau, although there may be no infringement of trade mark (unless the

Apple logo had been registered in miscellaneous services class), there would probably be an action in passing-off because many people might think that the computer bureau was somehow connected with the computer company. Examples of marks turned down on these grounds are:

- HUNTSMAN − earlier mark SPORTSMAN (both cherry brandy)
- An application showing a picture of three pigs was refused because of a prior word mark THREE PIGS BRAND (bacon)

However, in *Coca-Cola Co. of Canada Ltd.* v *Pepsi-Cola Co. of Canada Ltd.* [1942], it was held that PEPSI-COLA was not too close to COCA-COLA because the suffix COLA was a word that had become common and descriptive of a type of beverage.

Creating a false impression

This should not present any major difficulties in the context of computers, although a dating agency which wanted to use a service mark 'COMPUTADATE', but did not have a computer, might fall into this category. Examples of marks refused on these grounds include DAIRY GOLD for a synthetic margarine and JARDEX for a poisonous disinfectant when there was already a meat extract called JARDOX.

Exception − honest concurrent use

An exception to the rules concerning deceptive marks is contained in section 12(2) of the 1938 Act. This applies where two companies have used identical or similar marks for at least five years or more in all honesty and have built up goodwill in ignorance of the use of the mark by the other company. Even though one is registered, the second may be accepted for registration, especially if there is little danger of confusion between the two.

Applications for registration of a trade mark are made to the Patent Office in London and the services of a trade mark agent may be helpful. The fees for registration are relatively modest (presently just over £100) but this must be multiplied by the number of classes for which registration is required. Initially, registration is for 7 years and may be renewed, ad infinitum, for further 14 year periods. Many trade marks first registered under the Trade Marks Act 1875 are still in use, testifying to the importance of trade marks, including Britain's No.1 trade mark, the BASS red triangle mark.

PASSING-OFF

In many ways, the law of passing-off is a common law version of trade mark law. It protects business goodwill and safeguards the public from deception by giving a right of action against anyone who tries to pass off his goods or services as those of someone else. One trader might try to 'cash in' on the goodwill and reputation of another trader by dressing up his goods in such a way that they look like those of that other trader. There is a large overlap between trade marks and passing-off and in many cases, passing-off will also involve infringement of a trade mark. Passing-off is particularly useful if there is no trade mark to be infringed; perhaps a trader or manufacturer has used a mark for several years without registering it as a trade mark. The mark may not qualify for registration of a trade mark or the act complained of might fall outside the scope of trade marks; for example, if it relates to a way of doing business.

The following example shows the application of passing-off. A computer retailer has been operating for three years under the name of 'COMPUTER EQUIPMENT SALES' and has a chain of stores in the South of England. The retailer has acquired a reputation for low prices and efficient service. Recently, another retailer has opened a store in the South of England and uses the name of 'COMPUTER EQUIPMENT SALES AND SERVICE'. Neither name is registered as a trade mark; in fact the names would be refused registration because they are too descriptive of computer retailing generally and would make it difficult for other traders to describe their business activities. As there is a danger that people will be confused and might deal with the second retailer thinking that they are dealing with the first, the first retailer should be able to obtain an injunction preventing the second retailer from continuing to use the name he has chosen. If the first retailer has only been in business a short time before the second retailer opens his store then it is unlikely that anything can be done. This is because there has not been sufficient time to build up a reputation connected with the name and so there is little danger that the public will be confused. Similarly, if the second trader's store was in North Wales, it would be unlikely that the first trader's business would be affected.

BASIC REQUIREMENTS FOR A PASSING-OFF ACTION

Before the plaintiff can suffer the type of damage caused by passing-off, he must have a reputation. He must be able to show that his name, mark, 'get-up' or something distinctive about his business will be associated with his goods by the public. If a trader has just started in business he will not succeed in a passing-off action but a newly registered trade mark has immediate protection.

The ingredients necessary to a successful passing-off action were described in *Erven Warninck Besloten Vernootschap* v *J Townend & Sons (Hull) Ltd.* [1979]. The plaintiffs made a liqueur called advocaat which came to be well known. It was made from brandewijn, egg yolks and sugar. The defendants decided to enter this market and they made a drink called 'Keeling's Old English Advocaat' which was made from Cyprus sherry and dried egg powder, an inferior but cheaper drink. This captured a large part of the plaintiffs' market in the United Kingdom. It was held that, because of the reputation the plaintiffs' product had gained, it should be protected from deceptive use of its name by competitors even though the goodwill was shared by several traders. There was a misrepresentation made by the defendant calculated to injure the plaintiffs' business or goodwill and an injunction was granted in favour of the plaintiffs. Lord Diplock laid down the essentials for a passing-off action:

1) a misrepresentation
2) made by a trader in the course of trade
3) to prospective customers of his or ultimate consumers of goods or services supplied by him
4) which is calculated to injure the business or goodwill of another trader . . . and
5) which causes actual damage to a business or goodwill of the trader by whom the action is brought.

Most of these points are self explanatory but the first one, the misrepresentation, requires further discussion.

THE MISREPRESENTATION

The misrepresentation is not necessarily limited to an exact copy of the name or 'get-up'. It may be sufficient if it imputes a quality in something which applies to an already well-known product, an important factor being whether the public will be deceived. In deciding this it is not necessary to consider whether members of the public who are knowledgeable about the product are deceived, it may be sufficient if members of the public who have very little knowledge of the product concerned are likely to be deceived. In *J. Bollinger* v *Costa Bravo Wine Co. Ltd. (No.2)* [1961], an injunction was granted to prevent the use of the name 'Spanish Champagne'.

As mentioned earlier, a misrepresentation does not have to be confined to a name or mark. The tort of passing-off is wide enough to encompass other descriptive material such as slogans and visual images associated with an advertising campaign if this material has become part of the goodwill of the plaintiff's product. The recent advertising campaign by IBM, using the Charlie Chaplin character, is an example. The test is whether the plaintiff has acquired an intangible property right for his product deriving from the distinctive nature of this material recognized by the market. In applying the test, the courts have to bear in mind the balance between the plaintiff's investment in the product and the protection of free competition.

COMMON FIELDS OF ACTIVITY

If the businesses concerned in a passing-off action operate in different fields of activity, it will usually be assumed that there is less danger of confusion and thus less danger of damage to the plaintiff. For example, in *Granada Group Ltd.* v *Ford Motor Company Ltd.* [1973], the GRANADA television group could not prevent the Ford Motor Company calling one of their cars a Ford GRANADA; the court held that there was no danger of confusion because of the different fields of activity, namely television and cars. However, in *Lego U.K. Ltd. v Lego M. Lemelstrich Ltd.* [1983], the Lego company, which makes children's construction kits comprising coloured plastic bricks, was granted an injunction against the manufacturers of coloured plastic irrigation material preventing them using the name 'Lego' as part of the description of the material. The plaintiff was able to show that there was a real danger of confusion and damage to its reputation.

There is no copyright in a fictitious name and an action in passing off is unlikely to be of much help if the defendant simply uses that name. Many such names are used on all types of goods to help sell them, usually by the way of licence agreements. The real test, as always, is whether the public are likely to be deceived by the use of the name and in applying this test it is important to consider the fields of activity involved; do both parties operate in the same or different fields? In applying this test it appears that the public are not generally to be expected to have a knowledge of character merchandising. An example is provided by the case of *Wombles Ltd. v Wombles Skips Ltd.* [1977]. Wombles are fictitious animals from a TV series noted for their cleanliness, and for cleaning up litter and putting it to good use. The plaintiff company owned the copyright in the books and drawings of the Wombles and their main business was granting licences so that manufacturers, in return for a fee, could use the Womble characters to promote their goods. They granted one such licence for wastepaper baskets. The defendant formed a company to lease builders skips for rubbish. After considerable thought and remembering the Wombles' clean habits, he decided to call his company Wombles Skips Ltd. In finding for the defendant, the court held that there was no common field of activity and, therefore, no danger of confusion.

REMEDIES FOR PASSING-OFF

Remedies available are injunctions, including interlocutory injunctions, and damages. An account of profits may be available as an alternative to damages. The damages are assessed by considering the harm done to the plaintiff's reputation and the lost sales of the plaintiff's product as a result of the passing-off. The most desirable remedy is an injunction, preventing the other person or business from continuing to use the disputed name or style.

Chapter 9
Designs

Designs are relevant to computer hardware. Computer equipment may be designed in such a way that it is aesthetically pleasing as well as functional, there may be something novel about the design which falls short of the scope of patents. Examples of these are: an attractive outer case for a computer monitor; a useful case for computer disks with built in carrying handle; a desk for a computer or an effective printer stand. A considerable amount of effort may have been expended on the design of such items so that they perform their intended function efficiently or are visually attractive so that they will sell in large numbers. It is only fair that such efforts should be rewarded by preventing others from simply copying them and this is the province of rights associated with designs.

Unfortunately, this area of law is far from straightforward and the Copyright, Designs and Patents Act 1988 has done little to simplify matters. To add to the confusion, there are now two forms of right relating to designs; one is subject to registration, the other not. *Registered designs* are provided for by the Registered Designs Act 1949 (amended by the Copyright, Designs and Patents Act 1988) whilst a new right, the *design right* is introduced by the Copyright, Designs and Patents Act 1988. The history of designs and their relationship with copyright is an interesting study in its own right and in many cases an original design was capable of dual protection under the 1949 Act as a registered design and, through any drawings of the design, under the Copyright Act of 1956 as an artistic work.

Drawings are prepared for most designs and drawings are protected by copyright as artistic works, irrespective of artistic quality. Before the 1988 Act, anyone copying a design would infringe the copyright in a drawing made for the design, even though that person had never seen the drawing, because making a three-dimensional copy of a two-dimensional work infringed the copyright in the latter (and vice versa). The only proviso was that a layman would be able to recognize the one from the other. For example, in *British Leyland Motor Corpn. Ltd.* v *Armstrong Patents Co. Ltd.* [1986], the defendants made replacement exhaust pipes for the plaintiff's cars by copying the shape and dimensions of the original pipes, a process known as 'reverse engineering'. The plaintiffs claimed that the exhaust pipes made by the defendants infringed the copyright in the original drawings of the exhaust systems, although the defendants had never had an opportunity to look at these drawings. This argument was accepted by the House of Lords but they refused to allow the plaintiffs to assert their rights under copyright law. They said that car owners have an inherent right to repair their cars in the most economical way possible and, for that purpose, are to have access to a free market in spare parts.

Until the 1988 Act, all a person had to do to gain copyright protection for a design was to make a drawing of the design in such a way that the design could be recognized from the drawing (as long as the design did not relate to a spare part). As copyright protection for an artistic work endures for at least 50 years (25 years if the work is commercially exploited, for example, by mass-production: section 52, Copyright, Designs and Patents Act 1988), and the protection under the Registered Designs Act 1949 used to last for 15 years, it was little wonder that there was not a massive rush to file registration applications. However, the overlap between designs and copyright has been partly eliminated by section 51 of the Copyright, Designs and Patents Act which states that it is not an infringement of any copyright in a design document or model recording or embodying a design for anything other than an artistic work (or a typeface), to make an article to the design or to copy an article made to the design. In this context, 'design' has the same definition as for the purposes of the *design right* and a design document includes a drawing or other documents such as specifications, photographs and *data stored in a computer*. This means that industrial designs must fall within either the design right or be registered as a design to be protected. It is no longer possible, in most cases, to rely on copyright in any drawings or computer data relating to the design.

Many of the intricacies of the law of designs have little relevance to computer technology and a complete discussion of the rights is outside the scope of this book. The following description of the two forms of right is thus necessarily brief and the emphasis is on computer equipment rather than attempting to give a detailed account of design law.

REGISTERED DESIGNS

Section 1 of the Registered Designs Act 1949, as amended, defines registerable designs as being:

> . . . features of shape, configuration or ornament applied to an article by any industrial process, being features which in the finished article appeal to and are judged by the eye . . .

This is concerned with aesthetic aspects and it is not sufficient that the article simply looks pretty or pleasing but the eye appeal of the article should be such that persons acquiring or using the article do so because of the appearance of articles made to the design. By section 1(3), a design shall not be registered if the appearance of the article is not material; that is, if aesthetic considerations are not normally taken into account to a material extent by persons acquiring or using articles made to the design. In addition, to be registerable, the design must be new (section 1(2)). Examples are a new shape of coffee cup or a new transfer pattern applied to plates or attractive and novel computer furniture, and with such objects the appearance of the object is important to a person buying it. Even if a person is buying desks for computers or word processors for an office, the appearance of the furniture is a major factor influencing the choice. However, an attractively designed computer will not fall within the scope of registered designs because a person buying a computer is more interested in the performance of the computer; its appearance is not important to a material extent.

Certain things are excluded from registration such as a method or principle of construction, or features of shape or configuration dictated solely by the function the article has to perform, or which depend upon the appearance of another article of which it is intended to form an integral part. Methods or principles of construction are verging on patent law, whilst eye-appeal resulting from function, or from fitting with another article is excluded because it is an indirect effect. Eye-appeal must be something which has been deliberately achieved. The proprietor (owner) of a design is normally its author, the person who creates it, unless the author is acting in the course of employment or has been commissioned, for money or money's worth, to create the design. If the design has been generated by a computer in circumstances where there is no human author, the person making the arrangements is treated as the proprietor of the design. The right lasts for 5 years initially from the date of registration but may be renewed in 5 year stages up to a maximum of 25 years.

THE NEW DESIGN RIGHT

Like copyright, this right is automatic and does not depend on registration but, unlike registered designs, there is no requirement for the design to have eye-appeal, although if it does, it is not barred from protection as a design right. The result is that the design right will apply to both functional and aesthetic articles and, hence, there is an overlap with registered designs. The potentially longer duration of registered designs is the main reason why a design which lies in this overlap should be registered.

A 'design' in the context of a design right is, by section 213 of the Copyright, Designs and Patents Act 1988, an original design being:

'the design of any aspect of the shape or configuration (whether external or internal) of the whole or part of the article.'

This definition is not too dissimilar to that relating to registered designs. This design right applies to all manner of industrial designs whether or not the design relates to the article's function. The requirement of originality is satisfied if the design is not commonplace in the design field in question (section 213(4) of the Copyright, Designs and Patents Act 1988).

As with registered designs, there are exceptions to design right protection. The first exception, a method or principle of construction, is common to

both rights. The second exception is subdivided into features of shape or configuration of an article which:
i) enable the article to be connected to, or placed in, around or against, another article so that either article may perform its function, or
ii) are dependent upon the appearance of another article of which the article is intended by the designer to form an integral part.

These exceptions are significant for manufacturers and suppliers of spare parts. The former part of the exception applies to 'functional' spare parts which have to be a particular shape to fit another article. An exhaust pipe for a car will fall into this part of the exception. Any piece of computer equipment which has to be fitted to some other equipment, such as a replacement 'card' (printed circuit board mainly containing integrated circuits) which has to be a certain shape, or have a certain type of connector, in order to fit into a computer will also fall into the first part of the exception. This exception is directed at rationalizing the *British Leyland* case and it allows for the fact that persons who buy items of equipment may need replacement parts in time and should be able to obtain spare parts on a free market at reasonable cost. If a design right monopoly were to be granted to spare parts, manufacturers of cars, washing machines, computers, etc. would be able to control the supply and price of spare parts and might be tempted to abuse their monopoly position.

The second part of the exception would apply to spare parts such as replacement body panels for cars where the design is dictated by the appearance of the car but it is unlikely that many computer spare parts will fall into this category. An example of computer equipment which falls into the 'functional' exception (i.e. the first part of the exception) is a soundproof box for a printer (acoustic hood). The shape of the box is determined largely by the shape and size of the printer and the box is placed around the printer so that it can perform its function of reducing the decibel level emanating from the printer. The 'appearance' exception (i.e. the second part of the exception) could only apply if the soundproof box and printer, when taken together, could be considered to be an integral unit. Generally, there is a small overlap between designs and copyright; for example, a design for a one-piece printer hood made by a process involving casting might be protected as a sculpture (which includes a cast), which is a category of artistic works. However, if there is such an overlap, section 236 of the Copyright, Designs and Patents Act 1988 removes design right protection, leaving copyright as providing the only legal remedy against unauthorized copying. Surface decoration is another exception because this lies within the scope of registered designs.

With registered designs, the person creating the design is known as the *author* but, and for no explicable reason, the person creating a design which is subject to a design right is known as its *designer*. The owner of a design right is the designer unless he creates the design in the course of his employment or has been commissioned by someone else. There is no requirement for the commissioner of a design to have paid money or money's worth to be the owner of the right. A computer-generated design belongs to the person making the arrangements necessary for the creation of the work. Design right lasts for fifteen years from the end of the calendar year in which it was first recorded in a design document (which includes storage in a computer), or an article was made to the design, unless articles have been made available for sale or hire within the first five years in which case the right lasts only a further ten years.

The result of the provisions relating to duration is that the owner of the right can only have a maximum of 10 years to exploit the design commercially. This period will be reduced if the owner fails to market articles made to the design within the first five years. Effectively, and in a commercial sense, the right lasts for 10 years with the owner being given a five year breathing space within which to bring articles made to the design to the market place.

Chapter 10
Semiconductor products

Integrated circuits, commonly known as 'silicon chips' or, simply, 'chips', are of tremendous importance to the computer industry. Without the miniaturization that they bring, the powerful personal computer of today would have remained an impossibility. Integrated circuits are made from layers of materials by a process which includes etching using various 'masks' (templates) which are made photographically. Alternatively, electron beam machines are used. The simplest integrated circuit consists of three layers, one of which is made of semiconductor material. A semiconducting material, in terms of its ability to conduct electricity, is one which lies between a conductor such as copper and an insulator such as rubber. Examples of semiconducting materials include silicon, germanium, selenium and gallium arsenide. A wafer of semiconductor material is coated with a layer of silicon oxide (an insulator) and the electronic components (for example, transistors) are formed by a process of diffusion (chemically doping the semiconductor material with impurities through holes etched through the oxide). Finally, an aluminium coating is applied which is partly evaporated using a mask, leaving behind the interconnections between components formed in the semiconductor layer.

The patterns formed by the processes of etching and/or evaporation of the conductor make the electrical circuitry of the integrated circuit. These patterns represent the circuit design. The processes involved in the making of integrated circuits fall within the province of patent law and the first patents for integrated circuits were filed in the late 1950s, the most important one being developed by Noyce of the Fairchild Semiconductor Corporation in 1959. Licences were readily available and in 1961 the first chips were available commercially. Now that the early patents have expired and much of the know-how lies in the public domain, it is essential that the considerable effort that goes into the design and development of new integrated circuits is protected. New types of integrated circuits are unlikely to be patentable for lack of novelty because many are simply more efficient or miniaturized forms of well-known electronic circuits.

SEMICONDUCTOR DESIGN RIGHT

One view was that integrated circuits were protected by copyright through drawings or photographs as most of the masks used in the manufacture were produced photographically and would be protected as photographs. However, this was uncertain because of the requirement in the 1956 Copyright Act for a non-expert to recognize the circuit as being a three-dimensional reproduction of the drawings or photographs. As a result of an EEC Directive, the Semiconductor Products (Protection of Topography) Regulations 1987 were made and came into force on 7th November 1987. These regulations gave a right (called a 'topography right') in the layout of an integrated circuit. However, with the advent of the Copyright, Designs and Patents Act 1988, it was decided to replace these regulations with an amended version of the new design right by the Design Right (Semiconductor Regulations) 1989, which came into force on 1st August 1989. The new right, referred to hereinafter as the 'semiconductor design right' draws heavily from Part III of the Copyright, Designs and Patents Act 1988 which deals with the unregistered design right but with some differences as far as semiconductor topographies are concerned (see Chapter 9 for a general description of the unregistered design right). The manner in which this has been done is most inept and we now have the situation where some sections of the 1988 Act are different depending on whether they are being applied to semiconductors or other articles. References below to the 1988 Act are to the Copyright, Designs and Patents Act 1988 as it applies to the semiconductor design right.

The 1989 regulations are similar to the 1987 regulations in several respects; for example, it is the topography of a semiconductor which is protected being, by regulation 2, a design which is either:

(a) the pattern fixed, or intended to be fixed, in or upon
   (i) a layer of a semiconductor product, or
   (ii) a layer of material in the course of and for the purpose of the manufacture of a semiconductor product, or
(b) the arrangement of the patterns fixed, or intended to be fixed, in or upon the layers of a semiconductor product in relation to one another.

A semiconductor product is defined as:

an article the purpose, or one of the purposes, of which is the performance of an electronic function and which consists of two or more layers, at least one of which is composed of semiconducting material and in or upon one or more of which is fixed a pattern appertaining to that or another function.

These definitions are not very helpful as they are somewhat tautologous but despite that it is fairly plain that all integrated circuits will be covered by the regulations. If the description of integrated circuits given earlier is now considered, it can be seen that the requirements are met; there are two or more layers (usually three), one layer is made of a semiconducting material and a pattern is fixed upon it for the purpose of performing an electronic function. Normally, the ingenuity which requires protection is in the circuitry represented by the patterns formed by the conducting materials, but the regulations are wider in the sense that they will apply in situations where the ingenuity lies not so much in the horizontal patterns themselves but in the vertical arrangement of layers.

Incidentally, the printed circuit boards commonly found inside most electronic equipment, ranging from transistor radios to computers, are not protected by these regulations because, although comprised of layers (usually two), neither layer is made from semiconductor material. The board is made of insulating material and a conductor which is etched away leaving the circuitry to which electronic components are later soldered. Generally, however, printed circuit boards will be protected, through their preparatory drawings, by copyright. A single electronic component such as a silicon diode or a transistor is not protected because they possess no topography within the meaning of the regulations.

To be protected, the semiconductor topography must be original and it is not original if it is commonplace in the design field in question at the time of its creation (section 213 of the 1988 Act). 'Original' is liberally interpreted in copyright law; however, the requirement that the topography is not commonplace is likely to lead to a much narrower interpretation. Additionally, there are qualification requirements based on the citizenship or domicile of the creator (or his employer or commissioner) of the topography or the person by whom and country in which semiconductors containing the topography are first marketed. These qualification requirements are wider than with other unregistered designs and there are also reciprocal arrangements with several non-European Community countries such as the United States, Switzerland and Japan. One reason why the 1989 regulations have been passed is to satisfy the United States as to the protection offered in the United Kingdom, otherwise there might have been some doubt as to whether topographies derived from the United Kingdom would have been afforded protection in the United States.

Ownership of the semiconductor design right is dealt with by amending section 215 of the 1988 Act. The first owner of the right is the designer unless the design is created in pursuance of a commission or in the course of employment in which cases, the commissioner or the employer respectively are the first owners of the right, subject to any written agreement to the contrary. If the right arises by reference to the first marketing of the article, such as where a semiconductor topography is designed by a Brazilian in Brazil but is marketed in the United Kingdom by an importer, then the importer will be deemed to own the semiconductor design right. By section 215 of the 1988 Act, the designer is the person who creates the design and in the case of a computer-generated design, the designer is the person by whom the arrangements necessary for the creation of the design are undertaken. The recognition of computer-generated topographies is a useful improvement on the 1987 regulations.

The semiconductor design right is, by section 226(1) of the 1988 Act, the exclusive right to reproduce the design by making articles to that design or by making a design document (which includes data stored in a computer) recording the design for the purpose of enabling such articles to be made. A person doing either of the above infringes the right whether he does it in relation of the whole or a substantial part of the topography. There are important exceptions to infringement connected with non-commercial, research and educational purposes. The regulations have one very unusual effect in that it is permissible to make a reproduction of a topography for the purpose of analysing or evaluating that topography or the concepts, processes, systems or techniques embodied in it, by section 226(1A) of the 1988 Act. Furthermore, by section 226(4), it is not an infringement of the semiconductor design right to create another *original* topography as a result of such analysis or evaluation or to reproduce that other topography. Therefore, a form of 'reverse engineering' is positively encouraged allowing the knowledge gained from an inspection of an existing topography to be used as the basis of a new topography. In practice, a limiting factor will be the requirement for the new topography to be original; that is, not commonplace. On reflection, this exception is probably justified on the grounds that to provide otherwise might inhibit innovation in this fast moving field where the existing technology is being built upon all the time whilst property rights still subsist in that existing technology. However, this runs counter to basic principles of intellectual property rights; such an activity with respect to a copyright work would probably infringe copyright because any derivative work would contain a copy of a substantial part of the first work. It will really depend on how the word 'substantial' is interpreted in terms of the semiconductor design right. For the reverse engineering provisions to have any real effect, the word 'substantial' would have to be interpreted in a quantitative sense which would run counter to copyright law. However, if an infringement of a topography right also infringes copyright, such as if a photographic mask is reproduced or a copy is made of computer data recording the design, the semiconductor design right is suppressed leaving remedies to be pursued under copyright law only, by section 236 of the 1988 Act.

The duration of the semiconductor design right depends on if and when the topography is commercially exploited. Normally, by section 216 of the 1988 Act the right endures for ten years from the end of the year in which it was first commercially exploited (anywhere in the world). However, if the right is not commercially exploited within fifteen years of the creation of the topography, the right expires fifteen years from the time the topography was first recorded in a design document or the time when an article was first made to the design, whichever is the earlier. These rules mean that it might benefit the owner of a topography right to sit on that right until such time as it can be exploited to its full potential, so long as this is done a reasonable period before the first fifteen years have expired. However, given the speed of development in the industry this is unlikely to be a great advantage as there is a danger that the product will be obsolete before it has been exploited. As with the unregistered design right as it applies to other articles, the semiconductor design right is automatic and does not require registration. Bearing this in mind (and the same applies to the unregistered design right generally and to copyright works) it is worthwhile keeping good records of the development of the topography so that the date it was created can be proved in a court of law. This is to prevent a copier claiming that he was the first to develop the topography in question. By regulation 9 of the 1989 regulations, licences of right are not available in relation to semiconductors as they are with other designs (such licences are normally available in the last five years of a design right).

REMEDIES

Remedies for infringement are as for the design right generally and are injunctions, damages and accounts of profits 'or otherwise' (section 229 of the 1988 Act). Additional damages are also provided for as they are for copyright infringement and the unregistered design right generally. Orders for delivery and destruction are also available. In the case of innocent infringement (i.e., the defendant did not know and had no reason to believe that the semiconductor design right subsisted in the article), damages are not available although other remedies may be, such as an account of profits.

Secondary infringement, such as where a person imports or deals with infringing copies of semiconductors, does not apply if they have already been marketed in the United Kingdom or any member state of the European Community by or with the licence of the owner of the right or other person entitled to do so. This means that someone importing or dealing with infringing copies does not infringe the right if semiconductors incorporating the topography in question have already been lawfully sold or hired within the EEC. Of course, there may still be an infringement related to making the semiconductors.

Chapter 11
International implications and summary

INTERNATIONAL IMPLICATIONS

Bearing in mind the international nature of business markets, the territorial scope of intellectual property rights is a serious issue to those creating and developing computer hardware and software. Some forms of intellectual property rights fare better than others when it comes to their subsistence and enforcement in other countries. With the United Kingdom membership of the European Community, it is to be expected that there should be some degree of harmonization with our European trading partners and recent legislation in the United Kingdom has been influenced by this. For example, the Patents Act 1977 went some way towards achieving compatibility, and the consolidation of moral rights in copyright law which is a traditional European concept, reinforces the move towards European commercial unity. However, on a world-wide scale there are many difficulties, and some countries, notably in the Middle East, fail to appreciate the significance of intellectual property. World-wide legal protection of invention and innovation is still a long way from being realized, although countries which include the major producers and users of intellectual property have strong laws protecting the same.

Copyright is subject to two main international conventions by which reciprocal protection is granted between members. The conventions are the Berne Convention and the Universal Copyright Convention and the United Kingdom is a signatory to both. This means that any work of copyright protected under the Copyright, Designs and Patents Act 1988, and previous legislation, is also protected in all the countries which are members of these conventions and that includes most of the major developed countries. In some of these countries, a copyright notice is required (for example, in the United States of America) and it is for this reason that the familiar copyright symbol, © (a 'c' within a circle), is used. To be valid the symbol must be shown with the year the work was created and the name of the copyright owner, though alternatives to the symbol are allowed, such as the unabbreviated word 'Copyright'.

The territorial scope of patent protection is determined by the application procedure. The applicant may apply for a United Kingdom patent, a European patent to be granted for three or more countries under the European Patent Convention or a 'world-wide' patent for one or more of the 39 member countries under the Patent Co-operation Treaty. The more countries for which patent protection is sought, the more expensive the operation becomes but the expense may be worthwhile if it is intended to exploit the invention internationally. At the moment, trade marks may be registered in individual countries but there are moves to develop an integrated European system, although this will present difficulties as the same or similar marks may already be registered in different countries by different proprietors.

Some areas of intellectual property discussed in this Part of the book have little, if any, international scope and are restricted to the United Kingdom. Prime examples are the law of confidence, as demonstrated by the failure to prevent the publication of the 'Spycatcher' book in Australia, the tort of passing-off and the new design right.

SUMMARY

The law has developed, somewhat slowly it might be claimed, to take account of computer technology and to protect ideas and innovation concerning the technology. However, the importance of such protection has been recognized by U.K. legislators and judiciary and, as a result, computers and computer software are reasonably well protected from counterfeiting and piracy. The civil remedies available to owners of intellectual property rights have been supplemented by criminal sanctions, showing the seriousness with which Parliament views these matters. Certainly, without strong protection, the computer industry would seem a poor area in which to invest, and foreign investment and the resulting jobs created would be lost to the United Kingdom.

Although this area of law is diverse and complex, it should be noted that, frequently, these various rights overlap and several different rights may each serve a purpose during the life of a product from inception to marketing. For example, in the case of a new piece of computer equipment, the law of confidence is all important in the early stages as it is being developed and evaluated. Then, as specifications and drawings are produced, the law of copyright comes into play and gives parallel protection. When a patent is granted in respect of the equipment, the law of confidence drops from the scene to be replaced by patent law and, possibly, trade mark law if a registered mark is to be used with the equipment.

This parallel and overlapping protection is most relevant to the computer industry. For example, imagine that a new computer has been designed. It is to be sold with and includes software which is 'hard-wired' (firmware) resident on integrated circuits inside the computer, in addition to software on magnetic disk. The computer has a new type of keyboard and an attractive design embossed on the monitor case which also carries the manufacturer's stylized name. The following rights may be relevant to this computer system:

- *Patent* Being new, the computer may incorporate some new and patentable inventions

71

- *Copyright* The software on disk and the programs stored on the integrated circuits (firmware) and all accompanying documentation are protected under copyright law
- *Semiconductor regulations* The topography of the integrated circuits containing the firmware
- *Trade marks* The stylized name may be registered as a trade mark
- *Registered design* The embossed pattern may be a registered design
- *Design right* The new type of keyboard may fall within the scope of the new design right

Key aspects to be remembered with respect to intellectual property rights are the importance of confidence, especially concerning employees and potential business partners, the usefulness of keeping a documented record of the development of an idea or invention so that its origin can be verified and the value, sometimes unexpected, of making drawings. Finally, although the legal enforcement of intellectual property rights is an expensive business, delay or dalliance can be disastrous and the possibility of obtaining some legal remedies, such as interlocutory injunctions may be prejudiced by delay. There follows a list of practical suggestions concerning ways in which the protection of intellectual property rights can be enhanced.

PRACTICAL SUGGESTIONS

Copyright

1. Those writing and developing computer software should distribute the computer programs in object code form only. They should also consider embedding the names of programmers or the company name within the program code; this can be extremely useful evidentially if a software pirate denies copying. Software, as it is written and developed, can be deposited with an independent person (for example, a bank manager or solicitor) who can verify important dates such as when the software was first written and when it was modified. Contractual arrangements should be made with respect to freelance workers and the ownership of the copyright in anything they produce.
2. Users of software should confirm that they may make back-up copies of any programs they have acquired. If back-up copies are permitted under any licence agreement, the number of back-up copies made should not exceed that agreed. Licensees of software should not assign or transfer their rights if the licence agreement prohibits this. If the agreement allows assignment conditional upon certain matters being complied with, it is essential to make sure that these conditions are met. Software users should operate secure and efficient housekeeping systems to reduce the danger of unauthorized copies being made of programs.
3. Software developers and users of software should clarify any doubts

concerning the ownership of any output produced by the use of the computer system in question.

Confidence

4. An air of confidence must be maintained during negotiations between those with new ideas for software, computer systems, etc. and potential manufacturers, investors and the like.
5. Confidence can be reinforced by contractual provision in respect of employees and freelance workers.
6. It is essential that any ideas and development work concerning a possible future patent application are kept absolutely secret and confidential.

Patent

7. The use of an experienced patent agent is highly recommended if a patent application is being considered.
8. Although a patent is a very powerful form of intellectual property, it is worth considering whether the invention involved can be kept secret indefinitely as an alternative to seeking a patent.
9. It may now be easier to obtain a patent for an invention which includes a computer program despite the apparent exception of computer programs from the scope of patent law. It needs to be borne in mind that the computer program will be protected by copyright law regardless of the patent situation.

Trade marks and passing-off

10. Distinctive names or marks are very powerful marketing devices. Those manufacturing or marketing computer software or hardware are advised to register a distinctive name or mark as a trade mark, and not to rely on the law of passing-off which requires a reputation to have been established. Computer bureaux can now also register a service mark.

Design law

11. Although this is a complex area of the law and subject to much speculation, as regards the various overlaps between artistic, aesthetic and functional designs, if a design has been made which has some degree of eye-appeal, an application for registration should be made.
12. Manufacturers and distributors of spare parts for computer equipment should familiarize themselves with the 'must-fit' and 'must-match' exceptions and their scope. *See* pages 62–3, *supra*.

Part II
Computer contracts

Contracts for the acquisition and use of computer hardware and software are dealt with in this part. Many such contracts are not sale contracts as such but are licence agreements; this is particularly so with respect to computer software where the owner of the rights subsisting in the software grants licences to customers, giving them permission to use the software in return for a licence fee.

Following the introductory chapter, Chapter 12, the fundamentals of the law of contract are discussed and related to computer technology. Then, in subsequent chapters, particular types of computer contracts are described, i.e.: contracts for the writing of computer software; 'off-the-shelf' software licences; agreements between software authors and publishers and, finally, hardware contracts. Where appropriate, other areas of law are discussed such as the law of tort and consumer protection law. Chapter 18 contains a checklist of terms normally to be found in contracts concerning computer hardware and software.

Chapter 12
Introduction to computer contracts

Contracts for the acquisition of computer equipment and software present special problems, many of which flow from the unique nature of computer technology. For example, we cannot see or touch a computer program running in a computer, all we can do is experience its effects through a peripheral device such as a monitor or a printer. It may be possible to read a listing of a computer program and perhaps make some sense of it but, certainly to many people who have to use computer programs, they take on a quasi-mystical nature as they are, after all, intangible. It is the difficulty in coming to terms with the nature, effects and implications of computer equipment and software that is a direct cause of many of the contractual problems associated with computers.

The case of *Brownton Ltd.* v *Edward Moore Inbucon Ltd.* [1985] provides an example of the financial implications of misunderstandings between the parties to a contract involving computer systems. A firm of commodity brokers sought advice from a computer consultant on the installation of a computer system. The consultant recommended a particular system which was installed in 1978. Unfortunately, the system never worked properly, was quite inadequate for the brokers' needs and was eventually scrapped. The consultant had charged over £66,000 for his work and the computer system had cost in the region of £75,000. The brokers claimed damages, for breach of contract, of over £250,000 based on the wasted expense and the difference in price between the system obtained and a new system that would be capable of doing the work. Later, the brokers submitted better particulars and claimed that an alternative computer system capable of carrying out the work would cost in excess of £1,100,000. Eventually, a settlement of around £300,000 was reached.

A fictitious example can further illustrate the difficulties. A company wants to install a computer system in one of its departments which has previously had to use slow, laborious (but reliable) manual methods. The initial decision to do this is probably based on some vague notion that a computer system will increase efficiency, or perhaps because all its competitors have installed computer systems. The company may already have a mainframe computer with a data processing department and the data processing manager might suggest that some potentially suitable software packages be evaluated and that obtaining a ready-made package should be considerably less expensive than writing one from scratch. The first problem is to decide how the available packages should be evaluated and by whom. The people in the company who will have to run the system, the manager or director in whose department the system will be installed ought to be involved in the selection process, but these people are unlikely to have much knowledge of computers and computer software although they may be familiar with word processing and spreadsheet systems running on micro-computers.

The data processing manager and other computer professionals, either within the company or brought in from outside as consultants, will have an important contribution to make to the decision. But, although they will have an intimate knowledge of computers, they will probably not have a deep knowledge of the particular application of the suggested software. Their priorities will differ. The computer people will want to know how the proposed software will fit in with their portfolio of software, whether it will require additional computer equipment, how well it will be maintained, how portable it is and so on. Then a lack of communication and understanding may occur between the computer professionals, the legal advisers, the ultimate users and the supplier of the software resulting in the purchase of a system which is cumbersome, does not provide all the information the users now realize they would have liked and which runs far too slowly to be of any practical use. The software company which supplied the package is not unsympathetic but claims that it was just not given clear and sufficient guidance as to what was expected of the software. The software company may even suggest that the problems will be overcome if a new mainframe computer is obtained, at a cost of £500,000, solely for running the new software. An allegation that the problem lies with the client's own computer installation might be difficult to refute.

It is at this stage that the contract is carefully examined, perhaps for the first time, and the company obtaining the software realizes, too late, that as far as it is concerned, the contract is little more than worthless and does not provide adequately for the situation. There may follow a refusal to make the final payments and the ensuing legal struggle is predictable. Data processing personnel and independent computer consultants must educate department heads and legal advisers as to the implications and dangers involved in acquiring computer equipment and software. Departmental heads and legal advisers, for their part, must be prepared to ask questions of their computer advisers and, even more importantly, to listen to the answers.

The point of the above story is to demonstrate the importance of the parties knowing precisely what is to be expected in terms of performance and the standards required. The role that the equipment or software is intended to fulfil must be clearly identified and quantified, a comprehensive and precise specification must be drawn up. The lack of or defects in the specification are probably at the heart of most disputes resulting from the acquisition of computer equipment and software.

The importance of choosing the most appropriate hardware and software should not be underestimated and, as a corollary, a contract which provides a reasonable and fair machinery for identifying responsibilities and resolving disputes needs to be settled. A mistake in the choice of equipment or software coupled with a poor contract can be disastrous for a purchasing company. The problems are not all one-sided, however, as it may be that a supplier of equipment or software has to fall back on contractual remedies. If the acquiring company refuses to provide, or is incapable of providing clear instructions, if it refuses to accept and/or pay for the equipment or software, if it tampers with the programs, misuses them and allows employees to copy them freely, the supplier will need to take action. The company making the acquisition will need to decide: how the contract can protect it if the equipment or software fails to perform as it should; about maintenance and training; what to do if the software or hardware infringes a third party's copyright or patent.

In the next chapter, the basic legal consequences of computer contracts will be described. The nature of the contract, contractual and tortious liabilities and the use of exclusion clauses will be considered. Then, individual terms which may be found in various types of computer contracts will be discussed in subsequent chapters with a view to avoiding the disasters.

Chapter 13
Fundamentals of computer contracts

NATURE OF THE CONTRACT

Software

A start will be made by looking at computer software, which is far from easy to classify both in contractual terms and in terms of the applicability of various statutory controls over contracts. The most common method of acquiring computer software is by way of a licence which is granted by the software publisher to the person or company acquiring the software, giving permission to use the software in return for the licence fee, i.e., the 'price'. The licence may be for a fixed, perhaps renewable, period of time or there may be no mention of duration, in which case it can be assumed that the licence will last as long as the software is subject to copyright protection. The software publisher will prefer to grant a licence because he will want to retain the copyright in the software and be free to grant licences to others. The licence may be exclusive which means that the software publisher cannot grant licences to others in respect of the software; but, more usually, the licence will be non-exclusive so that the software publisher will be free to grant licences to anyone else he wishes to. An exclusive licence will be appropriate between an independent software writer and a software publisher who undertakes to market the programs on behalf of the writer; this type of arrangement and its contractual implications will be examined in a later chapter.

The special nature of computer software, and the fact that software is usually acquired by means of a licence, has several legal implications. To begin with, the Sale of Goods Act 1979 does not apply to computer software. This Act is very important in the commercial world; in addition to being, in general, a very comprehensive regulator of contracts of sale it implies important terms into contracts such as requirements that the goods must match their description, be of merchantable quality, be fit for their purpose and that the seller has the right to sell the goods. But, 'goods' are defined by section 61(1) of the Act as including:

all personal chattels other than things in action and money.

It seems unlikely, even if the copyright is transferred with the computer programs, that an intangible computer program resident on a magnetic disk or in a computer chip is a personal chattel, because copyright is a 'thing in action' like company shares or a money order, to be contrasted with the more tangible 'things in possession' such as motor cars or computers. Copyright is thus excluded from the definition of goods. The result of this is that the terms contained in the Sale of Goods Act which are implied into a contract for the sale of goods will not apply to a computer software contract. This is unfortunate as these implied terms are a very useful weapon for the buyer and, in the case of consumer sales, the implied terms cannot be excluded or modified at all. In non-consumer sales the implied terms can only be so excluded or modified if the terms purporting to do this are reasonable in accordance with the Unfair Contract Terms Act 1977 sections 5–7.

Beside the programs the software package will usually include magnetic disks on which the programs are stored and assorted documentation and the Sale of Goods Act might apply to these ancillary items. One way of interpreting the agreement, in the absence of anything to the contrary, might be that the programs themselves are subject to a licence agreement but the manuals, disks etc. are subject to a collateral sale of goods contract. Bearing in mind, however, that the most important items will be the actual programs, the law is not going to do much to help fill in the gaps in a contract or give some basic protection to the person acquiring the software. It is doubly important therefore that the contract includes terms concerning the quality of the software.

The Supply of Goods and Services Act 1982 implies terms into contracts under which the property (ownership) in goods passes, and also into contracts for the hire of goods and contracts for services. Some of the terms implied are similar to those implied by the Sale of Goods Act. Examples of contracts governed by the Supply of Goods and Services Act are hybrid contracts, i.e., those which involve part services and part goods such as a contract for the painting of a portrait. In this particular instance the service is the actual act of painting, the goods are the canvas and frame. The Act also governs a contract purely for services, such as a contract for a haircut. Has the Sale of Goods and Services Act any relevance for computer software contracts? As far as 'goods' are concerned, the situation is the same as with a sale of goods contract because the definition of goods excludes things in action, of which copyright is an example. The 1982 Act may be relevant, however, if an independent computer firm or a programmer is engaged to write a computer program as this should come within the meaning of 'service'. The draftsmen of the Supply of Goods and Services Act elected not to attempt to define 'service', probably in deference to the very wide variety of services offered both to consumers and to businesses. So, there is good reason to believe that a contract for writing a computer program will fall within that part of the Act dealing with the supply of services, i.e., sections 12 to 16. The fact that goods such as manuals and floppy disks may also be transferred does not prevent the contract from being a contract for the supply of services (section 12(3)).

Expert systems and other types of software which provide advice could, arguably, be construed as supplying a service and thus fall within the ambit of the Supply of Goods and Services Act 1982. If this view is taken by the courts, bearing in mind that 'service' is not defined in the Act, it will result in the appropriate terms from the Act being implied into a contract for the supply of such computer software systems. The dealer who supplies an expert system may be deemed to be supplying a service (i.e., providing the advice available from the system) even though others, such as the experts who provided the knowledge used in the system and the makers of the system, are responsible (in a non-legal sense) for how the system operates. This is because by section 12(1) of the Supply of Goods and Services Act 1982, a 'contract for the supply of a service' means:

> . . . a contract under which a person ('the supplier') agrees to carry out a service.

The implied terms contained in the Supply of Goods and Services Act 1982 are only applicable in the context of a contract and whilst the dealer supplying the expert system is a party to the contract with the customer, the experts and the maker of the expert system are not. The latter two may, however, be liable under the law of negligence if the system is defective and causes loss.

The only question remaining is whether the dealer has agreed to 'carry out a service'. By supplying expert systems, the dealer has enabled the advice-giving service to be performed and in some respects it is similar to the position where a supplier sub-contracts all or part of the work. The customer relies on the dealer to provide a suitable and effective system and, consequently, there is a duty on the dealer to select and recommend a suitable system (*see Stewart v Reavell's Garage* [1952], discussed in Chapter 14). Therefore, dealers marketing expert systems should satisfy themselves as to the veracity and reliability of these systems and their suitability for particular customers. Dealers may also wish to consider including appropriate and reasonable exemption clauses in their supply contracts with respect to advice-giving computer systems.

What are the terms implied by the Supply of Goods and Services Act? Section 13 implies a term that the supplier, if acting in the course of business, will carry out the service with reasonable care and skill. This restates the previous position at common law, that a person who holds himself out as being prepared to carry out a service is expected to exercise a level of skill that could be expected of a reasonably competent member of the relevant trade. Therefore, if a firm engaged to write a computer program fails to measure up to the standards that would normally be expected from able computer programmers and the program turns out to be sub-standard then, prima facie, the firm will be liable in contract. It does not matter that the firm's employees tried their best, the question is: does the program meet this objective standard?

Another term implied by the Supply of Goods and Services Act 1982 concerns the time for performance. Again, this only applies to suppliers acting in the course of business. Section 14 states that, in the absence of an agreed time for performance or an agreed formula to determine the time for performance, the supplier will carry out the service in a reasonable time. The Act also says that what is reasonable is a question of fact; that is, it depends on the facts of the case. The case of *Charnock* v *Liverpool Corporation* [1968], gives an example of an unreasonable time. The defendant garage was liable in damages because it took eight weeks to repair a motor vehicle when a normally competent garage would have taken about five weeks. A contract for the writing of computer programs should have detailed provisions about completion times and all section 14 does is to provide a net to catch those instances where there has been an oversight. What is a reasonable time will depend on the nature of the programs and their complexity, taking into account the time required for testing and acceptance.

Section 15 of the Act states that, unless the contract fixes the payment or a method of calculating payment, the supplier will be paid a reasonable amount. Usually, the contract will mention the fee, but this provision might be useful if the supplier takes on additional work at the request of the other party and no mention is made at the time of agreement of the charge for this extra work. It means that the supplier cannot, much as he might like to, charge an unreasonably high price.

Hardware

As far as computer equipment (hardware) is concerned, this may be purchased outright or hired. If purchased, then the Sale of Goods Act 1979 will apply and the usual terms involving merchantable quality, fitness for purpose, etc. will be implied into the contract, subject to any valid exclusion clauses. If the supplier goes beyond the mere supply of the equipment and carries out some work such as installing the equipment, the Supply of Goods and Services Act 1982 will apply, as discussed above. If the contract is for the hire of the equipment, then the Supply of Goods and Services Act will apply, whether or not installation or other services are provided by the supplier. An agreement which is described as a lease or a rental is essentially a contract of hire and a hire agreement is one under which the possession of the goods passes to the other party but the property in the goods (the ownership) remains with the supplier. 'Hire' does not include hire purchase agreements which are covered by the Supply of Goods (Implied Terms) Act 1973 which implies similar terms into the contract as does the Sale of Goods Act 1979. The relevant provisions in the Supply of Goods and Services Act 1982 regarding hire agreements include implied terms about the right of the supplier to transfer possession of the goods, correspondence of the goods with their description and implied terms about quality and fitness for purpose. These terms are mostly very similar to the equivalent ones in the Sale of Goods Act.

NEGLIGENCE

Negligence is part of an area of law known as tort. It imposes legal liabilities on a person who has acted carelessly. Under certain circumstances a person will be liable to another for failing to exercise a required duty of care. In the case of consumer goods, such as a table lamp, if the negligence of the manufacturer causes them to be defective, then the person injured as a result will be entitled to damages. A claim in negligence does not depend on the presence of a contract, so if the person injured is someone other than the buyer, then that person can still sue. The buyer should be able to sue on the basis of breach of contract if the item is defective and fails to comply with implied terms such as those concerning merchantable quality and fitness for purpose.

To be able to sue in negligence, three essential ingredients must be present; they are:
a) a duty of care owed to the injured party;
b) a breach of that duty of care;
c) consequential loss, that is loss which is a direct and natural result of the breach of duty of care.

The landmark case on negligence is *Donoghue* v *Stevenson* [1932], in which the plaintiff had been bought a bottle of ginger beer by a friend in a café. The bottle was made of opaque glass so that the contents could not be seen. The café owner poured part of the contents into a glass which the plaintiff drank. The plaintiff's friend then poured out the rest of the contents and a decomposed snail flowed out of the bottle. The plaintiff suffered shock and severe gastro-enteritis as a result of the revolting sight and the fact that she had already swallowed some of the ginger beer. The plaintiff could not sue in contract because she was not a party to the contract; it had been her friend who had bought the drink. But, nevertheless, the House of Lords held that a manufacturer who sold food or medicine or the like in containers of a nature that the distributor or ultimate purchasers or consumers could not discover the defect by inspection is under a legal duty to the ultimate purchaser or consumer to take reasonable care that the article is free from defect likely to cause injury to health. This duty of care is owed to any person who might be contemplated to be injured by the act or omission of the manufacturer. Negligence can be thought of as an early form of product liability (*see post*) and has developed over the years to its present wide scope, although this is tempered by some extent by the growth of insurance.

What is the significance of the tort of negligence as far as computers and software are concerned? Although it is unlikely that decomposing snails will be found within the workings of computers, it is possible to come across computer 'bugs'; and there may still be some further nasty surprises. At first sight it may seem unlikely that computers and computer software could kill or cause serious injury, but negligent liability does not stop at personal injury but extends to damage to property in addition. Computer equipment runs on electricity so there is always the danger of electrical shock and, if this results from negligence, then there is a strong possibility of an action in negligence. But, what if a large passenger aircraft has to be fuelled ready for flight. A computer program is used to calculate the amount of fuel required; this is based on information such as the number of passengers, the weight of baggage, the flight distance and prevailing winds, etc. Then, because of a hitherto undiscovered 'bug' in the computer program, less fuel is loaded than required, with the result that the aircraft runs out of fuel over mid-Atlantic. It is possible that the company writing the computer program was negligent in its testing of the program. The total size of the claims resulting from such an incident might quite well be enormous, even though the computer program itself may have only cost a few hundred pounds.

The fact that negligence lies without the need for a contract is important both for computer program writers and manufacturers of computer equipment. If a program is licensed by a publisher, the program author could be liable in negligence even though he is not a party to the licence agreement. In the case of computer hardware, a person suffering loss or injury as a result of the negligence of the manufacturer will have a claim in negligence against the manufacturer regardless of the fact that the equipment was bought from a dealer.

There are limitations, however, to the scope of the law of negligence and for a claim in negligence to succeed, certain ingredients (*see* p. 84, *ante*) must be present. A person writing a computer program, or a company manufacturing computer equipment will not necessarily be potentially liable to the world at large in negligence; they will be liable, however, to those whom they could contemplate being adversely affected by any negligent act or omission of theirs. A further limiting factor that works against a plaintiff is that it is he who bears the burden of proof; he has to show that the defendant was negligent and this is not always easy to do. There may be an exception if the event causing the injury or damage could only be reasonably explained by assuming there had been negligence. This is known to lawyers as '*res ipsa loquitur*', i.e., 'the thing speaks for itself'. If you are hit on the head by a pot of paint whilst walking under a ladder you would not be asked to show the precise act of negligence that caused the paint to fall; it goes without saying that someone had been negligent. This is the exception, however, and normally the plaintiff must show the negligent act or omission.

Even if negligence is proved, the amount of damages awarded may be reduced if the plaintiff has contributed in a causal sense to the negligence. If a computer has been badly made and is an electrical hazard then, if the person who has been electrocuted had tampered with the machine, the damages awarded may be reduced in proportion to the extent of his contribution to the accident. Fortunately, death or personal injury resulting from the use of a computer is a rare occurrence, but other forms of loss or damage might be more common, and, e.g., in a business context where a computer may be used to assist with decision-making, there is a strong probability that a financial loss will be blamed on the computer. However, an action based solely on economic loss is unlikely to succeed.

PRODUCT LIABILITY

Related to negligence are the product liability provisions contained in the Consumer Protection Act 1987. Under the Act, an ultimate consumer can claim against the producer of a defective product regardless of the lack of a contractual relationship between the consumer and the producer and without having to show the basic requirements for an action in tort. Part I of the Act deals with product liability and stems from the Council of European Communities Directive on Product Liability, 1985 (85/375/EEC). A 'product' is defined by the Act as being any goods including electricity and includes a product comprised in another product whether a component part or a raw material. A computer would therefore come within the meaning of product but computer software will be outside the scope of this part of the Act.

The producer of a defective product will be liable for damage resulting wholly or partly from that defect. Distributors and retailers selling 'own brand' goods can be liable if they can be said to be holding themselves out to be the producer. If a person imports a product, in the course of business, into a country belonging to the European Community from outside the Community in order to supply the product to another, then that importer will be regarded as the producer for the purposes of determining liability by section 2 of the Act. This might have implications for the many companies which import computers made outside the European Community especially the 'clone' importers who affix their own name to the equipment. If one of these machines is defective and someone is injured as a result, then the importer/distributor will be liable under the Act, apart from any remedies available against him under contract. The Consumer Protection Act also makes a supplier liable if he fails to identify the producer within a reasonable time, having been asked to do so by the claimant.

A defect is defined by reference to the expectation of safety in the product and this relates to property damage as well as death and personal injury. A computer with an exposed unearthed metal chassis would fall short of the expectation of safety. There are certain defences available, an important one of which is the 'state of the art' defence. This means that the defect is judged in the light of the scientific and technical knowledge at the time the product was under the control of the person seeking to rely on the defence. This particular defence was optional in the EEC Product Liability Directive but has been adopted in the United Kingdom; it seems sensible because standards of safety change over time and what might seem perfectly acceptable now might be considered grossly unsafe in a few years time. The development of the motor car is an excellent example of these shifting standards and expectations.

Computers, especially micro-computers and terminals with monitors, have been claimed to be harmful to the health of the operator because of radioactive emissions although at the present time there does not appear to be any conclusive proof that a real danger to health exists. If, however, a definite association were to be found between the occurrence of skin cancers or miscarriages and the continued use of computer monitors, then computer manufacturers and importers who continued to make or sell equipment giving off such dangerous emissions would be liable under the Act. There may also be implications under the Health and Safety at Work etc. Act 1974 if an employer persists in requiring his staff to use such machines. The producers would have to consider fitting some device such as an ionization screen to absorb the rays, and in the absence of a technological way of overcoming the problem, they might be forced to withdraw the product until such time as a solution could be found. The product liability provisions contained in the Consumer Protection Act came into force in 1988 and although it is a little early to be certain, the implications and effects of these provisions could be enormous for all manufacturers including those making computer equipment. Thus, if a computer accessory manufacturer makes a device improving the safety of computers, this might imply that computers not fitted with such devices fall short of the expectation of safety. At the very least, a manufacturer should be constantly watching for such developments in the industry which might shift the threshold of the expectation of safety.

By section 5 of the 1987 Act, the liability covered by Part I of the Act extends to:

a) death or personal injury,

b) damage to or destruction of any item of property (including land) other than the defective product itself (there is a lower threshold of £275 before a claim can be made) provided that the property:

    i) is the type normally intended for private use and consumption, and

    ii) it is used mainly for the private use or consumption of the person claiming.

Therefore, in dealings between businesses, the product liability part of the Act will only apply to defective products causing death or personal injury. As far as property damage is concerned, the provisions are really aimed at the consumer market, so, if you buy a home computer as a Christmas present for your uncle and, because of a fault it catches fire and causes £1,500 of damage to his house, then your uncle will have a claim under the 1987 Act against the manufacturer of the computer for the damage to the house and furniture. Personally, you may have a separate claim against the retail outlet because the computer was not of merchantable quality under the Sale of Goods Act 1979.

BREACH OF CONTRACT

If a party to a contract breaks one or more of its terms, the remedy depends on the status of the particular term or terms which have been broken. The aggrieved party may want to repudiate (cancel) the contract and recover any money he has paid out as well as any other expenses. Alternatively, he might prefer to hold the other party to the contract but would like some compensation for the breach and if the breach concerns a minor term this is usually the better solution. However, the injured party usually does not have a free choice as the law lays down rules determining and limiting the scope of remedies.

Traditionally there are two types of terms in contracts, these are 'conditions' and 'warranties'. The distinction is important because breach of a condition gives the other party the right to repudiate the contract and claim damages. For example, consider a contract to deliver a computer by 'the 1st June at the latest'. Even though the buyer has regularly pressed for delivery, there is still no sign of the machine by the end of August. Undoubtedly, the buyer can treat the failure to deliver as a breach of a condition and he can cancel the contract as time for delivery is usually construed as being a condition; *see Hartley* v *Hyams* [1920]. Additionally, the buyer can claim damages which would be equivalent to the difference in cost of buying another similar computer elsewhere and any other expenses and losses he has been put to as a direct consequence of the breach, with the proviso that he mitigates his losses, that is, he keeps them to a minimum. The buyer may have wanted the computer to expand his business and he will be able to claim the resulting loss in profits, provided the seller knew or should have known of this; that is, it was in the reasonable contemplation of the parties.

On the other hand, a breach of warranty allows the aggrieved party to claim for damages only. The contract is still in force and must be completed by both parties. They must both perform the remainder of their agreed duties under the contract. For example, if a supplier has agreed to deliver a computer system and the contract states that the terminals are to be a deep yellow colour but, instead, he delivers a computer with lemon coloured terminals, this will amount to a breach of warranty unless there is some special reason why the deep yellow colour was specified. The buyer will be entitled to damages only and he will still have to pay the purchase price of the computer, although he may be able to set-off a sum representing the damages. Damages are assessed on the basis of the damage naturally arising from the breach and in the contemplation of the parties. In the example given, the damages would be little more than nominal.

In *Koufos* v *C. Czarnikow Ltd.* [1969], a ship was chartered by sugar merchants to transport a cargo of sugar. The shipowners knew that there was a sugar market at the port of destination but did not know that the merchants wanted to sell the sugar immediately on its arrival. The ship deviated from the agreed voyage and arrived about 10 days late and in the meantime the price of sugar had fallen and the merchants lost over £4,000. It was held that this loss should be recoverable from the shipowners because they should reasonably have contemplated that the delay would have resulted in a loss. The shipowners knew there was a commodity market at the destination and that prices would be liable to fluctuate so that any delay could lead to a diminution of the value of the cargo. Unfortunately this does not appear to work the other way; the shipowners would not be entitled to any share in a windfall profit if the market value of the cargo increased dramatically and was sold for much more than if it had arrived on time.

How does the basic principle that damages are based on the losses that were within the contemplation of the parties when the contract was made work in the context of computers? Suppose that you run a computer bureau and carry out ordinary data processing work. You decide to expand the business and buy a more powerful computer to be delivered by a certain date. You tell the supplier that you need the computer to carry out some additional data processing but neglect to inform him that you are negotiating a very lucrative top secret government contract on the basis of having the new computer. If the computer is delivered late, then you would be entitled to damages based on the loss in profits in the normal course of business but you would not be entitled to anything should you lose the government contract. This is simply because the supplier did not know, and could not reasonably be expected to know of this potential contract. A buyer should therefore consider informing a supplier of the uses to which the equipment or programs will be put, especially if they are unusual.

The distinction between conditions and warranties is not always clear. Sometimes a contractual term lies in a grey area between the two. If the term is broken, then it will be classified in the light of the facts surrounding the breach and it will depend on the facts as to whether the breach goes to the root of the contract. If it does, then the term will be effectively promoted to the rank of condition with all that entails, otherwise it will be classed as a warranty. These intermediate terms are called 'innominate' terms and their nature is determined retrospectively, after a breach. The case which paved the way for this approach was *Hong Kong Fir Shipping Co. Ltd.* v *Kawasaki Kisen Kaisha* [1962], in which it was held that a term implied in a hire contract for a ship that it must be seaworthy was such an innominate term. The nature of the breach determined the nature of the contractual term. For example, if the ship had a 5 degree list and was badly leaking, it would be totally unseaworthy and this would be a breach of a condition enabling the hirer to repudiate the contract. However, if the breach concerned some trifling defect, perhaps a mere technicality, which could be put right very quickly and easily, the term would be classed as a warranty.

For example, if a word-processing program is acquired which is claimed by the supplier to be a 'professional package' and it does not have a built-in thesaurus, this might be considered a breach of warranty. It cannot be truly said that the breach goes to the root of the contract if the program has all the other usual features normally found in powerful word processing systems. However, if the package does not include features such as right-justification and block editing facilities this would be more serious and could make the system virtually useless in a business environment. Such a breach would go to the root of the contract and would be a breach of a condition, giving the person acquiring the program the right to cancel the contract and recover the cost of the system plus any direct losses.

This way of looking at terms and not deciding their status until there has been a breach is very useful as it gives a welcome degree of flexibility to contracts, although it could be criticized for introducing uncertainty. There may be some terms however which are obviously conditions, e.g., if the contract is for the delivery of a particular make of computer, and the seller attempts to deliver a different make altogether, this would clearly be a breach of condition.

What sort of terms in computer contracts could be described as innominate terms? Suppose that a contract is made for the provision of a network to link individual computers together, a term in the contract stating that the network will support at least 16 micro-computers. If there is then serious degradation of performance when 15 or more machines are in use but otherwise the network is fine, this might be regarded as a breach of warranty. On the other hand, if it turns out that the network fails when more than 7 machines are in use, the term would be regarded as a condition.

Sometimes a term can start as a condition, become a warranty and then revert to a condition. In *Rickards* v *Oppenheim* [1950], the defendant wanted a body built on his Rolls-Royce chassis and he agreed that the plaintiffs (from whom he had purchased the chassis) could use a sub-contractor to do this specialised work which should have been completed in March 1948. The work was not complete by that time, and although time for delivery is usually a condition, the defendant did not cancel the contract as he was entitled to do, but continued to press for delivery, thereby waiving his right to cancel. In the end the defendant gave an ultimatum. He said that the car must be ready by 25th July 1948 or he would refuse to take delivery after that date. The car was not ready by that date, so the defendant bought another car elsewhere and claimed back the price he had paid for the chassis. It was held that when time for delivery is of the essence of a contract for the sale of goods (that is, a condition) and after the stipulated time has elapsed the buyer waives his right to cancel by pressing for delivery, converting the term into a warranty, he may later give notice setting a reasonable deadline, once again making the time for delivery a condition of the contract.

It is common to find provisions for late delivery and late payment included in contracts. The contract might state that the supplier will pay £150 per week if he delivers late, or that the buyer will pay interest at 0.75% above the current bank base rate, should he be late in making payment. Pre-determined damages, known as liquidated damages, are frequently found in contracts. 'Liquidated' simply means that the damages or the method of calculating them are fixed and agreed. Liquidated damages are to be distinguished from a penalty. Liquidated damages are a genuine pre-estimate of the loss resulting from the breach, whereas a penalty, which might be out of all proportion to the loss suffered, will rarely be enforced by the courts. The stipulation of liquidated damages for breach of a particular term contradicts the possibility of that term being a condition; therefore, terms backed by liquidated damages will usually not be regarded as conditions, unless the scale of the breach is considerable.

In practice, many terms will be innominate terms, in which case it will only be possible to determine whether breach of the term allows a party to repudiate the contract in the light of the actual facts of the breach. Provisions concerning the performance of a computer system, how fast the programs work in practice, the degree of compatibility with other equipment are likely to be innominate terms. Provisions which will probably be conditions from the beginning deal with aspects such as the time for delivery and the description of the actual computer concerned. Time for payment is usually treated as being a warranty unless the contract states otherwise or the circumstances suggest a different interpretation; see for example, section 10(1) of the Sale of Goods Act 1979.

MISREPRESENTATION

If you are negotiating with a salesman with a view to acquiring computer software, he may make statements regarding the software and its performance. It is not unknown for a salesman to describe the product in glowing terms and you would expect him to highlight the best features. Sometimes, he can go too far; he may be anxious to make a sale and make statements which are simply untrue in an effort to try to induce you to buy the product. Some statements are so wild that no one is expected to take them seriously; these are sometimes referred to as salesman's 'puff'. Examples abound in the secondhand motor trade; for example, an ageing car may be described as being 'immaculate'. Such statements are not to be taken seriously and the courts would not support a case brought on them. Less wild statements, however, if untrue, may give rise to remedies. The standing of the statement needs initially to be determined and it may be elevated to the rank of contractual term if the courts consider on the facts that this was the intention of the parties. If this happens then normal contractual remedies are available to the aggrieved party if the statement turns out to be untrue.

If the statement does not become incorporated into the contract it is said to be a representation; something said in the course of the negotiations leading up to the contract itself. It may well induce the other party to conclude the contract, in which case a remedy may be available on the basis of misrepresentation if the statement turns out to be untrue. Obviously, if the party to whom the representation is made knows that the statement is untrue he will not have any remedy. He has entered into the contract with eyes open to the true facts; the statement itself will not have influenced him.

There are three forms of misrepresentation, i.e., fraudulent, negligent and innocent. If the representation has been made fraudulently or recklessly (not caring whether or not it is true), then at common law the remedy of rescission is available (setting the contract aside as if it had never been made at all), together with a right to recover any money laid out. Fraud may be difficult to prove, the person making the statement may simply say that he honestly believed, at the time he made it, that it was true. The Misrepresentation Act 1967, as amended by the Unfair Contract Terms Act 1977, made the situation more satisfactory. Rescission is the standard remedy for misrepresentation but this may cause hardship; therefore, in the case of negligent or innocent misrepresentation, a court may award damages in lieu of rescission by section 2 of the Misrepresentation Act. This is important because rescission is an equitable remedy and as such will only be ordered by the courts if the aggrieved party has acted promptly. Formerly if the aggrieved party had already accepted the goods; the very fact of acceptance would mean that rescission would not be available. In a fictitious example a company buys a computer. It is important that this computer is directly compatible with its existing equipment and the supplier confirms in good faith, before the contract is made, that the computer is compatible although the contract itself is silent on the matter. Some weeks after accepting delivery and paying for the computer, it is found that, although the computer works well in every other respect, it is not compatible with the company's other machines and cannot reasonably be made so. Before the 1967 Act, the company acquiring the computer would have had no remedy for this innocent misrepresentation as it would be too late to have the contract set aside. Now the courts would be likely to award damages instead which might be considerable in this example. The better approach would have been for the company to insist that a term was inserted into the contract to the effect that the computer to be acquired must be compatible with the existing equipment.

EXEMPTION CLAUSES

An exemption clause is one which excludes or restricts the liability of a party who is in breach of contract. Exemption clauses can be sub-divided into exclusion clauses and limitation clauses. An exclusion clause gives the party relying on it total exemption for the breach whereas a limitation clause limits liability to a specified amount. An example of an exclusion clause is where a supplier totally excludes his liability under the contract for late delivery if this is caused by circumstances beyond his control such as industrial action. An example of a limitation clause is where a supplier of computer software limits his liability for faulty software to the licence fee he has received for that software.

When people draft contracts they are usually keen to limit or exclude their liabilities and yet wish to ensure that the other party is absolutely bound to perform his part of the contract. Such one-sided contracts were fairly common in the past (they are by no means extinct now) particularly in circumstances where there was an inequality of bargaining power. An ordinary individual buying a product from a supplier who had a virtual monopoly in the product had little choice but to accept the terms imposed on him or manage without the product. A golden principle in contract was 'freedom of contract', meaning that the parties should be free to agree whatever terms they wished and this is acceptable where two powerful companies are negotiating a contract in a free market. Contractually weaker persons, such as consumers, however, suffered in such a situation. However, over the years, Parliament and the courts have intervened to mitigate the harshness of the situation and certain terms are now implied into sale of goods and similar contracts, whilst exclusion clauses have been disapproved of by the courts especially if such clauses are demonstrably unfair.

The courts developed techniques to limit the effects of exclusion clauses, including the interpretation of an ambiguous clause to the disadvantage of the party seeking to rely on it. For example, in *Andrews Brothers (Bournemouth) Ltd.* v *Singer & Co. Ltd.* [1934], the plaintiff ordered a new Singer car from the defendants. When the car was delivered it was found to have done some 550 miles. The defendants sought to rely on an exclusion clause which stated that liability for terms implied by statute was excluded; one of these terms was that goods must comply with their description. The contract, however, repeatedly described the car as a 'new Singer car'. It was held that because the car was referred to in the contract as a new car, this was an *express term* and since the exclusion clause sought to exclude liability for *implied terms* only, the defendants were liable. The exclusion clause was of no effect for this breach of an express term. The plaintiff was awarded £50 in damages.

Exemption clauses are also controlled by statute. The Unfair Contract Terms Act 1977 limits the extent to which liability can be excluded or limited for breach of contract, or for negligence, or under the terms implied by the Sale of Goods Act 1979 and other legislation containing similar provisions, such as the Supply of Goods and Services Act 1982. Sections 2–4 of the Unfair Contract Terms Act apply to contractual terms or notices which attempt to exclude or restrict liability for negligence and breach of contract. For example, business liability for death and personal injury resulting from negligence cannot be excluded or limited at all by section 2(1) and, in the case of other loss or damage, liability can only be excluded or restricted where the term or notice purporting to do this satisfies a test of reasonableness: section 2(2). Section 3 of the Act prevents exclusion or limitation of liability arising from a breach of contract where the injured party deals as a consumer, or on the other's written standard terms of contract. There are also other provisions to prevent a party claiming he is entitled to render a contractual performance substantially different from that which was reasonably expected from him, or rendering no performance at all, of the whole or part of the contract.

By Schedule 1, section 1(c) of the Act, the provisions contained in sections 2 to 4 do not extend to any contract:

> so far as it relates to the creation or transfer of any right or interest in any patent, trade mark, copyright, . . . or other intellectual property.

A software licence does not grant an interest in the copyright but gives *permission* to use the software. It is debatable whether this permission can properly be described as a 'right or interest' in the copyright; if it can be so described then sections 2–4 of the Unfair Contract Terms Act 1977 do not apply to software contracts and this is the most likely interpretation. Other important provisions of the Unfair Contract Terms Act relate to the implied terms under the Sale of Goods Act and similar legislation; these will apply to computer hardware but will be largely irrelevant as far as computer software is concerned because computer software does not come within the definition of goods. Therefore, the Unfair Contract Terms Act is helpful as far as contracts for hardware are concerned but has little relevance for software contracts. The following paragraphs consider the problem of exclusion clauses in software contracts.

Before the Unfair Contract Terms Act 1977 came into force, the courts developed, somewhat erratically, the doctrine of 'fundamental breach' as a way of curbing the worst excesses of exclusion clauses. *Pinnock Bros.* v *Lewis & Peat Ltd.* [1923], concerned a contract for the purchase of copra cake. When delivered, it was discovered to be poisonous because it had been contaminated with castor oil. It was held that it was not copra cake at all but a substance quite different from that contracted for and, because of this, the sellers could not rely on an exclusion clause purporting to exempt them from liability. Later, it was said that where there had been a fundamental breach of contract, that is, if one party fails to carry out his part of the bargain at all or attempts to render a performance totally different from that contemplated, then that party could not rely on an exclusion clause (*see Karsales (Harrow) Ltd.* v *Wallis* [1956]). However, recently, the courts have taken a more laissez-faire attitude to exclusion clauses and fundamental breach on the basis that the parties should be free to agree that there should be no liability under the contract even for a fundamental breach, if that was their desire; *see Photo Productions Ltd.* v *Securicor Transport Ltd.* [1980]. This case concerned the law before the implementation of the Unfair Contract Terms Act 1977, but the impact of this Act on exclusion clauses was in the minds of their lordships. Nevertheless, the doctrine of fundamental breach may still have some utility when it comes to controlling exclusion clauses in contracts which do not come within the scope of the Unfair Contract Terms Act.

Section 8 of the Unfair Contract Terms Act provides that a clause in a contract which purports to exclude or restrict liability for misrepresentation will only be effective if it satisfies the requirement of reasonableness. The burden of proof is on the person seeking to rely on the clause. If a computer salesman claims that the computer he is selling will run a particular software package and this claim turns out to be untrue, it will be for the company selling the computer to show that any exemption clause it hopes to rely on passes the test of reasonableness. The test is laid out in section 11 of the Unfair Contract Terms Act 1977 which requires that the term be:

fair and reasonable . . . having regard to the circumstances which were, or ought reasonably to have been, known to or in the contemplation of the parties when the contract was made.

This is a nebulous requirement which gives the courts room to manoeuvre and to take the facts of a particular case into account.

To complete this discussion of exclusion clauses it should be noted that, by section 7 of the Unfair Contract Terms Act 1977, liability for defective products under Part I of the Consumer Protection Act 1987 cannot be excluded or limited by any contract term.

Chapter 14
Contracts for writing software

If an organization requires additional or new computer software, there may be several options open to it. Appropriate software may be available as an 'off-the-shelf' package or the organization may employ its own computer staff who can develop the software. In other circumstances, it may be advantageous to have the software written or adapted by a software house, a firm specializing in particular types of computer software. The following fictitious situation is typical of instances when software will be developed under a contractual agreement.

A company owns a large mainframe computer or a system of networked micro-computers and a new computer software system is required. There may be no suitable package available 'off-the-shelf' or, if there is a such a package, it would need to be modified to run on the particular computer configuration. The latter situation is fairly common and fraught with difficulties. The company has decided against attempting to write the programs or using freelance programmers and analysts and is going to use a specialized software house which has a high degree of expertise in writing programs for the particular application. The company undertaking to write or modify software will be described as the 'software house' in this chapter. It may well be that the software is already available for some computer systems but not yet for the company in the example; however, the software house will be only too pleased to modify the programs accordingly. In this situation it is essential to be especially careful otherwise the software house might conduct experiments and development work at the expense of the company needing the modified software. We will now turn to the terms commonly found in a contract for writing computer software.

DEFINITIONS

The very first clause is likely to deal with a description of the parties to the contract and appropriate definitions relating to the software and the equipment on which the software will be installed. Apart from being a word-saving provision in that the client's full business name can be abbreviated throughout to CLIENT or CUSTOMER, the definitions clause can usefully describe terms such as software and hardware and thus assist with the interpretation and construction of the agreement. Consequently, any expressions defined here should be defined precisely and comprehensively.

LICENCE AGREEMENT

What will the software house give the 'buyer' in return for the price? On the face of it a set of programs and associated documentation is what will be provided, but will the software house really *hand over* the programs? This will be highly unlikely and an important term usually states that the software is being licensed; the contract is, first and foremost, a *licence agreement*. A licence is a permission to do something; in terms of computer software, a licence is a permission to use the software. Without this permission, use of the software would be an infringement of the copyright subsisting in the software. The software house will undoubtedly want to retain the ownership of the intellectual property rights in the programs and the documentation, for its business is selling software and it will want to sell the programs elsewhere. If it is especially important for the company acquiring the software that it is not to be sold elsewhere, it should insist on an *exclusive licence* which is likely to be much more expensive.

Important points to check will include the duration of the licence and its scope (sometimes, the licence will be silent on the matter of duration). Because a licence is a mere permission to do something which would otherwise be unlawful, it does not give any proprietary interest in the software. The implications of this are twofold:

1. The licence should be for a fixed duration or there should be some provisions for termination of the licence. If the licence appears, on the face of it, to be perpetual, this contradicts the nature of a licence and it might even be implied that the agreement is not a licence but an assignment of the rights in the software. However, it is more likely, in the absence of any express reference to duration, that the licence will endure as long as the copyright subsists in the software. The wording of the whole agreement should give a clue as to which interpretation is correct.
2. The licence agreement should state whether the licence can be assigned to a third party. In the absence of any provision covering this aspect, it would appear that the licence is transferable, depending on the circumstances.

The scope of the licence is very important. Is it permissible to run the software on several computers or just one particular computer? If the acquiring company is part of a group of companies; can the programs be used throughout the group or just within the one company? Can the software be transferred to another company? All these questions should be considered and discussed with the software house in the light of the contract and the intended uses to which the software is to be put. The possibility of expanding computing facilities and usage in the future must not be overlooked.

THE CONTRACT PRICE

As the agreement will be almost certainly in the nature of a licence, the sum of money owed should be termed a licence fee. However, this fee is often described as the price and will frequently include other things such as training and tangible items such as disks and documentation. The word 'price' will be used therefore, bearing in mind that this will include a once and for all licence fee which will usually make up the largest part of the overall price. Wherever possible the question of price should be tied down precisely and, in addition, the contract should provide some machinery for calculating the cost of any extra work or services provided other than those which the software house has agreed to provide as its consideration for the contract. There may, for example, be unanticipated problems with the computer equipment or the client may change his mind half-way through the work so the contract should include hourly rates for programmers, analysts and others.

If a lump-sum price is agreed, it should be clear from the contract exactly what this includes, whether maintenance and training are included, whether the price includes the documentation, and if so, how many copies. What about the cost of the media such as magnetic disks and tapes? If the payment is to be made in instalments when are they due? If they become due on the performance of certain stages of the work, can these stages be clearly identified? For example, the contract might provide for payment of two-thirds of the total price when certain specified programs are operational and draft documentation has been provided. If the client is late paying, does the contract include provision for charging him interest? What if the client shows no intention of paying? It is in the interests of both parties that there should be no ambiguity as far as time for payment is concerned.

It may be that the software house feels unable to quote a firm price from the start perhaps because the client's computer equipment is unusual or unfamiliar. Some software companies may actually refuse to be tied down to a fixed price particularly if the work involves modifying existing software to run on unusual equipment. If the software house refuses to quote a fixed price the reason for this should be ascertained. Is it because the software house is tackling something beyond its capabilities or are there acceptable reasons? Is it genuinely difficult even for an experienced company to forecast the amount of work and the time-scale because of the complexity of the work? One way round this problem is to ask the software house, or preferably a competent and independent consultant, to carry out a feasibility study. This will enable the viability of the project to be determined before the parties are committed, and then the actual amount of work involved, and thus the price, can be more accurately predicted. The cost of the feasibility study, however, can be a considerable addition to the overall cost of implementing the software.

If the work involved in writing the software is substantial, the possibility of obtaining quotations by competitive tender should be considered, but if this course is chosen, specialist advice should be sought as to the specification and other aspects of the contract. The company inviting tenders is taking upon itself the responsibility for the feasibility of the project and the quality of the documentation provided to the tenderers. If the specification is inadequate, any software house awarded the contract will be able to point to this in its defence should the programs fail to be satisfactory, or use the deficiencies as a basis for claiming additional payment. Therefore, this approach can only be recommended for companies who have access to the necessary professional expertise. A major problem with comparing quotations and tenders is that it is unlikely that all those submitting will have put their bids together on the same basis. The chances are that some or all will have modified the specification in some way or another in spite of a request not to diverge from the specification. Some of those quoting may be unable to obtain a particular piece of equipment or software tool and will offer an alternative, or they may offer an alternative simply because it is cheaper and they hope this will make their quote more attractive. Although it could be argued that initiative should be rewarded, in fairness to the others quoting, all should be asked to reconsider their quotes in the light of the alternative should it appear to be worthwhile considering.

SPECIFICATION

The topics of quotations and tenders lead naturally to the question of the specification. Whether the company acquiring the software, or the software house itself, writes the specification there are several important points to be made in respect of it. The specification is the main provision in the contract which concerns the performance and capabilities of the software. It should be a detailed description of what the software is, what it will do and how quickly it will do it. The specification may well be contained in a separate document or be an appendix to the contract, but it must be noted that it is of crucial importance being the yardstick by which the software will be measured in the case of a dispute about the character and performance of the software.

The three most important items which the specification should include are:
  i) a detailed description of the tasks the software will perform,
 ii) the equipment on which the software will run, and
iii) how quickly the software will carry out the operations involved, bearing in mind any networking and multi-user situations.

The client may have little knowledge of the mysteries of computer science and will hope to receive some guidance on these matters from the experts writing the programs. But here, as anywhere else, the client should contemplate seeking independent advice unless he has his own computer professionals to consult. There are real dangers at this stage of over-optimism by both parties, plain misunderstanding or just a difference in emphasis of priorities. A great number of retrospectively ill-founded assumptions can be made about performance; computer programmers and analysts cannot be expected to know all the intricacies of the client's business, the nature of which may call for very fast information processing.

If the client does rely on the software house to supply a system that will do a particular job, he can expect that the software house will bring a certain degree of expertise to bear upon the work and will perform its part of the contract in a workmanlike manner. Companies in the business of writing computer systems are impliedly holding themselves out to possess a minimum level of skill and experience when it comes to writing their particular type of system, and the courts have long been prepared to imply such a duty in contracts for supplying services, such as in the case of hairdressers, garages and the like. A contract to write or adapt a computer system is analogous to such contracts. In *Stewart* v *Reavell's Garage* [1952], a customer relied on a garage to re-line the brakes on his 1929 Bentley. The garage obtained a quotation from a sub-contractor; the quotation was recommended to the customer who agreed to it. The work by the sub-contractor was carried out in a way unsuitable for Bentley cars and because of this the customer crashed the car, causing £362 worth of damage. It was held that, because the customer had relied on the garage to repair the brakes in a suitable and efficient manner and because the garage owed a duty to provide good workmanship and materials of good quality so that the braking system would be reasonably fit for its purpose, the garage was liable for the faulty work, even though the work itself was carried out by a sub-contractor. The garage had a duty to select and recommend a suitable sub-contractor. An equivalent duty of care and skill is now implied into service contracts, where the supplier of the service is acting in the course of business, by section 13 of the Supply of Goods and Services Act 1982. However, liability for loss resulting from failure to exercise reasonable care and skill can be excluded or limited subject to the provisions in the Unfair Contract Terms Act 1977.

In terms of computers, if you have a particular computer and approach a company to write software for that computer, the company has a duty to bring a reasonable amount of skill to the task and to supply software that will be fit for its purpose. If your computer is particularly demanding about the nature of the software it will run, or it has a strange operating system, then you can expect the software house to use its skill in taking such matters into account. If it sub-lets part of the work, it is under a duty also to select a sub-contractor capable of carrying out the work in a like manner. The software house cannot avoid liability for defective software merely because it has asked you to agree to the particular sub-contractor recommended by it. An example of a sub-contract is where a software house, contracted to write an accounts package, uses another specialist firm or, perhaps freelance programmers to carry out part of the work. The software house owes a duty to the client to choose the specialist firm and the freelance programmers carefully.

Other matters to which the specification should address itself include details of what information will be entered to be used by the programs and how it will be entered. Will entry be by keyboard, optical character reader, from magnetic disk or through a modem? Will the entry be of an interactive nature, in which case can the programs operate quickly enough? What results and reports are expected from the system and is there any likelihood of further reports being required once the programs have become established in use? What files, temporary and permanent will be created? Is access to be controlled by passwords and if so, is a hierarchical systems of passwords required?

The feature of computer systems which lies at the root of many disputes is the speed of operation. Computers work at fantastic speeds, measured in microseconds but they have a great disadvantage in that they are set up, on the whole, to process information in serial fashion, a piece at a time. The human brain, because of its massive parallel processing capabilities, can easily outperform a computer, and, when given real work to do, computers are anything but fast. Therefore, it is essential that the specification contains information about the speed of the software in use, e.g., response times at the keyboard (2 seconds can seem an eternity), the time taken to sort items into order, the time taken to compile and print reports. These timings should indicate the effect of multiple concurrent use of the same files and the fact that the equipment might be carrying out other demanding work at the same time. The specification should also describe the portability of the software, i.e., can it be run on other equipment with little effort or will a major 'refit' be needed? The client should ask questions about the effect of a future change of or a modification to his computer equipment. Another problem might concern the compatibility of the software with other systems run by the client; can data be easily transferred from the new system to the client's existing computer systems and vice versa?

TIME FOR COMPLETION

A contract for writing computer programs and preparing associated documentation whilst fundamentally different in character from a contract for the sale of goods is, however, analogous to a building contract. The performance of the contract is not a single event but rather extends over a period of time. This fact alone brings some doubt to any assumption that time is of the essence of the contract. We have already seen that although time for payment is not usually a condition in a commercial sale of goods contract, time for delivery is. But, if we contract with a builder for the construction of a house, we would not expect that we could repudiate the contract if the house was completed a day late and the position is similar with contracts for writing computer software. A delay of a few days might give rise to a claim for damages but would be unlikely to give the client the right to cancel the contract altogether, although if completion is very late, the client may well be entitled to cancel. Writing computer software carries with it a degree of unpredictability and the client should be aware of this, especially if he is planning his business operations around a particular completion date. Unexpected problems frequently arise which can add considerably to the overall time for performance, just as construction projects are often delayed because of unanticipated problems with the sub-soil which has to support a new building, requiring extensive changes to be made to the design of the foundations.

In case the software is completed late, it would be sensible to have some contractual provisions to cover this situation rather than argue about the damages. The usual method of dealing with late completion is to include a term which gives the client a right to liquidated damages. These damages may be quantified as a certain sum of money for every week completion is late, e.g., £200 per week. But, the sum must be a genuine pre-estimate of the financial losses which the client will suffer as a result of the delay and it must not be in the nature of a penalty. The courts will not enforce a 'penalty clause'. An example of acceptable liquidated damages would be an estimate of the loss of profits arising from the late completion. Sometimes, it may be in the client's interests to offer a bonus for early completion.

It is not always easy to determine when completion has taken place. The software might have been installed on the client's computer and be working, but requires some further work to be carried out. The programs may be finished but the documentation is only available in draft form. It is clear that problems might arise concerning when completion takes place and it is advisable to define completion in the contract. Does it include testing and documentation? What, if anything, does the client have to do to signify his acceptance of the software? What is the effect of completion on payment, do all outstanding monies become due? The concept of substantial completion could be used whereby upon substantial completion a large percentage of the agreed price becomes due with the moiety retained by the client until the remaining work has been completed. Substantial completion should of course be defined if this approach is used.

If completion is late, this will not necessarily be the fault of the software house. The completion of the work could be late as a result of the inaction of the client in providing information necessary to the continuation of the work or the client might fail to provide on time the facilities required by the software house. The contract should clearly state what facilities the client must provide and when he must provide them. The contract should also contain machinery providing that the software house will be entitled to an extension in the time for completion as a result of the client's default in his duties under the contract and be recompensed for the additional expense incurred. Ideally, the contract should include rates or a formula to help determine such additional costs.

MAINTENANCE OF AND ENHANCEMENTS TO THE SOFTWARE

No matter how much skill and care has been put into the writing of the software or how much testing has been carried out, the odds are overwhelmingly in favour of it containing errors or, colloquially, 'bugs'. Some of these bugs might not appear for a considerable period of time and they may be discoverable only under a very rare combination of factors. If a bug does appear this will normally be a breach of warranty and the client can expect that the software house will correct the error. Naturally, the latter will wish to limit responsibility to correct such errors to a specified period of time. It is therefore important that the contract takes account of the maintenance of the software. A compromise might have to be struck; perhaps the software house will be happy to rectify errors in the programs and manuals free of charge for a period of time and thereafter they will still be prepared to offer this service for a fee.

A software house will frequently offer an ancillary contract for maintenance for which the client will have to pay. It would be reckless to eschew a maintenance agreement and the cost of it should be allowed for in the overall budget for the work. It would be very difficult to engage another company to work on the software and, indeed, the software house will probably insist that the software is not to be modified by anyone other than itself. A maintenance agreement may also provide for enhancements and updates to be made available to the client which can be very useful because software is continually being developed and having new features added.

As mentioned above, the software house is unlikely to be willing to allow third parties, or even the client himself, to interfere with the software. The person modifying the programs might make a poor job of the work and this would reflect badly on the software which could acquire a bad reputation as a result. If the client considers it very important to be allowed to modify the software himself, this should be discussed before the contract is made and a suitable term incorporated. If agreed to, it will be essential that the client receives a copy of the source code so that he can make the modifications and the contract must clearly provide for this. The contract should also cover questions of copyright ownership in the modifications, the assignment of modifications and whether the software house has any rights in those modifications.

ESCROW

It is worthwhile considering what happens if the software house goes out of business. Will the client be able to maintain and modify the software or find another company to do this for him? If the software house has only supplied the object code this will be very difficult, if not impossible. The liquidator or a company taking over the software house's business may obtain the source code and expect to be paid by the client for a copy. If the software house is taken over, the new parent company might refuse to support the software yet not be willing to make the source code available. Some contracts provide for a legal device known as *escrow* which is invaluable in such situations.

Escrow describes a situation where the software house deposits, with an independent person, a source code copy of the programs together with copies of all the documentation and flowcharts relevant to the design and development of the software; in short, all the materials that will enable a third party to take over the maintenance and further development of the software. The independent person (the 'stakeholder') holding these materials is instructed not to divulge them to anyone and to keep them generally secure except in very special circumstances. If a specified event occurs, such as the software house going out of business or being unable to continue to support the software, then the stakeholder will release all the materials to the client who will then have all the information he needs to arrange for the software to be supported. Escrow works in the form of a guarantee or as insurance, should something unfortunate happen to the software house. The stakeholder must obviously be someone who can be absolutely trusted in the performance of his duties under the escrow arrangement and the details of the agreement need to be carefully thought out. It is better if the client pays his fees, perhaps annually in advance, with the condition that the materials will be returned to the software house if a payment becomes overdue by a certain period of time. If the client pays, this puts the client in a clear contractual relationship with the stakeholder and could prevent complications either with a liquidator, or if the software house should go out of business owing the stakeholder his fee. An organization which provides an escrow service is the National Computing Centre.

The implications of mergers and take-overs will need to be carefully dealt with; the new company might want to carry on business as usual, keeping the source code from the client, for reasons connected with confidentiality. The basic test determining whether to pass on the source code and other materials subject to an escrow agreement should be the permanent inability, for whatever reason, of the software house to continue to support the software.

COPYRIGHT AND OTHER INTELLECTUAL PROPERTY RIGHTS

The contract may impose duties on both parties associated with intellectual property rights. The software house will be anxious to prevent unauthorized copying of the programs and will want its techniques kept secret. The client will want to be able to use the software with impunity, without interfering with the rights of some third party who might seek an injunction to prevent the client using the software. The client will also be worried about the fact that some of the software house's staff will have gained a detailed insight into his business. The law of copyright and to some extent, the law of confidence will give some protection to the software house should the programs or the ideas contained therein be copied or plagiarized, but problems of proof and evidence may make it desirable to place a contractual duty on the client to prevent copying or unauthorized disclosure of methods. This duty will run in parallel to any duties imposed by intellectual property law, but the contractual approach will be useful because it will draw the client's attention to the existence of these rights and the importance of making his employees aware of them and the consequences of infringing them.

The client's employees may make, surreptitiously, copies of the programs and pass these on to others. If the software house discovers these copies, it has remedies available under copyright law to prevent the use of these copies by the recipients and their further transmission to others, but it might be difficult to prove that the copies originated from the client. A unique serial or code number could be embedded in the programs identifying the software as being that given to the client and if the client is made aware of this and the consequences he may be more careful. The contract may state that the licence is to be terminated forthwith should copies of the programs find their way into the hands of third parties without the permission of the software house. This will not preclude the software house from seeking remedies for infringement of copyright, a fact which is often expressly stated in computer software contracts.

Another aspect of intellectual property rights concerns the possibility that the software might infringe a third party's copyright or other right such as a patent. Whether or not the infringement is deliberate will not usually be relevant. The client could have been using the software quite happily for a number of years when the software house is successfully sued for infringement of copyright by some third party. That third party may then decide to pursue all the clients of the software house who are using the infringing software and seek injunctions to prevent them continuing to use the software. Even if the client is not troubled in this way by the third party, the software house will be prevented from continuing to support the software. It may be that the third party will be happy to allow the client to continue to use the software in return for a licence fee. But, in any case, the client should satisfy himself that there is a term in the agreement with the software house covering the infringement of intellectual property rights belonging to others. The term should give the client an indemnity against the event of legal action being taken against him as a result of the software infringing these rights. The term should be widely drafted so as to include all forms of intellectual property rights such as copyright, patents, trade marks, etc. The costs and implications of suddenly being unable to use an item of software might be quite enormous and it is likely that the software house will hope to limit its liability under this head, perhaps to the amount of the licence fee.

On the subject of confidentiality, the client will want a term included strengthening and extending the common law duty of confidence. He will want to prevent the software house's employees divulging details of his business methods and techniques and other confidential information such as client accounts, debtors and creditors. It is inevitable, if the contract is for a substantial amount of work, that the employees of the software house and any freelance staff they use will be exposed to confidential information. Without such a term in the contract, the client may be lacking legal recourse, especially if the confidential nature of materials involved is not otherwise made clear. The software house too may have worries about confidentiality, it may have developed special techniques for writing and testing software which the client's staff might see when the software is installed and tested; a contractual term imposing a two-way duty in respect of confidentiality should be included in the contract.

LIABILITY

Computer software is widely used to assist in decision-making processes in business. A decision to engage upon a particular line of action may be based upon an interpretation of the results of running a computer program; for example, a construction company might submit a bid for a motorway contract worth many millions of pounds; the bid total will have been calculated by estimators using a computer program. If there is an error in the program, the total might be miscalculated by £1 million; this could mean that the company loses the scheme because their bid is too high, or worse still, they win the contract by too great a margin and make a substantial loss.

The software house will be very keen to limit its liability if the software proves to be defective. The software house will attempt to limit or exclude its liability for defects in the software by the insertion of a suitably drafted exemption clause. The exemption clause will be controlled by the Unfair Contract Terms Act 1977; that is, in contracts between businesses, the clause will be subject to the requirement of reasonableness. The software house will usually attempt to limit its liability to the cost of replacing the software or remedying the defect. This may seem unsatisfactory from the client's point of view, but the software house would be foolish not to limit liability in this way; the potential claims could far outweigh the payment it receives for the software. It would expose itself to the possibility of enormous claims and not only for actual defects, there is also the possibility of a client misinterpreting the results obtained from running the programs and blaming this on a lack of clarity in the instructions. The insurance aspect will be important as far as the courts are concerned when considering the validity of such a limitation clause. How far would it be reasonable to expect the software house to take out insurance against a claim for defective software? It is unlikely that insurance companies would be keen to issue policies for unlimited claims at a reasonable premium.

ARBITRATION

It is prudent to include provision in the agreement for arbitration whereby a dispute between the parties will be referred to an arbitrator, an independent expert, who will rule on the dispute. Arbitration is a commonly used method of resolving disputes without having to go to the courts. The parties to the contract appoint an independent third party who will listen to both sides and then make a ruling. Arbitration is less formal than a court hearing, although the basic rules of evidence and procedure are adhered to, and it has the advantage that the arbitrator, unlike a judge, will be an expert in the technical matters involved. In a dispute involving computer software, the arbitrator would be expected to have considerable knowledge of software engineering and be a leading member of the computer profession. Another advantage of arbitration over a normal court hearing is that arbitration should be, in principle, quicker and cheaper, although this is not always so. Arbitration hearings can be fairly formal involving the calling of many expert witnesses.

It is common for arbitration clauses to state that the arbitrator's decision shall be final and binding on the parties, and the courts will seldom interfere with an arbitrator's decision unless he has erred on a point of law. A court will usually accept the arbitrator's evaluation of the facts of the case as being conclusive. If the contract provides for arbitration, neither party will be able to take a short cut to the courts because a judge will insist that the arbitration procedure is adhered to in the first instance.

A disadvantage of arbitration is that the arbitrator will not have the depth of legal knowledge of a high court judge and an arbitrator will, consequently, be more likely to err on a point of law or procedure, for example, an arbitrator might admit evidence which should be inadmissible. Although a judge will not usually have the technical expertise of an arbitrator, judges by their training and experience have the knack of getting to the kernel of a dispute and are able to concentrate on the important issues without being sidetracked. However, it must be said that, in practice, arbitration works extremely well and the standard of arbitrators, who belong to the Chartered Institute of Arbitrators, is very high. If an arbitration clause is included in the agreement, the machinery for selecting an arbitrator should also be dealt with, the usual practice being to appoint an arbitrator agreed upon by the parties, or failing such agreement, a person to be nominated by the British Computer Society who hold a register of suitably qualified arbitrators.

OTHER TERMS

A contract for the writing or modification of software will undoubtedly contain other terms dealing with matters such as the training of the client's staff, termination of the licence and misrepresentation. These will be dealt with in the following chapter which covers 'off-the-shelf' software.

Chapter 15

Licence agreements for 'off-the-shelf' software

This is software which is acquired as a ready-made package. It is mass-produced software obtained from a dealer and includes familiar packages such as word processing systems, spreadsheets and databases. As with other types of software, the person acquiring the software does not buy the software or the copyright in the software but merely obtains a licence to use the package. The licence will often be of indefinite duration although there may be some provision for termination, such as if the person acquiring it, i.e., the customer, contravenes some term in the licence agreement which is stated to determine the agreement. A term requiring the customer not to transfer the software to a third party could be an example. Strictly speaking, the licence cannot endure longer than the duration of the copyright in the software because when the copyright expires, the software effectively falls into the public domain and can be used freely without requiring permission. Some licence agreements allow the customer to terminate the agreement unilaterally simply by destroying all the copies of the programs and documentation, although why he should want to do this is hard to understand.

Many of the points raised in the preceding two chapters will also apply to 'off-the-shelf' packages; so, the agreement should state the scope of the licence, its transferability, liability for defects and cover copyright issues. A common feature with software originating in the United States is the 'shrink-wrap' licence. The customer pays the dealer the licence fee and receives a sealed pack containing the program diskettes, the documentation and the licence. The contract is made at the time the customer pays and the dealer signifies acceptance, perhaps by taking the money and handing over the package. At the time the contract is made the customer will not have seen the licence but, when he opens the package, the customer will probably find that the agreement will state that the very act of opening the package indicates acceptance of the terms of the licence. There may also be a notice to this effect on the outside of the package. In English law, the attempted introduction of a term after the contract has been made will be ineffective. However, many of these software packages derive from the United States and the licence agreement usually specifically states that the contract is subject to the laws of some State such as New York or California. This could cause problems but for the fact that usually the licence also states that if the customer does not agree with the terms he can return the software forthwith to the dealer and recover the licence fee. Anxious as he will be to try the software out, discarding empty box and licence, the customer should give the licence a brief inspection to make sure there is nothing nasty lurking there. It will probably turn out that the licence contains nothing exceptional and will include terms protecting the software company's interests with respect to the copyright of the software and limiting its liability for defects.

MISREPRESENTATION AND DEALERS' PROMISES

The identity of the parties to the licence agreement needs to be considered. The software company producing and distributing the package is the licensor, that is, the party granting the licence. The dealer from whom the software is obtained is the agent of the software company and it is his job to bring about the contract between the licensor and the customer who is known as the licensee. Because the dealer is the software company's agent, he has the authority, express or implied, to bind the software company contractually and this should not lead to problems. The dealer, however, may have misled the customer about the nature and performance of the software; he may, deliberately or otherwise have made false claims which have induced the customer to obtain the software. Usually, the licence agreement will contain a term to the effect that the software company will not be bound by anything which the dealer says in the pre-contractual negotiations and that the licence itself contains the entire agreement between the parties to the exclusion of anything else. In English law, such a term would be subject to the reasonableness test by section 8 of the Unfair Contract Terms Act 1977. If, however, the contract is one which is to be construed according to, e.g., the laws of New York State, rather than attempting to sue for misrepresentation in New York, the better course of action might be for a potential customer to satisfy himself of the quality and suitability of the software, and not to take disproportionate notice of the dealers' promises. In such a case the legal maxim 'caveat emptor' (let the buyer beware) applies. The vast majority of software deriving from the United States is of a very high standard but, if the customer is uncertain, it is as well to check with some existing users of the software or in some of the many excellent computer journals and publications which carry out comparative tests on these software packages. However, it should be borne in mind that sometimes magazines fail to be truly objective and may omit to test some particular software.

BACK-UP COPIES OF PROGRAMS

As we have seen in Chapter 4, technically speaking, the making of back-up copies of computer programs is an infringement of copyright unless the owner of the copyright has given permission to do this. The licence agreement should therefore mention back-up copies and it is usual for the contract to state that the client can make a specified number of copies of the programs for back-up purposes. In fact, it is advisable to make a copy of the programs to use as a working copy, retaining the original disks in a safe place. There is always a danger, however, of proliferation of copies of the programs and the customer should guard against this and indeed a sensible approach to this matter is required from both sides. Copy-protected computer programs can be inconvenient to use and could cause problems in the case of sudden failure of a disk, and on the other hand, the customer should operate good housekeeping systems and make sure that unauthorized copies of the programs do not find their way into the hands of third parties.

INTEGRATION AND UPGRADES

The customer should check how well, if at all, the software will integrate with other computer systems and whether data can be easily transferred to and from the software. Will the software run satisfactorily on the customer's hardware? What is the position if the customer decides to upgrade his equipment, will the software still be usable? What if a better version of the software is made available in due course; can the customer trade-in his old system or will he have to pay the full licence fee for the new version? These are the type of questions someone contemplating an off-the-shelf system should consider, even though some of the events described might seem unlikely at the time, they have an unfortunate habit of becoming relevant later and if a customer is in doubt it is better to err on the side of flexibility.

TRAINING AND SUPPORT

Training is an aspect which is often overlooked. A computer dealer may offer training under a separate contract between himself and the customer. The quality of the training obviously will be important as will the provision of refresher courses. A final point concerns 'hot-line' support. Will the dealer be prepared to provide an emergency call-out service if there is a problem related to the use of the software, such as trying to interface a word processing package with a new printer? In a case like this, the software itself will not be at fault, it will be a matter of installing the software in the correct manner for the particular printer. A dealer will charge for this type of support and the rate he requires will depend, amongst other things, on the speed of call out expected by the customer.

Chapter 16
Contract between software author and publisher

Not all software is developed directly by companies marketing the software. Frequently, a software author, whether a person, team or company will prefer to deal with a software publishing company, already well established, with a good reputation and a high volume of sales. This may prove to be the most satisfactory way of exploiting the software. The software author will therefore consider granting a licence to a software publishing company permitting the latter to market the product on the basis of agreed royalty payments. Usually, the licence will be exclusive, which means that the author will grant the publisher the sole rights to deal with the software. An important side-effect of an exclusive licence is that the licensee, the software publishing company, will have rights under copyright law as if it owned the copyright itself; the software publisher can sue for infringement of copyright directly without reference to the author. Indeed, this is usually desirable as far as the author is concerned as he may not have the resources to mount an infringement action himself.

PAYMENT

A very important provision in the agreement will concern payment, how it will be calculated and when it will become due. Usually, the software author will be paid on the basis of royalties; it may be a fixed sum for every unit sold, or it may be expressed as a percentage of the price charged for the software. Less commonly, the author will be paid a lump sum for granting the exclusive licence, although this should be avoided unless there are special circumstances. The quantification of royalty payments must be precisely defined in the licence agreement. If royalties are based on the price of the software, is this the retail price or the payment the software publisher receives from a dealer? The author should look at the agreement and ask questions such as: what happens if the software publisher does not try very hard to market the product? What if the software publisher suddenly decides to distribute the software at a cut price? How does the software author know that the sales figures disclosed by the publisher are correct? Has the author the right of access to the publisher's accounts and sales information? How frequently will payments be made and what is the position if the publisher is consistently late in making payment? What if the publisher decides to stop marketing the software package, does this terminate the agreement? Finally, can the author terminate the agreement and, if so, under what circumstances?

TRAINING, MAINTENANCE AND DEFECTS

Other matters that will require the attention of the author and publisher include questions of training and maintenance and who is responsible for undertaking it. If the author is to be responsible, will he be paid anything for his work or is it included in the royalty payments? If the software publisher has to correct subsequent defects in the software, will the author be charged? Related to such questions is the need for the licence agreement to state clearly exactly what the author has to provide and when he has to provide it.

CONFIDENTIALITY

The author should satisfy himself that the software publisher is fully aware of the confidential nature of elements of the software. The author may provide the publisher with the source code and the specification, including flowcharts, for the software. The agreement should spell out the duty of confidentiality in respect to these materials, reinforcing the common law duty. If the author has access to the publisher's information about sales and marketing techniques, a reciprocal duty could be placed on the author.

LIABILITY

The relationship between the author, publisher and ultimate customer is shown in Figure 3.

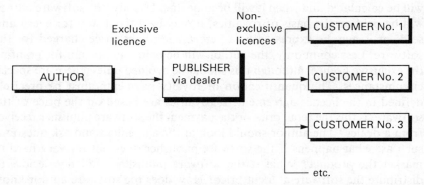

Figure 3   Licence arrangement between author, publisher and customers

The author grants an exclusive licence to the publisher giving the publisher the sole right to produce copies of the software and to market them. The publisher 'sells' the software through a dealer, granting non-exclusive licences to the customers. The dealer is a 'middle-man' whose only role in this context is to act on behalf of the publisher to bring about the contract (the licence agreement) between the publisher and the customer. The author and ultimate customers are not in a contractual relationship, but the law of negligence operates without the need for a contract as long as there is a duty of care owed by one person to another. The author will therefore want to be protected against any claims for losses to ultimate customers caused by defects in the software. The publisher will probably protect himself by having a suitably drafted exclusion or limitation clause in his licence agreements with the customers. The author should ask the software publisher to draw up any such term in the licence agreement with the ultimate customers in language wide enough to give some protection to the author, bearing in mind the legal controls on exclusion clauses.

Other terms will be relevant in these forms of agreements, dealing with matters such as definitions, items provided, specification, delivery, liquidated damages, copyright and arbitration and reference should be made to the previous two chapters for further details of these aspects.

Chapter 17
Hardware contracts

Computer hardware may be purchased outright or hired. Much of what has already been discussed in relation to computer software contracts, in particular contracts for the writing or modification of software, will apply to contracts for the acquisition of hardware. Very often, the purchase of or hire of computer equipment will include software, such as operating system software, computer programming languages, utility programs or applications programs. These items of software will be subject to collateral licence agreements.

Computer software is important; the choice of the software best suited to the client's requirements is critical and when it comes to setting up a computer system de novo, in a company or business that has not used computers before, the decisions regarding the selection of software are of primary importance. The secondary decision should then be to determine the type of computer equipment which will be most suitable for running this software, not forgetting other important considerations such as future growth, the impact of the computing operations and the future of the software packages and computer equipment. Will the company manufacturing the computer continue to develop and support it in the longer term?

If the client already has some computer equipment and software, this will influence any decisions about obtaining new hardware. Compatibility with the existing equipment will be important and some compromises may have to be made. The aim should be that in three or five years time, the decision will still seem to have been a good choice.

PERFORMANCE

The performance of software is directly related to the computer's performance. The speed of operation of the computer will be very important and a contract for the purchase or hire of computer equipment should make reference to this. The purchaser must satisfy himself as to the performance of the equipment, bearing in mind the environment in which the equipment will be working. Simple benchmark speed tests may not provide a very good picture of the computer's performance if it will be used to carry out many different tasks at the same time, with multiple concurrent access to data files. The client should think about the operating system and whether it is a common one able to run a large variety of applications programs. Another point which might be relevant is the maximum number of data files the computer will permit to be in use at the same time.

MAINTENANCE AND UPGRADES

The contract should state exactly who does what in terms of installation and initial testing. Once the equipment is installed, how well will the supplier support it? Maintenance will probably be provided for by a separate contract, renewable annually, and the client should check this contract to see what it has to say on the point of speed of response to a breakdown. If repairs have to be made to the computer equipment, does the client have to pay for parts or labour or both and is there a minimum call out charge? The maintenance contract may provide for the loan of alternative equipment whilst repairs are carried out and if it does not so provide, it could be worth asking why not.

Sooner or later, the computer equipment will become obsolete as faster, more powerful equipment is continually being developed. This can have one of two consequences. First, the new equipment is better in so many respects and so different that there is no possibility of upgrading the old equipment to the new standards. It is then a matter of making do, standing by the existing equipment, consolidating it and adding improvements when they become available with a view to reviewing the situation in a year or two, when the quality and performance of the new equipment has been fully tested by others. The general acceptance of equipment amongst the computer world is very important. Sometimes, a new computer will catch on and sell in volume and this will then encourage the leading software companies to produce appropriate software for the new machine, making it an even more attractive proposition. Once a new computer attracts the attention of the software companies it is well on its way to becoming established. It is very tempting to stay with the market leaders when buying computer equipment.

A second consequence of the announcement of new, improved equipment is that it may be possible to upgrade the existing equipment to those standards, as the new equipment may be in the form of an upgrade. When buying computer equipment, it is worthwhile finding out what the manufacturer's attitude is to his existing customers regarding upgrades or new equipment. Will the improved equipment be sympathetically priced as far as existing customers are concerned? Will a generous trade-in be allowed on the old equipment or is there a good secondhand market for the manufacturer's equipment? Does the manufacturer have a history of upwardly compatible machines or does he bring out new equipment that is totally unlike the old equipment? Does he change operating systems continually? Ideally, the manufacturer should have a policy of building on his past products. It must be borne in mind that there is a dichotomy here for manufacturers. A manufacturer will want to attract new customers and, to do this, the equipment must be up to date and make use of the latest technological developments. On the other hand, the manufacturer will owe a moral duty to his loyal customers to maintain some degree of compatibility. The history of computing is one of constant change and of abandoning out-of-date equipment and the person or company considering purchasing a computer or other computer equipment would do well to bear this in mind. There is little that can be done contractually, apart from insisting that the supplier (it will be the supplier and not the manufacturer who will be a party to the contract unless the supplier and manufacturer are one and the same) will continue to support the equipment for a reasonable period of time, regardless of whether it is later withdrawn from the market place.

If the equipment is hired, problems of obsolescence are less important providing the hirer is not committing himself to an unduly long period of hire. Hiring is often referred to as leasing; there is no particular significance in this because a lease contract and a contract of hire are basically the same. The duration of the agreement will be important as will be the presence of any term in the agreement concerning termination and the relevant circumstances. If a much better piece of equipment is suddenly available, the hirer may wish to terminate the agreement quickly so that he can avail himself of the new equipment. The company hiring the equipment out will obviously want some form of compensation should the hirer want to return the computer equipment before the normal time and it requires a sensible compromise.

LEGAL CONTROLS

Statutory safeguards are more in evidence when it comes to hardware contracts. For example, the Sale of Goods Act 1979 will apply because a computer or other related equipment comes within the meaning of 'goods'; a computer is a personal chattel. This means that the important terms such as compliance with description and merchantable quality will be implied into a contract to purchase a computer. Certain terms implied by the Sale of Goods Act 1979 are implied into all contracts of sale whilst others only apply where the seller sells in the course of business. Compliance with description is an example of the former whilst merchantable quality is an example of the latter. Most of the contracts under consideration in this book will be in the course of business. Similar terms will be implied into hire contracts by the Supply of Goods and Services Act 1982. These implied terms can be excluded or limited in the case of a non-consumer sale but only in so far as the exemption clauses purporting to do this meet the requirement of reasonableness as provided for by the Unfair Contract Terms Act 1977, sections 5−7.

A final point to consider is that there is a possibility that the computer hardware or the software sold with it infringes some intellectual property right. The hardware itself could infringe a patent whilst the software might infringe a copyright. The client should make sure that the contract contains a term indemnifying him in case this should happen. However if, as will usually be the case, the contract is governed by the Sale of Goods Act 1979, there will be remedies available to the buyer if he is prevented from using or hindered in his use of the equipment because it infringes another person's rights. By section 12(1), there is an implied *condition* that the seller has the right to sell the goods and, by section 12(2), there is an implied *warranty* that the buyer will enjoy 'quiet possession' of the goods. Section 6 of the Unfair Contract Terms Act 1977 provides that section 12 of the Sale of Goods Act 1979 cannot be excluded or restricted by reference to any contractual term. If a company buys a computer and, at the time of the sale, the computer infringes a trade mark or patent, then the seller is in breach of section 12(1) of the Sale of Goods Act 1979. Because this is a condition, the buyer can repudiate the contract and claim back the purchase price, plus damages for any consequential losses he has suffered (provided they are not too remote). In *Niblett Ltd.* v *Confectioners' Materials Co Ltd.* [1921], it was held that because goods, when sold, infringed a trade mark, this entitled the buyer to repudiate the contract.

It may happen that equipment does not infringe a patent when it is sold but does so infringe a patent soon afterwards, perhaps because at the time of sale a patent application, made by a third party, was being processed. When the patent is granted, the third party may commence an infringement action against the buyer of the equipment. This occurred in a case involving road marking machines, *Microbeads A.C.* v *Vinhurst Road Markings* [1975], where it was held that:

(a) there was not a breach of section 12(1) because, at the time of the sale, the seller had every right to sell (the patent could not be enforced at that time), and

(b) the seller was in breach of section 12(2), the implied warranty as to quiet possession, and was liable to the buyer in damages.

There is always a danger that computer equipment or software will infringe a third party's rights (even if it is inadvertent) because of the rapid development of new hardware and software. The remedies in section 12 of the Sale of Goods Act 1979 are useful but it is advisable to make specific contractual provision for the eventuality. For example, in a situation like that in the *Microbeads* case, the buyer may prefer to be able to repudiate the contract rather than being limited to damages only.

Chapter 18
Summary and checklist

Many potential pitfalls in contracts for computer software and hardware have been discussed in the previous chapters and also how they can be avoided or at least assuaged by careful consideration of the terms of the contract. The rapid rate of change in the computer industry, whilst bringing great improvements to computer technology, has also contributed to the scale of the problems. Tales of incompatibility and abandoned systems are commonplace and the effect of bad decisions coupled with poor contracts can be quite horrendous, contributing to the downfall of the client's business. Choice of computer equipment and software is a very crucial decision and often is given far too little thought.

When looking at a contract for computer equipment or software, the golden rule is to be suspicious and sceptical. Awkward questions should be asked and their answers sought by reference to the contract. The contract needs to be assessed in the light of such questions as:

- What if the software contains bugs?
- What if the computer breaks down in the middle of the wages run?
- What if the client copies the programs and sells the copies?
- What if the programs run too slow to be of any practical use?
- What if the computer becomes obsolete and the manufacturer washes his hands of it?

It is so easy to be over-optimistic when acquiring computers and software, especially for the first time − and it is essential to have a long, hard look at the contract and even to be a little bit cynical about it. Both parties to a contract for hardware or software should be prepared to look at that contract from the other's point of view and be prepared to negotiate an agreement giving a fair balance of responsibilities and liabilities.

Table 2 indicates the purpose and relevance of contractual terms to the four types of agreement specifically covered in this part of the book.

Table 2 Checklist of terms normally found in computer contracts

• indicates that this term will normally be present in the particular form of agreement

Term	Purpose	Bespoke	Off-the-shelf	Author/publisher	Hardware
			Software		
Definitions	To clarify and assist with the interpretation of the contract.	•	•	•	•
Form of agreement	Describes the nature of the contract, e.g. sale contract, licence or lease agreement.	•	•	•	•
Assignment/ transfer	States whether the subject-matter of the contract can be assigned or transferred to third parties.	•	•	•	if leased
Items provided	List of items included in the contract, e.g. manuals, disks, etc. Also, any facilities to be provided by the client.	•	•	•	•
Price or licence fee	The price to be paid or the method of calculating the price. Instalment details and when they are due.	•	•		•
Royalties	The 'price' paid to an author usually based on a percentage of sales. The formula for calculating royalties should be clearly stated as should details of the timing of payments.			•	
Specification	Describes in detail the quality and content of the subject-matter of the contract. Of special note is performance.	•		•	•
Delivery	Defines the time when the subject-matter of the contract will be delivered or will be available. Delivery may be by instalments.	•		•	•
Liquidated damages	To quantify the damages payable in the event of late performance of all or part of the contract.	•		•	•
Acceptance	To define what the client has to do to signify acceptance of the software or hardware.	•		•	•
Use	The scope of the uses to which the client can put the software or hardware.	•			•
Maintenance	Expresses the duties of the supplier to correct errors in the software or faults in the equipment. May be subject to a separate agreement.	•	•	•	•

Table 2 (contd)

Term	Purpose	Type of contract/agreement			
		Software			Hardware
		Bespoke	Off-the-shelf	Author/publisher	
Enhance-ments	Outlines whether subsequent improvements to the software or hardware will be available and whether they will be charged for. Enhancements may be available as part of a maintenance contract.	•		•	•
Modifica-tions	States whether the client can modify the software or hardware without recourse to the supplier. If permitted, ownership of rights in any modifications must be stated.	•	•	•	•
Training	Describes responsibility of supplier for training the client's staff in the use of the software. May be a separate agreement with a dealer.	•	•	•	
Copyright, etc.	Defines the client's duty to prevent unauthorized copying or transmission of the software or trade secrets relating to the software or hardware.	•	•	•	•
Escrow	The machinery for the provision of a source code version of the programs and all relevant documentation to the client in the event of the supplier ceasing to support the software.	•		•	
Confiden-tiality	States the supplier's duty not to divulge confidential information concerning the client's business.	•		•	•
Liability	To limit the liability of the supplier in the event of defects (bearing in mind the effects to the Unfair Contract Terms Act 1977).	•	•	•	•
Indemnity	To protect the client if the subject-matter infringes a third party's copyright, patent or other right.	•	•	•	•
Staff poaching	To provide contractual remedies should either party offer employment to a member of the other's staff.	•			•
Termination	Describes under what circumstances the contract can be terminated. There should be provision for termination by either party.	•	•	•	Hire contracts

Table 2 (contd)

Term	Purpose	Type of contract/agreement			
		Software			
		Bespoke	Off-the-shelf	Author/publisher	Hardware
Applicable law	Denotes the country or state whose law will be used to settle disputes. Bear in mind that Scots law is substantially different from English law.	●	●	●	●
Arbitration	The machinery for settling disputes without recourse to the courts by appointing a suitably qualified arbitrator.	●	●		●

Part III
Computers and crime

Computer technology has opened up a whole new area of criminal activity, but the response of the legislators and the courts has appeared to be half-hearted. An important factor when developing and extending criminal law, much more so than in the case of the civil law, is the scope and width of the newly prohibited act or omission. The criminal law is involved with issues concerning civil liberties and personal freedom. The act of 'hacking' provides an example. If the unauthorized access of a computer system is made a criminal offence, this means that hacking (without committing any subsequent act such as fraud or erasing computer data) will be subject to the criminal law, whereas trespass to land, a physical analogy with computer hacking, can only be dealt with by using the civil law. It has been argued that the law should not make such a distinction, and that computers should not be better protected from 'trespass' than physical property.

Attempts to strengthen the criminal law are often delayed or frustrated by the consideration of civil liberties and personal freedom. There are problems too with the detection of computer crime and with the purpose to be achieved by labelling particular activities as being criminal. If the purpose is seen to be deterrence, then the law should be enforceable and a good proportion of offenders should be detected and punished severely. An activity should not be made a criminal offence merely to placate a worried computer industry by showing that 'something is being done'.

In this Part of the book, the present state of the criminal law as it relates to computer technology is discussed and possible changes to the criminal law are described, where appropriate. One point to be remembered when reading the following chapters is that the actions described will sometimes give rise to liabilities under civil law. For example, if a hacker makes a copy of some of the information stored on a computer system, he may be infringing the copyright subsisting in that information and may also be in breach of confidence if he divulges it to others. Similarly, a fraudster transferring funds will be guilty of the civil law tort of conversion.

In addition to considering the legal position regarding computer crime, practical suggestions are given to reduce the risk of becoming a victim.

Chapter 19
Introduction

The advent of computer technology has brought many kinds of opportunities and some of these, not surprisingly, are of a criminal nature. Computers may facilitate the commission of 'old-fashioned' crimes such as fraud or counterfeiting, and new activities, which are potentially criminal, have been created, for example, computer hacking (gaining access to a computer system without permission). Contrary to popular belief, the law in general is reasonably well equipped to deal with computer crime, although it must be said that, in this respect, the criminal law is fragmented and poorly organized. The choice of offence with which to charge someone suspected of computer-related crime is not always a simple matter. This is largely because the criminal law takes little account of computer technology directly and few criminal offences have been created to deal specifically with the phenomenon of computer crime. The biggest stumbling-block, in practical terms, is detection and a considerable amount of thought must be given to the security of any computer system as in this case prevention is better than cure.

By far the greatest threat to a computer system comes from within, i.e., from employees. The largest computer fraud ever attempted, which concerned the transfer of $70 million, involved an employee of the First National Bank of Chicago. Even when computer crime is detected and the persons involved are prosecuted and convicted, the penalties imposed seem relatively trivial when compared with other forms of criminal activity. In 1989, a teenage bank cashier who transferred nearly £1 million into his own and a friend's bank account received only one year's youth custody.

The diversity of criminal activities associated with computers is remarkable and has given rise to a new vocabulary, e.g., computer hacking, time-bombs, logic-bombs and viruses. These terms will be defined at the appropriate sections of this Part of the book, the purpose of which is to describe the criminal offences associated with computers, what remedies are available at law and to suggest how the threats posed by these activities can be avoided or, at least, minimized. First, in Chapter 20, the offences popularly described as 'computer fraud' are considered. In Chapter 21 the activity known as hacking is examined followed, in Chapter 22, by the law of criminal damage which might apply to a situation where a person erases data from a computer system or leaves a virus on a system which later corrupts or deletes information. Other forms of criminal activity are also discussed such as blackmail, forgery and counterfeiting and offences under copyright law, in Chapter 23.

It is extremely likely that a criminal prosecution for any form of computer crime will involve evidence produced by or associated with computer equipment; for example, a print-out of a computer file or a log of computer use and the implications of this, as far as the admissibility of evidence is concerned, are discussed in Chapter 24. Practical suggestions to prevent computer crime are made in Chapter 25 and, finally, a summary of offences, their maximum penalties and scope is presented in tabular form. The practicalities of bringing a criminal prosecution are first briefly outlined.

THE PROSECUTION OF CRIMINAL OFFENCES

Before specific offences are examined, it will be useful to describe, very briefly, the normal procedure for prosecuting offences, the classification of offences and the different modes of trial.

When a criminal offence has been committed, the normal procedure is for the police to be informed (the police detect very little crime themselves but depend on the public bringing incidents of crime to their notice). The police will then investigate the crime and, if they suspect a particular person or persons of having committed the crime, they may then pass the case over to the Crown Prosecution Service which decides whether to prosecute and what charges to bring. In coming to its decision, the Crown Prosecution Service uses guidelines which include the possibility of securing a conviction and the public interest. If the decision is made to proceed, the accused will appear before a Magistrates' Court where, depending on the nature of the offence and other matters, either his case will be dealt with, or he will be committed for trial to the Crown Court. It is still possible to bring a private prosecution if, for example, the Crown Prosecution Service declines to act. Also, other bodies may bring prosecutions such as local authority Trading Standards Departments and the Department of Social Security. Bringing a private prosecution is, in most cases, an extreme action, but it may be relevant in computer crime if the official bodies fail to take an interest in prosecuting certain behaviour, due perhaps to a lack of understanding of the problems involved or a feeling that the civil law offers sufficient remedies. Though this latter point may be true, it does not have the deterrent effect that a successful criminal prosecution can have.

Criminal offences are heard in either the Crown Court or in Magistrates' Courts. The latter tend to deal with the less serious offences which make up the vast majority of criminal cases. Offences are classified according to how they may be tried. Relatively minor offences, such as exceeding the speed limit, may be tried only in Magistrates' Courts and these offences are described as being *summary* offences. Serious offences such as murder and robbery can only be tried in the Crown Court and these are called *indictable* offences. In between these two types of offences, there are a vast number of intermediate offences which can be tried in either a Magistrates' Court or in the Crown Court; these offences, of which theft is an example, are called *triable either way* offences. These may be tried summarily, in a Magistrates' Court or, on indictment, in the Crown Court. Most of the offences which will be described in this Part of the book fall into this category; they are offences which are triable either way.

When an offence is classified as being triable either way, the choice of mode of trial initially rests with the magistrates. They may decide that the nature of the case is such that it should be tried in the Crown Court; for example, if it is a serious example of the offence. If the magistrates decide that the case can be heard in their court, the accused person then can decide whether to proceed in the Magistrates' Court, or to elect trial at the Crown Court. Certain other factors are important in deciding on the mode of trial apart from the seriousness of the offence. For example, the magistrates might consider that the accused, if found guilty, is deserving of a punishment greater than they can award (although they can commit a convicted person for sentence by the Crown Court), or the accused might think he stands a better chance of acquittal before a jury.

The maximum penalties available in Magistrates' Courts need to be mentioned. Providing the relevant statute does not contain a lower maximum, for a single offence the magistrates may send a person to prison for a term not exceeding 6 months and/or impose a fine not exceeding £2,000. Other sentencing powers are available to the magistrates such as discharging the offender, imposing a probation order, ordering the offender to perform community service, etc. In the context of computer crime, the use of imprisonment and fines are the most likely punishments, although other forms of sentence may be appropriate in some circumstances.

Chapter 20
Computer fraud

Computer fraud makes headline news and it is thought that the number of cases of fraud detected and prosecuted are just the tip of the iceberg. It is impossible to determine the scale of computer fraud but rumours abound about massive frauds which are not prosecuted by the victims (usually large financial institutions) because of a fear of publicity. It does not help a bank's image of solid dependability to have employees prosecuted for computer fraud at regular intervals. All the major financial institutions throughout the world use computers to carry out their business and vast sums of money are transferred by computer. As far as the criminal is concerned, the creation of an account in his own name, followed by instructions via a computer terminal to the main computer to transfer large sums into that account is much more attractive than walking into a bank with a shotgun. There seems to be a feeling that to commit fraud by using one's own brains to defeat a computer system is something to be applauded and is not really serious crime. However, this form of crime causes great anxiety in the commercial world and is considered by the authorities to be very serious. The maximum penalties available are quite heavy and computer fraud can be dealt with by prison sentences of up to 10 years.

TYPES OF COMPUTER FRAUD

The phrase 'computer fraud' is used to describe stealing money or property by means of a computer, i.e., using a computer to obtain, dishonestly, property (including money and cheques) or credit or services or to evade dishonestly some debt or liability. It might involve dishonestly giving an instruction to a computer to transfer funds into a bank account or using a forged bank card to obtain money from a cash dispenser.

The types of activities described as computer fraud can be considered to be of two main types: data frauds and programming frauds. In the first type, unauthorized data is entered into a computer or data that should be entered is altered or suppressed. The main distinguishing factor in this type of fraud is that it is computer data, either input or output data, which is tampered with. Data fraud is probably the most common (it is the most commonly *detected*) type of computer fraud and is relatively easy to carry out. Some sub-species of data frauds are described below.

a) Entry of unauthorized instruction

A person dishonestly entering an instruction causing the computer system to transfer money from one account to another is an example of this form of fraud. The person entering the instruction may be an employee or may be an outsider who has gained access to the computer system without permission. If the person involved is an employee, he may be authorized to enter such instructions but has entered a particular instruction beyond the scope of his authority to do so, with a view to defrauding his employer.

b) Alteration of input data

Data which is legitimately entered into a computer is intentionally altered. For example, in one case, a data preparation employee entering overtime hours worked by employees into the company's computer system for calculating wages, falsely increased those hours so that some of the employees received more wages than they were entitled to. These employees and the person entering the hours were in collusion (Audit Commission, *Survey of Computer Fraud and Abuse*, H.M.S.O. 1987 at p.26). This form of fraud is very common, easily done and hard to detect unless periodic checks are made. Most organizations using computers are vulnerable to fraud perpetrated by employees authorized to enter data into a computer system and, consequently, care must be taken in the selection of such employees and an effective way of checking systems for the occurrence of fraud should be used.

c) Suppression of data

This particularly applies to output data; for example, printed reports generated by a computer system. These reports may be suppressed simply by tearing them up or not printing them out or, if printed, they may be altered. In either case, the motive will usually be to hide some criminal activity. For example, a person responsible for collecting money for a club might destroy computer print-out which would indicate that he had kept some of the money collected.

d) The computer as an unwitting accomplice

A computer system might be used to detect information which assists the criminal in the commission of his crime. For example; in the case of *R* v *Sunderland* [1983], an employee of Barclays Bank used the bank's computer to discover a dormant account and then forged the holder's signature to withdraw some £2,100. The employee of the bank used the computer in a very simple way to detect an account which had not been used for a long period of time but which had some funds in it. This was a simple but effective way of stealing money although, eventually, the scheme was discovered when the holder of the dormant account attempted to make a withdrawal and discovered that the account contained less money than it should have done. The employee, who was of previous good character, was sentenced to 2 years' imprisonment which was changed on appeal by the Lord Chief Justice who suspended 18 months of the sentence. He said:

> . . . other people like bank clerks and bank officials need very little reminding that if they commit this sort of offence they will lose their job and go to prison, albeit for a comparatively short time.

This case illustrates the vulnerability of some computer systems to criminal activities. Of fundamental importance in the design of any computer system, as mentioned several times in this book, is the attention given to passwords and security and the controls placed on employees.

None of the activities described above requires a great deal of computer expertise to carry out; they will often be committed by lowly paid employees engaged to perform relatively menial tasks such as data preparation and entry. Such frauds are fairly easy to detect by careful scrutiny, spot-checks and occasional manual checks. Strong security measures will also have a major deterrent effect, especially if they are performed in a high-profile manner.

The second form of computer fraud, which is much more sophisticated and more dangerous, is where someone alters a computer program. This type of fraud is much harder to detect than data fraud and reported examples are few and far between. In one case, computer programmers concealed a routine in a stock accounting system which suppressed certain details in reports generated, in order to reduce Value Added Tax liability (Audit Commission, *Survey of Computer Fraud and Abuse*, H.M.S.O., 1987 at p.58). Another example of this form of fraud which was discovered in West Germany and made famous in the film 'Superman III', involved the alteration of a program to collect decimal fractions of financial transactions, such as half-cents which were normally rounded down and ignored. Instead, these fractions were placed in an account opened by the perpetrator of the fraud.

Computer programmers, analysts and others involved in the commissioning or alteration of software present another source of danger in that many of them will have detailed knowledge about the security and password systems used and could pass such information on to persons intent on committing fraud. Because of their knowledge of the computer systems, computer staff are also susceptible to involvement with would-be fraudsters.

FRAUD OFFENCES

When discussing computer fraud, the word 'fraud' can be a little misleading, and the activities commonly described as computer fraud can involve criminal offences other than those traditionally described as fraud. Fraud comprises a collection of similar offences such as obtaining property or services by deception, false accounting, false statements made by company directors, suppression of documents and income tax fraud including cheating. Most of these offences are covered by sections 15–20 of the Theft Act 1968 and sections 1 and 2 of the Theft Act 1978. Income Tax and Value Added Tax fraud are dealt with by the Finance Acts although the common law offence of cheating is still available for offences relating to the public revenue, but with this exception, cheating was abolished by section 32(1) of the Theft Act 1968. Certainly, some of these offences may be carried out using a computer; for example, false accounting, but it is with respect to those offences requiring deception that the greatest difficulty lies. Often, the most appropriate offence to charge is theft. Although theft (section 1 of the Theft Act 1968) is not normally considered to fall within the 'fraud' group of offences, there is an overlap between theft and fraud and, depending on the circumstances, a charge of theft might be more likely to lead to a successful prosecution. First, the deception offences will be considered.

OBTAINING BY DECEPTION

At first sight, the offence of obtaining property by deception (section 15 of the Theft Act 1968) seems to be most appropriate to computer fraud as the criminal usually means to obtain someone else's money by a deception or trick; for example, by pretending to have authority to carry out some transaction on the computer such as transferring money. There is no problem stemming from the intangible nature of money, credits or cheques as section 4(1) of the 1968 Act states that property includes money and things in action, and a banker's cheque is an example of a 'thing in action'. This definition of property applies to the 1968 Act generally and therefore applies to section 15. There are several forms of deception provided for by the Theft Acts of 1968 and 1978 involving the obtaining of property or a pecuniary advantage or services, and the evasion of liability. So far as obtaining property by deception is concerned, section 15(1) of the Theft Act 1968 defines the offence as follows:

> A person who by any deception dishonestly obtains property belonging to another, with the intention of permanently depriving the other of it, shall on conviction on indictment be liable to imprisonment for a term not exceeding ten years.

Dishonesty is an important requirement and this affects the nature of the deception. The Theft Act 1968 further states that the deception must be 'deliberate or reckless', so if a person carelessly causes a computer system to transfer money into his own or a friend's account, he is not guilty of the offence as carelessness is not sufficient in this context.

In terms of computer fraud, the difficulty with this offence is that it requires a deception and this implies that it is an actual person that is being deceived, not a machine. In *DPP* v *Ray* [1974], Lord Morris said:

> For a deception to take place there must be some person or persons who will have been deceived.

Other case law does not help very much and the question was left open in one case involving an automatic car park barrier (*Davies* v *Flackett* [1973]). Bearing in mind that *DPP* v *Ray* was decided in the House of Lords, the better view is that the deception must work upon a human mind.

If a person gains access, whether with or without permission, to a bank's computer system and dishonestly instructs the computer system to transfer money from one account into another, then that person is 'deceiving' the computer or computer system; that is, he purports to have the authority to carry out such an act. Even if he has authority to transfer money from one account to another under normal circumstances as an employee would, that authority is nullified by his dishonesty. The main point is that it is the computer which is being 'deceived'. Under normal circumstances, no other human being is involved and, therefore, it would seem that the offence of obtaining property by deception is not made out. It would be different if, before the transfer was made, a message is displayed at someone's terminal requesting confirmation of the transfer. In that case, the other person would be subject to the deception as well as the computer and there should then be no difficulty related to the applicability of the offence of obtaining property by deception or any other offence involving deception.

The notion that a machine cannot be deceived is strengthened by the 1978 Theft Act which defines the offences of obtaining services by deception (services such as hiring a car or providing bed and breakfast) and evasion of liability by deception (such as where a debtor tells a lie to his creditor in order to be let off part or the whole of the debt), because the wording used strongly suggests that the deception must operate on the human mind. For example, section 1(1) states:

> 'A person who by any deception dishonestly obtains services from *another* shall be guilty of an offence.' [*emphasis added*]

This interpretation is reinforced by other language used in the statute. An example of obtaining services by deception in the context of computers is where a person makes an unauthorized use of a system which is normally paid for such as PRESTEL. The problem of who has been deceived still exists, but if the person has deceived some other person by saying that he has permission to use the terminal used to access the system, then the offence of deception will have been made out under section 1 of the Theft Act 1978. There is a requirement for the services to be subject to payment, so the same act with respect to a 'free' service does not involve the offence; for example, if a person, without permission, uses a computer system in a library to locate a particular book.

To summarize, an essential element for deception offences contained in the Theft Acts is that a human being has been deceived. In such a case, the deception could be simply by a person claiming to have permission to use a computer system to gain access to a terminal or by pretending to be someone else. Some related offences such as false accounting, where 'deception' is not an element of the offence, should cause no additional problems merely because the offence was committed by or facilitated by the use of a computer system.

CONSPIRACY TO DEFRAUD AND ATTEMPTS

Generally, a conspiracy is an agreement between two or more persons to carry out an unlawful act. Conspiracy may be statutory or common law. A statutory conspiracy is when a person agrees with another or others to embark upon a course of conduct which will necessarily involve a criminal offence by section 1 of the Criminal Law Act 1977 as amended by the Criminal Attempts Act 1981. An example is where two persons agree to steal a computer; both will be guilty of a conspiracy to steal the computer even if they do not go on to actually steal it. Statutory conspiracy requires that the proposed act is itself a criminal offence and, in the case of obtaining by deception, there remain difficulties relating to the concept of deceiving a machine as discussed above.

However, at common law, the offence of conspiracy to defraud may be available. It appears that, in this context, 'deceit' is not an essential element of the offence and in *Scott* v *Metropolitan Police Commissioner* [1975], Viscount Dilhorne said:

> . . . 'to defraud' ordinarily means . . . to deprive a person dishonestly of something which is his or of something to which he is or would or might but for the perpetration of the fraud be entitled.

In other words, it is not necessary to show that a person has been deceived. This common law offence is separate and distinct from the fraud offences in the Theft Acts, although in many cases, such as where two or more persons agree to obtain goods or services by impersonating others, the offence of conspiracy to defraud and offences under the Theft Acts will be committed if the course of action is carried through to its conclusion.

The consequence is that if two or more persons agree to dishonestly operate a computer, perhaps entering a password they are not entitled to use, to transfer funds to their own accounts, they will be guilty of a conspiracy to defraud even though no human being has been deceived. Of course, a limitation of the scope of this offence is that it requires an agreement between two or more conspirators and it cannot apply when only one person is involved. Nevertheless, the offence is a useful weapon in the fight against computer fraud, especially if the act of transferring the funds in question is not completed and the circumstances are not sufficient to warrant a charge of attempting to steal.

To be charged with an attempt, the person involved must have done an act which is 'more than merely preparatory to the commission of the offence' (section 1 Criminal Attempts Act 1981). The scope of the law of attempts is uncertain when it comes to computer fraud but it does not apply to conspiracies. It could be argued that a computer fraud which is not completed is an attempt to steal money. However, it depends on how far towards the completion of the theft the fraudster got and whether his actions or any of them were more than merely preparatory. It has been argued that a criminal attempt occurs when the person concerned carries out an act penultimate to the commission of the offence, i.e., the last act before completion. But, ultimately, the question is one for the jury to decide: it is a question of fact. Consider the case of an employee at a bank who decides, on his own, to transfer money to his own account from a customer's account. First, he switches on a computer terminal. Secondly, he enters the appropriate password to gain access. Then, he enters the instruction at the keyboard which causes the funds to be transferred. Finally, he draws the money out of his account. The problems arise when the bank employee fails to complete the offence of theft of the money for one reason or another. At what stage in the course of the events described does his actions become more than merely preparatory? A reasonable juryman might conclude that the offence of attempting to steal is not made out until the third act has been carried out, i.e., the entry of instructions which cause the computer system to transfer the money to the employee's account.

COMPUTER FRAUD AS THEFT

It might seem, from the above paragraphs, that, unless a conspiracy or attempt can be proved, a person who dishonestly convinces a computer that he is authorized to do something when he is not in fact so authorized, and makes the computer transfer money into his own bank account, commits an offence only if some other person has been deceived. Unless a human being has been subjected to the deception, it might seem that a charge of obtaining property by deception would not succeed, but the criminal law is not so easily defeated. Usually, the offence of theft will have been committed, regardless of the interposition of a computer. The offence of theft is defined in sections 1−6 of the Theft Act 1968 and section 1(1) states:

> A person is guilty of theft if he dishonestly appropriates property belonging to another with the intention of permanently depriving the other of it . . .

The words 'dishonestly', 'appropriates', 'property' and the phrases 'belonging to another' and 'with the intention of permanently depriving the other of it' all have special legal meanings which are set out in sections 2−5 of the Act. As far as computer crime is concerned, there is no real difficulty arising from the meanings of these words and phrases although the following points should be noted:

a) The definition of 'property' is very wide and will cover most things that can be stolen with the aid of a computer, but land does not usually come within the meaning of property nor do wild mushrooms or flowers, fruit or foliage on a wild plant.

b) Property is deemed to 'belong to another' if that person has control of it or has any proprietary right of interest in it.

c) 'Appropriation' is the assumption of the rights of the owner.

d) The 'thief' must intend permanently to deprive the other of the property, usually a mere 'borrowing' of an article is not theft, although it can be if, for example, it is for a very long period of time.

Point (d), above, is quite interesting. What is the position if a person gains access to a bank's computer system, draws money from various accounts and puts the money in his own account for a few weeks, collecting interest on the money, and then transfers the money back from whence it came, less the interest earned? Although there has been an appropriation (the person involved has assumed the rights of the owners of the money in the accounts), the account holders have not been permanently deprived of their money, it has merely been borrowed for a few weeks, what they have lost is the interest to which they would have been entitled. Clearly, there is no theft of the capital which has been returned intact, but what about the interest — has this been stolen? The interest did belong to another, that is the bank, but the bank paid it willingly under its normal terms of business, the appropriation has not been dishonest as far as the bank is concerned. After all, the bank has had the use of the capital for a period of time and the perpetrator of the 'fraud' will probably believe that he is not acting dishonestly as regards the bank.

The meaning of 'dishonesty' needs to be considered. The test used, derived from the case of *R* v *Ghosh* [1982], has two elements: first, was what was done dishonest according to the ordinary standards of reasonable and honest people? Secondly, did the person involved realize that what he did was dishonest by those standards? In the example above, where money is borrowed for a period of time for the purpose of collecting interest, the second limb of the test would be difficult to prove beyond reasonable doubt as regards the obtaining of interest from the bank. Certainly, the actions as a whole are dishonest and the actions should be criminal. The only way it appears that the above facts would give rise to criminal liability would be by regarding the true owners of the money used as having a proprietary right in the interest due on the money, but to hold that this is the case may be straining the language of the Theft Acts too far.

A case involving the borrowing of cinema films adds weight to the argument that a person who uses the computer to transfer funds temporarily into his own account does not commit the offence of theft. In *R* v *Lloyd* [1985], a projectionist at a cinema, in association with two others, removed films from the cinema for a few hours so that they could be copied and then returned the films so that no one would know what had occurred. The pirated copies of the films were then sold, making a considerable profit for the pirates. Here again a charge of theft (actually a conspiracy to steal in this case) was held to be inappropriate. Obviously, there was no intention permanently to deprive the owners of the films, nor was the copyright in the films stolen (it is not altogether clear whether copyright can be stolen). As mentioned earlier, borrowing can be theft if the period and circumstances are equivalent to an outright taking or disposal by section 6(1) of the Theft Act 1968, and this would be when the 'goodness' or 'virtue' in the thing taken had gone from it. Examples would include when a person borrows a radio battery intending to return it when it is exhausted, or borrows a bus pass intending to return it to the rightful owner when it expires. In the case of the films, however, there was still virtue in them when they were returned – they were still capable of being used and shown to paying audiences, so the pirates' convictions were quashed.

The fact that the owner of the copyright in the films had been deprived of potential 'sales' of the films by the circulation of pirate copies was not relevant to the offence of theft; nor would it be relevant in a case of the temporary transferral of funds whilst interest is collected. Although the lawful owner of the money (or other things such as shares and investments) has been deprived of the interest or earnings, it would appear that the law of theft cannot be invoked. However, the owner may be able to get some relief by obtaining damages in conversion at civil law. Depending on the circumstances, other criminal offences, such as abstracting electricity, may be committed by the person transferring the money etc.: *see* the following chapter on computer hacking.

A person committing fraud may have authority to use the computer system concerned. An employee whose duties include entering data into a computer system may alter that data to effect the fraud. Here, the employee is doing no more than carrying out his duties, albeit fraudulently. In other cases, an employee who has permission to use a computer system might use the computer in a manner beyond his normal duties. How does the law of theft deal with such cases? The concept of authority or consent is an important one in theft, for how can a person steal something if he has permission to take the thing? In *R* v *Morris* [1984], a case involving label-switching in a supermarket (that is, substituting one price tag with another stating a lower price) it was said that an unauthorized act was required for the appropriation necessary to constitute theft. Switching price labels is obviously not authorized by the supermarket. An employee who attempts to commit a fraud using computers will be doing something outside the scope of his authority to use the computer system, e.g., the person employed to input data into a computer system does not have authority to enter false data. If the other elements of the offence are present, such as an intention to permanently deprive, then theft will have been committed.

Another case which reinforces this approach is *Lawrence* v *Metropolitan Police Commissioner* [1972]. An Italian visitor to England hired a taxi and at the end of the journey gave the taxi-driver a £1 note for the fare. The taxi-driver said that this was not enough (the correct fare was just over 50p) and proceeded to help himself to an additional £6 from the visitor's wallet which was still open. The defence argued that the money had been taken with consent but it was held that the prosecution did not have to prove that the taking of the money was without the victim's consent. This is considerably wider than the *Morris* case and it is difficult to reconcile the two. However, even if the narrower view is taken, it is difficult to think of a case of computer fraud where the person will not be guilty of theft when he exceeds or otherwise compromises his authority to use a computer system. The fact that the computer system 'consents' to the transaction should not be relevant, as in the *Lawrence* case, because it is consent obtained by deception. The restriction of deception operating on a human mind should not be relevant in these circumstances.

OTHER OFFENCES INVOLVING FRAUD

Other offences which contain an element of fraud are provided for in the Theft Act 1968, e.g., false accounting (section 17), false statements by company directors, etc. (section 19) and the suppression of documents (section 20). There is nothing special about these offences in terms of computers except that their commission may be carried out with the aid of a computer. However, there may be problems associated with the admissibility of evidence in the form of computer documents and these evidential problems are discussed later in Chapter 24.

The remaining part of the common law fraud-related offence of cheating is of interest. Cheating was abolished by section 32(1) of the Theft Act 1968, with the exception of cheating with respect to offences relating to the public revenue. So, if a person makes a false declaration concerning his Income Tax or Value Added Tax, whether by using a computer or not, he will be guilty of the offence of cheating in addition to any offence under the Finance Acts. This dual liability is useful because there is little limitation on the penalty available for cheating which can consequently be used for more serious examples of revenue fraud. For example, in *R* v *Mavji* [1987], the accused had evaded Value Added Tax of over £1,000,000 and was charged with cheating; he was sentenced to six years' imprisonment and fined. If he had been charged under the Finance Act 1972, the longest sentence of imprisonment he could have received was 2 years. In the light of this case, it appears that no deception is required, the omission to make a tax return is sufficient. According to the Theft Acts, it appears that the offence of deception requires a human being to be deceived, but in the case of cheating there is no such requirement. This leads to the conclusion that if a person has a computerized accounts system which incorporates a Value Added Tax report generator, then suppressing or altering computer reports, and consequent failure to submit a return or submitting a 'doctored' return, means that the offence of cheating has been committed and the fact that a computer is implicated should not cause any difficulty.

Chapter 21
Hacking – the unauthorized access of computer systems

THE PROBLEM IN PERSPECTIVE

Computer hacking is the accessing of a computer system without the express or implied permission of the owner of that computer system. A person who engages in this activity is known as a computer hacker and may be motivated by the mere thrill of being able to outwit the security systems contained in a computer. A hacker may gain access remotely, using a computer in his own home or office connected to a telecommunications network.

Hacking can be thought of as a form of mental challenge, not unlike solving a crossword puzzle, and to date, the vast majority of hacking activities have been relatively harmless. Sometimes, the hacker has left a message publicizing his feat and this reflects the popular image of a hacker – a young enthusiast who is fascinated by computers and who likes to gain access to secure computer systems to prove his skills to himself or his peers. At worst, this form of hacking is no more than a nuisance. Many hackers are motivated by a sense of achievement; the very act of breaking into a computer system using their own mental effort is reward enough for them. There is a danger, however, that such 'innocent' hackers can cause damage to computer systems inadvertently.

However, there is a more sinister side to computer hacking. Many computer systems concern what might be called 'high-risk' activities such as the control of nuclear power stations, defence systems, aeroplane flight control and hospital records. The dangers stemming from hacking into these systems is self-evident and the potential for terrorism is worrying. As terrorists are unlikely to be deterred by the criminal law it is not just a matter of strengthening the law to deal with hackers. The key to overcoming the problems lies with those responsible for computer systems in high risk areas and it is essential that they do their utmost to make sure that the systems are as secure as possible. There is something to be said for the view that the enthusiastic young hacker has done the computer industry a great service by highlighting the deficiencies in the security aspects of many computer systems. Rather than subjecting these hackers to criminal proceedings, perhaps the computer industry should consider making use of their skill and expertise. In 1989, the co-founder of the Apple Computer Corporation made a donation to the University of Colorado for a computer hacking scholarship on the basis that it increased knowledge and understanding of computer systems.

Once the hacker has penetrated a computer system he may do several different things and the legal implications are determined by which of these are involved. He might read or copy information, which may be highly confidential, or he might erase or change information or programs stored in the computer system, or he may simply add something, such as a message boasting of his feat. He might be tempted to steal money or direct the computer to have goods sent to him, in which case what has been discussed in the previous chapter in terms of computer fraud is relevant.

By their very nature and relative susceptibility to unauthorized access, computer systems pose different problems from those encountered with information stored on paper. In the days before computers, sensitive information was kept locked away, in filing cabinets in locked rooms on the premises of the organization holding the data. This way, the sensitive information was relatively safe from being tampered with or copied. The biggest threat then would come from employees or burglars, but persons outside the organization would find it, on the whole, extremely difficult to gain access to the information. By contrast, information stored on a computer which is linked to a telecommunications system is much more vulnerable. It is analogous to paper files kept in locked cabinets but left in a public place. It is just a matter of finding the right key to fit the cabinet, and not only can a total stranger try the lock but, often, he can spend as long as he likes trying different keys with impunity until he finds one that turns the lock.

The House of Lords decision in the case of *R* v *Gold* [1988], highlights the problem of computer hacking and the danger of people gaining access to computer files without authorization. After the case, which seemed to conclude that computer hacking was not a criminal activity, per se, the computer industry was most dissatisfied with the scope of the criminal law and the perceived lack of haste on the part of Parliament to act. Concern at this position led to the Law Commission Working Paper No.110 on Computer Misuse (H.M.S.O., 1988), examining the scope of the law in terms of computer misuse generally and proposing alternative suggestions for legal changes directed at the problem of computer crime. However, as it stands, the law is not completely impotent when it comes to computer hacking and there are some areas of criminal law which might be available with which to combat computer hackers. Law can be very flexible but, when a new mischief appears, it is not always an easy matter to choose the most appropriate area of law with which to deal with it. There may be several areas of law which appear to have potential application, some will be better suited than others and the wrong choice of offence will be disastrous to a successful prosecution. In the *Gold* case it seems that the wrong choice was made.

If a hacker has broken into a computer system, what can the criminal law do? Criminal offences which may be relevant are those contained in the Theft Act 1968, the Criminal Damage Act 1971 and other less well known offences. In addition, the civil law can offer assistance in the areas of the law of confidence and copyright law (see Part I). After looking at the *Gold* decision in detail, these different areas of law will be discussed in terms of their scope and suitability as weapons to be used against hackers. Criminal damage offences, however, will be considered separately because they are of wider application. The Law Commission's recommendations for changing the criminal law to deal with hacking and other forms of computer misuse are discussed in Chapter 25.

THE CASE OF *R* v *GOLD*

Two computer hackers gained access to the British Telecom Prestel Gold computer network without permission and altered data. One of the accused also got into the Duke of Edinburgh's personal computer files and left the message: 'Good afternoon. HRH Duke of Edinburgh'. The accused were charged under the Forgery and Counterfeiting Act 1981 on the basis that they had made a *false instrument* falling within section 1. This states that a person shall be guilty of forgery if he makes a false instrument, with the intention that he or another shall use it to induce somebody to accept it as genuine, and by reason of so accepting it to do or not to do some act to his own or any other person's prejudice.

It was claimed that the false instrument was the CIN (customer identification number) and password. Section 8(1) of the Act states that a false instrument may be 'recorded or stored on disc, tape, sound track or other device'. However, their lordships suggested that 'recorded' or 'stored' connoted a process of a lasting and continuous nature from which the instrument could be retrieved in the future. In this case, the CIN and password were held only temporarily in the computer system whilst they were checked for validity and, after the check, they were eradicated totally and irretrievably.

The accused had been found guilty at the Crown Court, one being fined £750 and the other £600, but their convictions were quashed by the Court of Appeal and this was confirmed in the House of Lords. In the Court of Appeal, Lord Lane CJ said that the act of the accused in gaining access to the Telecom Gold files by what amounted to a dishonest trick was not a criminal offence. If the defendants' convictions had been upheld, the only rational interpretation of the effect of section 1 in the circumstances was that the defendants had deceived a computer. Bearing in mind that, in terms of the Theft Act offences, it does not appear to be possible to deceive a machine, the decision in the *Gold* case is eminently sensible. In effect, this was the wrong charge to bring and the defendants should have been charged with abstracting electricity and, possibly, criminal damage.

OFFENCES UNDER THE THEFT ACT 1968

As we have seen, the offence of theft is defined by section 1 of the Theft Act 1968 as a dishonest appropriation of property belonging to another with the intention permanently to deprive the other of it. If a hacker gains access to a computer system without permission and then makes a print-out of some information contained therein, has he committed theft? The fact that the owner of the information has not been deprived of it, because the hacker has only made a copy, is fatal to any charge of theft.

In *Oxford* v *Moss* (1978), it was held that confidential information does not come within the definition of property for the purposes of theft. The case concerned the 'borrowing' of an examination paper by a student before the date of the examination. Although the authority of the case is debatable, having been decided at first instance only, it is likely that it would be followed because the consequences of the decision are fundamentally sensible. After all, the owner still has the information unless the only copy was taken, but this is different from saying that the information is not property within the Theft Act. Property is defined as including 'money and all other property, real or personal, including things in action and other intangible property' and it could fairly be argued that confidential information comes within the meaning of 'other intangible property'. A better construction of *Oxford* v *Moss* is that the taking of the examination paper could not be theft because there was no intention to deprive the owner of it permanently. For this reason a hacker who simply reads or copies information has not committed theft. Similarly, in the Scottish case of *Grant* v *Procurator Fiscal* [1988], an employee who offered copies of his employer's computer print-outs to a competitor for £400 was acquitted. It was said that there was no authority for the proposition that the dishonest exploitation of the confidential information was a criminal offence. As a comparison, in Canada, there appears to be no difficulty in adjudging stealing confidential information as theft, as in the case of *R* v *Stewart* (1983).

If the information concerned is copied onto paper belonging to someone else, such as an employer, there will be an offence of theft committed with respect to the paper. Likewise, if a person copies information from a computer onto a disk which belongs to someone else and takes the disk, this would be theft of the disk if the other elements of theft are present such as the intention permanently to deprive the owner of the disk.

If the hacker goes further and not only makes a copy of the information but then, immediately after, goes on to erase the original from the computer system, is this more likely to be viewed as theft? The act of erasure will almost certainly be criminal damage as discussed later. In terms of theft, there will then be a dishonest appropriation of property belonging to another but is there an intention permanently to deprive the owner of that information? The difficulty here will be if the hacker believes that the owner has another copy of that information for if he does so believe there is no intention permanently to deprive. In the world of computers, additional security (back-up) copies of information are the rule and it would be reasonable for the hacker to believe that back-up copies have been made. Therefore, it would appear that unauthorized copying even coupled with the subsequent destruction of the original is unlikely to be theft.

There is an offence in the Theft Act 1968 which holds out more promise and that is the offence of abstracting electricity. The very act of hacking will result in the host computer (the computer 'hacked' into – accessed without permission) performing work as it retrieves information from its store. If that information is stored on magnetic disks, the disk drive heads will physically move, tracking across the disks, locating then reading the information which will then be moved into the computer's volatile memory by means of tiny electrical pulses. More electricity will be consumed in transmitting the information to the hacker's computer terminal. The total amount of electricity used to perform these acts will be small but, nevertheless, a definite amount will have been used as a result of the hacker's actions.

Section 13 of the Theft Act 1968 describes the offence of abstracting electricity as its dishonest use without due authority, or its dishonest waste or diversion. The offence is committed regardless of the amount of electricity so used and the only difficulty concerns the concept of dishonesty. There is no definition of dishonesty in the Theft Act 1968 for the purposes of section 13, but case law provides some guidance. The test of dishonesty which is used for the offences of theft and obtaining by deception derives from the case of *R* v *Ghosh* [1982], and there is no reason to doubt that the same test would apply to the offence of abstracting electricity. This test has already been described in the context of fraud in the previous chapter. Ultimately, the test must be resolved by the jury and whilst a jury would probably consider, objectively, that hacking was dishonest, the members of a jury might have more difficulty in deciding whether the accused hacker would realize that what he was doing was dishonest by the ordinary standards of reasonable and honest persons. It would depend to a large extent on the hacker's motives. If he did it for a mental challenge without wanting to do any real harm, then a jury would be likely to find the hacker not dishonest. On the other hand, if the hacker was attempting to commit some other crime, or taking revenge on a previous employer, a jury might be less inclined to acquit. The case of *R* v *Greenstein* [1975] illustrates one jury's perceptions of honesty: In this case the jury considered as dishonest the practice of 'stagging', which means applying for more shares in a new share issue than one can afford on the basis that the issue probably will be oversubscribed. Finally, it should be borne in mind that computer hackers are, by their very nature, fairly intelligent which means that they would probably realize that their actions were dishonest and in this case, a hacker would be committing the offence of abstracting electricity regardless of the nature of his actions.

COMMUNICATIONS OFFENCES

In certain circumstances, other offences may be committed by a hacker gaining access into a computer system without permission. Section 1 of the Interception of Communications Act 1985 makes it an offence to intercept a communication intentionally during its transmission through a public telecommunications system. This will only apply to a case where the hacker actually *intercepts* something, for example, the transmission of computer data over the British Telecom network. In most cases, the hacker will initiate the transmission and will cause the sending of the information. This offence, therefore, applies only to the situation where the hacker is 'eavesdropping', i.e., listening in for interesting communications to intercept.

Section 43 of the Telecommunications Act 1984 makes it a criminal offence to transmit messages which are grossly offensive, indecent, obscene or menacing by means of a public telecommunications system. Similarly, an offence is committed if false messages are sent by a person knowing of their falsity, or persistent use is made of the system for the purpose of causing annoyance, inconvenience or needless anxiety. The Act refers to messages, so if a pornographic diagram or picture is sent by the hacker, the offence might not be applicable. It could be argued, however, that a picture is just another way of conveying a message in which case section 43 of the 1984 Act would apply.

Menacing messages could be linked to the offence of blackmail (*see* Chapter 22) where the threat itself is transmitted by such means. The threat could concern the computer system, for example, where someone threatens to destroy information stored on the computer system. Alternatively, the threat may be of a less technical nature, for example, a threat to inform the Data Processing Manager's wife of his adultery. This offence under the Telecommunications Act will only be committed where a public system is used, such as British Telecom. It would appear that a hacker who sends just one false message will commit the offence if he knows that the message is false and transmits it for one of the purposes mentioned, for example, to cause annoyance. The same applies if the hacker persistently sends messages, whether true or false, with any of the motives mentioned above.

These offences are of limited scope only and will not apply to all cases of hacking. Often, a hacker will not transmit a message or if he does, it will not fall into any of the categories mentioned above. Sometimes, the hacker will only want to inspect information on the host computer. This offence would cover the situation where a person with a grudge, such as an ex-employee, wished to cause trouble and sent rude messages to be stored on his employer's computer system.

DATA PROTECTION ACT 1984

This Act and its implications are described more fully in Part IV. However, there may be some scope for the Act in terms of computer hacking and this aspect will be discussed here.

The Data Protection Act 1984 regulates the use and storage of personal data, i.e., information relating to individuals who can be identified from that information. The scope of the Act is limited to data processing apparatus as, by section 1(2), it states that it applies to data:

. . . recorded in a form which can be processed by equipment operating automatically in response to instructions given for that purpose.

A 'data user' is a person who holds personal data and must be registered with the Data Protection Registrar. Failure to register is a criminal offence, triable either way, carrying an unlimited fine if tried in the Crown Court, or a fine not exceeding £2,000 if tried in a Magistrates' Court.

If a computer hacker gains access to a computer system on which personal data is stored and then copies some of that data to his own computer, the hacker is guilty of the offence of holding personal data without being registered. Even if the hacker is registered under the Act, if he 'knowingly or recklessly' obtains personal data beyond the scope of his registration, he will still commit an offence. The above offences are not limited to computer hackers and will apply to any person.

Chapter 22

Damage to computer programs or data

CRIMINAL DAMAGE

An individual who gains access to a computer system and then erases information or programs stored in that computer system is guilty of criminal damage. The offence can be committed by a computer hacker or by a person who has permission to use a computer system, for example, an employee. Instances of criminal damage on a computer system will often involve employees. The offence may be carried out contemporaneously with the accessing of the computer system or it may occur after, as where a 'time-bomb' may have been placed in the computer system which will spring into action at a predetermined date and erase data stored on the computer system. A 'time-bomb' is simply some computer code which contains instructions to delete data from the computer system; the code itself is designed to check the computer date from time to time and when a predetermined date is reached, the code is activated and performs its task. It may even delete itself after doing its work, so destroying evidence of its existence. Employees may introduce these small programs which can do enormous damage if the employee is dismissed and unable to re-set the date at which the program will be activated.

Initially this chapter will consider the application of the Criminal Damage Act 1971 to cases where information of any type, including computer programs, is erased from a computer system. By section 1(1) of the Criminal Damage Act 1971, a person is guilty of an offence if, without lawful excuse, he destroys or damages any property belonging to another, and intends to do this or is reckless as to the possibility of its occurrence. The meaning of 'property' is obviously important as is the meaning of 'reckless'.

DAMAGE TO PROPERTY

Unlike the definition of property in the Theft Act 1968, the definition in section 10 Criminal Damage Act 1971 does not include tangible property. Data stored on a computer disk or tape cannot be directly seen or touched and is intangible and it would therefore appear that destroying or damaging information stored in a computer system is not criminal damage. At first sight, this seems to defeat the law of criminal damage, but there is a way around this problem by considering not the information itself, but the device upon which that information is stored. Usually, the information is stored on magnetic disks, tapes or cards or in silicon chips or on compact disks, or in terms of older technology, it may be stored on punched cards or paper tape. The type of storage medium is not important, but it is essential that the medium is tangible. If a person deliberately erases information stored on a computer disk, the disk itself is not physically damaged but it becomes of less value than it was before. Instead of being a useful computer disk containing programs or files of information it becomes a blank disk which is useless as it stands. The disk can be re-used and, perhaps, the data restored from a back-up copy but this may cause the owner considerable work. In such an instance has the person erasing the information committed the offence of criminal damage? In *Cox* v *Riley* (1986), the defendant, a disgruntled employee, erased computer programs stored on a printed circuit card which was used to control his employer's computerized saw. The defendant argued that he had not committed criminal damage because the programs were intangible and did not fall within the meaning of 'property' for the purposes of the Criminal Damage Act 1971. However, it was held that the printed circuit card itself was damaged by the erasure of the computer programs even though the card had not been physically damaged in any normal sense.

The decision may be interpreted on the basis that the card and the programs should be taken together as an entity in its own right as a programmed circuit card. This programmed card had been tampered with and was now a blank card and so the programmed card was damaged because it could no longer perform the tasks it was intended to do. It had been converted from a useful object to a useless one which would require a substantial amount of work to re-program it. Therefore, the act of erasing computer programs and data stored on disks, tapes or chips falls within the meaning of criminal damage.

A person charged with criminal damage may be tried in a Magistrates' Court or the Crown Court, depending largely on the value of the damage. If it is less than £4,000, the trial will be in a Magistrates' Court where the maximum term of imprisonment is six months. In the Crown Court, the maximum penalty for criminal damage is 10 years. The law has sharp teeth when it comes to criminal damage and there is no reason why persons indulging in destroying information stored on computers should be treated lightly. The consequences of their actions can be as severe as any other form of criminal damage. If a person commits arson or endangers life by his act of criminal damage then the maximum penalty available to the Crown Court is life imprisonment and damage to computer programs, or data stored on computer could conceivably have this type of effect. For example, a person who erases information on a computer system which controls a nuclear power station could well commit this more serious form of criminal damage, and it is rumoured that two patients died in a French hospital as a result of someone changing details of drug dosages stored in a computer system.

RECKLESS DAMAGE

The Criminal Damage Act 1971 states that the offence is committed if a person intends to cause damage or destruction to property or is *reckless* as to whether such damage or destruction might occur. The meaning and scope of the word 'reckless' is important in defining the limits of the offence; obviously, there is no difficulty if the person concerned has intended to cause the damage or destruction.

To examine the meaning of 'recklessness', it may be helpful to consider a possible chain of events. A person has gained access to a computer system, either with or without permission. He then proceeds to do certain things which could erase information, although he does not realize that this is a possible consequence of what he is doing. Typically, a computer hacker might erase information stored on a computer system because he does not fully understand the computer's operating system; he causes damage by mistake, not by intent. An employee who decides to abandon his normal duties and enters parts of the computer system he should not, perhaps out of curiosity, could also erase data inadvertently. The question is whether such unintentional damage constitutes a criminal offence; does it fall within the meaning of 'reckless'? In terms of the offence of criminal damage, 'recklessness' is when a person 'does an act which in fact creates an obvious risk that property would be destroyed or damaged and when he (that person) does that act he has either given no thought to the possibility of there being any such risk or has recognized that there was some risk involved and has nevertheless gone on to do it.' (*R* v *Caldwell* [1982].)

A basic requirement in establishing recklessness is that there is an obvious risk. If a person enters a computer system or part of a computer system with which he is unfamiliar, it is reasonable to suggest that there is such a risk. A file may be accidentally erased or corrupted by the use of a wrong or inappropriate command and given the variety of commands and instructions in operating systems, utilities and applications software, this is a very real danger. If the person then goes on to take the risk, whether aware of its existence or not, then, if there is subsequent damage or destruction of data which effectively reduces the value of the medium on which it stored, the offence is committed.

In most cases, a hacker or an employee who gains access into parts of a computer system without permission will run the risk of committing criminal damage even if there is no intention for this to happen. The only difficulty is where a person recognizes that there might be such a risk but concludes wrongly that the risk is non-existent or minimal; for example, he may have a certain amount of confidence in his own skill and may consider that he can overcome the risk. In this case, criminal damage will not apply. This gap in the scope of 'recklessness' is a result of case law and is regarded by some commentators to be unsatisfactory.

ADDITIONS OR ALTERATIONS TO DATA

Criminal damage applies to information and programs stored on a computer system by considering the storage medium itself to be damaged; that is, it has become less valuable, as a result. What is the situation if, instead of erasing data, additions or alterations are made to it? The only test to be applied is by reference to the medium; has it become less valuable as a result? Will it involve considerable work to restore it to its previous condition? To some extent, the answers to these questions depend on the nature of the additions or alterations. If they are minor and have no significant effect on the information or the performance of programs stored on the medium, it is unlikely that criminal damage will apply to such acts. However, if the additions or alterations are sufficient to spoil the usefulness of the medium and result in much work to put things back as they should be, a different conclusion will be reached.

It is probably with respect to additions that the greatest problem exists. If a person does not erase or alter information but simply adds to it by, e.g. simply leaving an unwelcome greeting, it can be argued that this is analogous to the work of 'graffiti artists' who use spray paint to apply their stylized initials or nickname on walls, buses and trains. These acts are clearly criminal damage even though the paint will, eventually, fade away and it is suggested that persons who leave messages and the like, the computer equivalent of graffiti, are guilty of criminal damage. The unwelcome addition damages the whole disk tape just as a wall can be damaged by the application of spray paint. In the latter case, the fabric and structure of the wall is unaffected but the visual information conveyed by the wall has been altered. If a person adds computer 'graffiti', it is submitted that this is criminal damage because the integrity of the storage media is totally dependent upon the information which is or is not stored on it.

COMPUTER VIRUSES

A recent phenomenon concerns so-called 'computer viruses'. These are usually small computer programs which are designed to spread throughout a computer system. They may 'attach' themselves to ordinary programs with the result that they are difficult to detect. Sometimes, viruses work simply by continually copying either themselves or other data until the computer storage medium becomes full, bringing the system to a standstill. More perniciously, the viruses may corrupt other computer programs or data. It may be some time before the presence of a computer virus is detected, by which time back-up copies of programs and data can become infected with the virus. It may be worth noting, as a salutary lesson, that it is rumoured that pirated software is the more likely type of software to contain a virus.

A person who deliberately (or recklessly) introduces a computer virus to a computer system will usually be guilty of criminal damage or attempted criminal damage. The purpose of a virus is to disable a computer system or to corrupt programs or files and make them unusable. The implications for the management of computer systems are twofold; first, that it is worth having a hierarchy of back-up versions of important programs and data and, secondly, making sure that software obtained for the computer system is from a reputable source. Unsolicited software should be treated with the utmost caution. Very recently, a large number of disks were distributed to various organizations purporting to give advice and information about 'AIDS' (acquired immune deficiency syndrome). These disks apparently contained a computer virus and the instructions stated that the programs and data should first be copied onto a hard disk. The so-called 'AIDS disks' were part of a blackmail plot in which it was suggested that damage would occur to all the information and programs stored on the hard disk unless a sum of money was sent to a box number in Panama. In many cases, the only way to eliminate the virus on a hard disk is to carry out a low-level format of the disk and replace the programs and data from back-up copies which it is hoped are unaffected. Specialized software is now available to detect and remove computer viruses.

BLACKMAIL

Blackmail is a serious offence and is triable only on indictment, that is, in the Crown Court. The offence is provided for in section 21 of the Theft Act 1968 and carries a maximum penalty of 14 years' imprisonment. Basically, a person is guilty of blackmail if, with a view to gain for himself or another or with intent to cause loss to another, he makes any *unwarranted demand with menaces*. The menaces are not restricted to threats of violence and include threats of action which is detrimental or unpleasant to the person to whom those threats are directed. An example is where a person threatens to reveal someone's previous financial difficulties unless that other person pays him some money. The 'protection racket' provides another example; that is, a shopkeeper's premises will be destroyed unless he makes certain payments.

So far as computers are concerned, a person would be guilty of blackmail who inserted a 'time-bomb' into a computer system and demanded money in return for details of how to disable the time-bomb. The fact that a computer is involved would be of no particular consequence apart from any difficulties concerning the admissibility of computer evidence, discussed in Chapter 24. If the owner of the computer system has already discovered and removed the time-bomb when the demand is made, it makes no difference, the offence has still been committed. The offence of blackmail will also have been committed even if the computer owner is not worried about the threat because he has a complete, up to date, set of back-up copies of everything likely to be affected.

The meaning of the word 'unwarranted' can cause problems. A demand is unwarranted unless the person making the demand does so in the belief that he has reasonable grounds for so doing and that the use of menaces is a proper way of reinforcing the demand. In most cases, the demand will plainly be unwarranted on the basis of this test, but there might be circumstances where this was not so. For example, a freelance programmer has carried out a substantial amount of work for a company which, he believes, has seriously underpaid him. In order to encourage the company to pay up, the programmer might tell the company that he has entered a computer virus into the computer system and he will unleash the viruses unless the shortfall in his payment is made up. It appears from case law that the accused must be judged by his own standards when it comes to the interpretation of 'unwarranted' and a jury might acquit the programmer if it feels that the programmer genuinely believes that he has reasonable grounds for making the demand and that the means he employs are proper, in his subjective opinion. Although this is somewhat unsatisfactory in that an accused person is being judged by his own moral standards, this is the current state of the law. However, a jury would be directed that the means cannot be proper if the action threatened is of a serious criminal nature such as murder or violence, but the position is less clear when it concerns criminal damage to a computer system.

Bearing in mind the serious nature of blackmail, any victim should not hesitate to inform the police. As with other forms of blackmail, a payment made to a blackmailer in return for not destroying computer data is likely to be followed by further demands in the future. Good security and comprehensive back-up systems are the best defences against this insidious form of crime. At the same time as committing blackmail, the blackmailer may also commit other offences such as abstracting electricity, criminal damage and offences under section 43 of the Telecommunications Act 1984.

Chapter 23
Miscellaneous offences

COPYRIGHT LAW

We have already seen that infringement of copyright can give rise to a wide range of civil law remedies such as injunctions, damages and accounts of profits. Copyright is unique amongst intellectual property rights in that it is also well served by the criminal law. Whilst patent law and trade mark law contain criminal sanctions, the rights prescribed by those branches of law are almost entirely enforced by the application of the civil law. Although it is true to say that the majority of copyright infringements will be dealt with in a satisfactory manner by the civil law, the criminal penalties available may be more appropriate in some circumstances.

Copyright law contains criminal penalties for most of the activities collectively known as 'secondary infringements'. The common denominator is that these activities can be thought of as being of a commercial nature and include the infringements of copyright commonly known as 'computer software piracy'; an example would be selling copies of computer software without the permission of the owner of the copyright in the software. The activities which attract criminal penalties are listed in Table 3 together with the appropriate maximum penalties.

As can be seen in Table 3, the scope of these criminal offences is fairly wide and will cover most forms of commercial exploitation. Of particular note is the fact that making an article designed to make copies is a criminal offence, as is being in possession of such a device if the intention is to make copies for sale or hire or use in the course of business. This would cover a piece of equipment specifically designed for this purpose but not a computer with a dual disk drive. Although the latter can be used for this purpose, computers are not designed for infringing copyright, they are designed for legitimate uses. The word 'article' is used in section 107(2) but is not defined in the Act in this context. Section 296 of the Act concerns devices and means to circumvent copy protection, but the word 'article' is not used here. It would seem unlikely that computer software designed to overcome copy protection, which facilitates the copying of other computer software, would fall within the meaning of 'article' and, therefore, producing such software may not be a criminal offence, although it would give rise to civil remedies. Alternatively, the software and the medium on which it resides might, taken together, be properly described as an article. The lack of clarity in section 107(2) is regrettable, although the purpose of this offence is probably to

Table 3 Criminal offences and copyright law

Offence (Copyright, Designs and Patents Act 1988)	Classification of penalty (see below)
Section 107(1). With respect to an article which the person concerned knows or has reason to believe is an infringing copy of a copyright work:	
a) making for sale or hire	MC/CC
b) importing into the U.K. (not for private and domestic use)	MC/CC
c) possessing in the course of business with a view to committing any act infringing the copyright	MC
d) in the course of a business –	
i) selling or letting for hire	MC
ii) offering or exposing for sale or hire	MC
iii) exhibiting in public	MC
iv) distributing	MC/CC
e) distributing otherwise than in the course of a business to such an extent as to affect prejudicially the owner of the copyright	MC/CC
Section 107(2). With respect to an article specifically designed or adapted for making copies of a particular copyright work where the person concerned knows or has reason to believe that it is to be used to make infringing copies for sale or hire or for use in the course of a business:	
a) making such an article	MC
b) being in possession of such an article	MC

Classification of penalties:

MC/CC – (triable either way). On summary conviction: imprisonment not exceeding 6 months and/or a fine not exceeding £2,000. On conviction on indictment: imprisonment not exceeding 2 years and/or a fine (unlimited amount)

MC – (summary trial only, i.e. in Magistrates' Court): imprisonment not exceeding 6 months and/or a fine not exceeding level 5 (presently £2,000)

control activities such as the making and use of plates for printing processes and the like and in fact, the Copyright Act of 1956 talked in terms of a plate for making infringing copies. However, as discussed later in this chapter, the supplying of software or devices to assist with the copying of computer software protected by copyright may be caught by the law of incitement.

The reason why the criminal law is relatively strong as regards copyright is the ease with which copyright works can be copied and the scale on which it can be done. It is a simple matter to copy most computer software even if it is copy-protected and, what is more, the investment required to do this and to market and sell the copies is relatively small. In contrast, to copy and sell an invention protected by patent law is likely to involve a substantial investment, requiring the acquisition of factory space, storage, expensive equipment, transport, etc. The scope and magnitude of criminal penalties have gradually been increased and strengthened to cater for the growing ease of copying with the advent of high speed photo-copiers, video recorders, twin-tape cassette players and computers.

The availability of equipment which facilitates copying has not gone unchallenged. In the United States of America the film industry attempted, unsuccessfully, to prevent the sale of the Sony Betamax video recorder. In the United Kingdom the record industry argued unsuccessfully that the sale of the Amstrad twin-tape cassette machine was an incitement to infringe copyright; *see Amstrad Consumer Electronics plc* v *The British Phonograph Industry Ltd.* [1986] and *CBS Songs Ltd.* v *Amstrad Consumer Electronics plc* [1988]. The way these machines were advertised did nothing to reassure the industry, using phrases such as 'you can even make a copy of your favourite cassettes', and it is true that most purchasers of such machines would use them to make unauthorized copies of music tapes and computer software, especially computer games on cassette tape. In the first *Amstrad* case above, it was held that supplying machines which would be likely to be used unlawfully to copy pre-recorded cassettes subject to copyright protection was insufficient to make the manufacturer or supplier an infringer of copyright. Neither could Amstrad be said to be authorizing infringement of copyright because it had no control over the way its machines were used once sold. In the latter case, it was held that a claim that Amstrad, by its advertising literature, was inciting others to infringe copyright gave no legal remedies. Amstrad had printed a small warning about infringing copyright in its literature and this was sufficient.

These two cases illustrate the difficulties in reconciling two distinct objectives, i.e., encouraging technical innovation and making it available to the public on the one hand and protecting the interests of those willing to invest in music, films, computer software, etc. on the other hand.

Incitement is a common law offence and, with the exception of incitement to commit murder, is not to be found in Acts of Parliament. This gives the courts some flexibility in applying and interpreting this area of law. Although Amstrad was not guilty of incitement to infringe copyright, there may be other situations where a conviction might be more likely. For example, in the case of devices and computer software specifically designed to circumvent copy protection, the makers and sellers of such gadgets and software cannot point to legitimate uses unlike the Amstrad and similar twin tape machines. They are designed to enable persons to make copies of software packages clearly against the wishes of the owners of the copyright in such packages. Indeed, as has been noted in Chapter 4, the Copyright, Designs and Patents Act 1988 specifically provides that civil law remedies should be available against persons responsible for the sale and distribution of such methods of overcoming copy-protection. It would appear that the criminal law offence of incitement may be available against such persons.

A pirate who copies or imports copied software with a view to selling it may also commit other offences apart from those under copyright law, depending on the circumstances. The Forgery and Counterfeiting Act 1981, the Trade Descriptions Act 1968 and section 25 of the Theft Act 1968 may be relevant. The pirate can also be pursued through the civil courts and the decision to pursue civil or criminal remedies, or both, will depend on the nature and scale of the infringement, the pirate's knowledge of the existence of copyright in the work and whether the pirate has any funds available to pay damages. It must be said, however, that criminal proceedings under copyright law have not been frequent. This might be explained by a lack of interest or understanding of the problem on the part of the police and Crown Prosecution Service or the possibility that these agencies perceive civil law to be a more satisfactory way of dealing with pirates. Nevertheless, the offences described below might be charged instead of, or in addition to copyright offences and Trading Standards Officers in particular, might be interested in offences concerned with the Trade Descriptions Act, especially if members of the public are being prejudiced by the pirate's activities.

FORGERY AND COUNTERFEITING ACT 1981

Section 1 of this Act states that:

> A person is guilty of forgery if he makes a false instrument, with the intention that he or another shall use it to induce somebody to accept it as genuine, and by reason of so accepting it to do or not to do some act to his own or any other person's prejudice.

We have seen that the application of this offence to computer hacking has been a failure. If a computer software pirate, however, makes copies of a popular package, dressing up the copies to look like the original and then selling them, he may be guilty of the offence contained in section 1 of the Act. It may seem strange to talk in terms of a 'false instrument' in relation to computer software, but section 8 of the Act describes a false instrument as including:

> 'any disc, tape, sound track or other device on or in which information is recorded or stored by mechanical, electronic or other means.'

It would seem that every form and method of storing computer software will fall within this definition.

It could be argued that the person who buys a pirate copy of computer software will not be deceived and that he will know that, in the circumstances, the software he is purchasing is an unauthorized copy, especially if the price is considerably lower than usual, but this does not matter. The Act requires that the pirate intends the customer to accept the copy as being genuine and in one sense the copy will be genuine as it will be a direct copy of the computer programs. The programs themselves are the genuine programs. Section 1 requires that someone should accept the false instrument as genuine resulting in that person *or another* being prejudiced. Therefore, it does not matter if the person buying the copy is not prejudiced, after all he will have obtained a copy which works as well as the genuine article, it is sufficient that someone else has been prejudiced. That someone else is the owner of the copyright subsisting in the programs who will have been prejudiced because he has lost a potential sale as a result of the pirate's activities. If the customer himself believes that the software is genuine, then the pirate can be charged with the offence of obtaining by deception (section 15, Theft Act 1968) which carries a maximum of 10 years' imprisonment, the same as under section 1 of the Forgery and Counterfeiting Act 1981. The choice between these two offences will have to be carefully considered in the light of the actual circumstances.

TRADE DESCRIPTIONS ACT 1968

By section 1 of the Trade Descriptions Act 1968, any person who, in the course of a trade or business, applies a false trade description to any goods or supplies or offers to supply goods to which a false trade description has been applied, is guilty of an offence. A 'trade description' includes an indication as to the person by whom the goods are manufactured. Therefore, if a computer software pirate makes copies of a software package, without the permission of the copyright owner, in such a way that the copies look like the genuine article, then the offence has been committed. A person who sells or offers such copies for sale will also be guilty of the offence. The rationale behind these provisions is to protect the public from being deceived into buying inferior goods, rather than protecting the interests of copyright owners. Prosecution is normally undertaken by Trading Standards Officers and the offence carries a maximum of 2 years' imprisonment and/or a fine if tried in the Crown Court, or a fine not exceeding £2,000 if the offender is convicted in a Magistrates' Court. The usefulness of this offence is that it is appropriate to pirated goods, including computer software, video cassettes, etc. sold in markets, often in the unofficial Sunday markets or car boot sales, which will be monitored by Trading Standards Officers.

The offence can only apply if the copy carries the name or mark of the genuine maker, or a name or mark which is extremely similar. So a pirate could avoid the consequences of this legislation if he takes care to use a different name for the software and its maker and uses packaging which is different.

If the maker of computer software uses a registered trade mark and many of the names of popular software packages and the names of the makers of the packages are registered trade marks, someone who applies a mark which is identical or nearly resembles the genuine mark or sells or offers for sale, etc. goods which bear that applied mark, is guilty of an offence under the Trade Marks Act 1938, as amended by section 300 of the Copyright, Designs and Patents Act 1988. The penalties for this offence are relatively severe, reflecting the problems of imported counterfeit goods, ranging from pedal cycles to T-shirts and including computer software. On conviction on indictment the maximum term of imprisonment is 10 years and/or a fine, whilst on summary conviction the maximum is 6 months imprisonment and/or a fine not exceeding £2,000. Computer software pirates would be well advised not to apply a trade mark or anything remotely resembling a trade mark to their pirated copies of software.

The offences mentioned in this chapter are not limited to computer software and could, just as easily, apply to hardware. For example, a person selling a computer which is identical to a well known make could, if he applies the trade mark to the machines, be guilty of both of the above offences.

SECTION 25 OF THE THEFT ACT 1968

In a fictitious example, a software pirate who is travelling by car to a market with a bootful of pirated software, is stopped on the way and the pirate copies are noticed. Has he committed an offence? He has not yet sold or offered any of the copies for sale. By section 25 of the Theft Act 1968, he may be guilty of 'going equipped to cheat' and 'cheat' means the same as obtaining by deception (section 15). Therefore, if the pirate intends to sell the software as genuine to obtain payment, he is guilty of the offence. The maximum penalty is three years imprisonment. It must be noted, however, that the software must look like the genuine article, and it must be packaged to look like the real thing so that potential customers will be 'deceived'.

Chapter 24
Evidential difficulties associated with computer crime

Evidence is a complicated subject, littered with rules and exceptions to rules. One of the rules governs the admissibility of hearsay evidence; that is, a statement made other than by a person giving oral evidence in the proceedings is not normally admissible of any fact or opinion contained in the statement. There are many exceptions to this harsh rule such as dying declarations, statements in public documents, depositions given before a magistrate, documentary evidence, etc. Without these exceptions, the person responsible for the statement in question must be able to stand up in court and confirm the statement. In the case of computer documents there has to be some exception to the hearsay rule as, in many cases, it will not be possible to identify the person or persons who entered the information concerned. This information may have passed through the hands of a chain of employees, several of whom could have entered the information in question. The law of evidence has to be flexible enough to cope with the realities of the modern business world, otherwise persons committing criminal activities (particularly those involving dishonesty such as fraud) would, in effect, be immune from prosecution. However, it must be recognized that computers are not infallible and some fundamental requirements have to be met before computer statements can be excepted from the hearsay rule.

The relevant statutory provisions are contained in section 69 of the Police and Criminal Evidence Act 1984, and in section 24 of the Criminal Justice Act 1988 which replaces section 68 of the Police and Criminal Evidence Act 1984. Section 24 applies to 'business documents'. In basic terms computer-generated documents (computer print-out) are admissible in evidence if created or received by a person in the course of a trade, business, profession or other occupation, or as the holder of a paid or unpaid office. Furthermore, the information contained in the document must have been supplied by a person having, or reasonably supposed to have, personal knowledge of it. An additional requirement is that the person who supplied the information cannot reasonably be expected to have any recollection of the matters contained in that information. This will obviously be the case in a large organization where employees are dealing with many transactions each working day. If, however, the person supplying the information can be identified and does remember it, then that person can give evidence of it, in which case his evidence will not be hearsay but will be first-hand and directly admissible.

Section 24 of the 1988 Act is subject to section 69 of the Police and Criminal

Evidence Act 1984 which states that a statement produced by a computer is not evidence of any fact stated in it, unless it can be shown that there are no reasonable grounds for believing that the statement is inaccurate because of improper use of the computer and that the computer was operating properly at all material times, or if not, any failure was not such as to affect the production of the document or the accuracy of the contents. Section 25 of the Criminal Justice Act 1988 gives the court a discretion to refuse to admit hearsay evidence, including computer documents, if the court is of the opinion that the statement ought not to be admitted in the interests of justice.

The application of these provisions has not proved easy for the courts and in the case of *R* v *Harper* (1988), the Court of Appeal laid down some guidelines. This case involved the interpretation of section 68 of the Police and Criminal Evidence Act 1984 which has now been replaced by section 24 of the Criminal Justice Act 1988, but the principles should be the same. If anything, section 24 is a less stringent provision. The guidelines suggest the following approach:

1) Section 24 of the Criminal Justice Act 1988 and section 69 of the Police and Criminal Evidence Act 1984 are not independent tests but should both be satisfied.
2) Although the 'personal knowledge' requirement of section 24 might prove difficult to show in practice because it may not be possible to identify the exact persons involved in a large organization, circumstantial evidence of the usual habit or routine regarding the use of the computer might suffice, based on a presumption of regularity. The same applies to the requirement that the person who supplied the information cannot reasonably be expected to have any recollection of the matters contained in the information concerned.
3) The trial judge should critically examine any suggestions that any prior malfunction of the computer or its software has any relevance to the reliability of the particular computer records submitted in evidence.
4) If the judge decides that the computer evidence is admissible, he should direct the jury that the weight to be attached to such evidence is a matter for the jury to assess.

These provisions are not notable for their clarity and the flowchart in Figure 4 will help to explain them. An example might also help to clarify the position. Joe Smith alters his Building Society passbook to show a balance of £1,000, when he should only have a balance of £100, and this is the figure recorded on the computer along with a record of his transactions. Joe is prosecuted for forgery and for obtaining by deception. The prosecution wishes to submit, in evidence, a computer print-out showing his account and transactions.

Referring to the flowchart, the first test is easily satisfied because the Building Society is acting in the course of business. The second test is more difficult because the employees of the Building Society who supplied details of the transactions entered into the computer system cannot be identified with any certainty. It can be presumed, however, from the regular business of the Building Society (i.e. the third test) that staff supplying the details

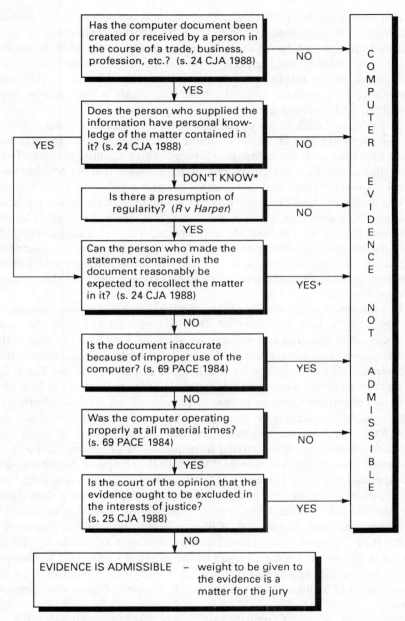

Has the computer document been created or received by a person in the course of a trade, business, profession, etc.? (s. 24 CJA 1988) — **NO** →

YES ↓

Does the person who supplied the information have personal knowledge of the matter contained in it? (s. 24 CJA 1988) — **NO** →

YES ←

DON'T KNOW*

Is there a presumption of regularity? (*R* v *Harper*) — **NO** →

YES ↓

Can the person who made the statement contained in the document reasonably be expected to recollect the matter in it? (s. 24 CJA 1988) — **YES+** →

NO ↓

Is the document inaccurate because of improper use of the computer? (s. 69 PACE 1984) — **YES** →

NO ↓

Was the computer operating properly at all material times? (s. 69 PACE 1984) — **NO** →

YES ↓

Is the court of the opinion that the evidence ought to be excluded in the interests of justice? (s. 25 CJA 1988) — **YES** →

NO ↓

COMPUTER EVIDENCE NOT ADMISSIBLE

EVIDENCE IS ADMISSIBLE — weight to be given to the evidence is a matter for the jury

* For example, the person cannot be identified.
+ In which case, the person may be able to give evidence himself.

Note: CJA – Criminal Justice Act, PACE – Police and Criminal Evidence Act

Figure 4   Admissibility of computer evidence in criminal proceedings

would have personal knowledge, at the time, of those details, so this provides sufficient circumstantial evidence. The fourth test, concerned with the recollection of the matters in the information, can be answered in the negative for it is self-evident that the persons who made the statement would not in the normal way be able to remember the information. If, however, there was something very unusual about it these individuals would be able to be identified and so could give evidence directly.

The fifth and sixth stages of the flowchart concern the use and operation of the computer system. In the example concerning Joe Smith there have been problems with the computer software which resulted in errors in the recording of certain transactions, but there is evidence that the problems were quickly overcome and that Joe Smith's account was not in use at the time of the problems. Also a computer hacker has penetrated the computer system but it is claimed that the system is now secure and, again, Joe Smith's account was not affected. On the basis of the foregoing, it is likely that the trial judge would allow the computer print-out to be submitted as evidence, but he would direct the jury that the weight to be attached to this evidence was a matter for them to assess in the light of the problems experienced with the computer system.

Once more, the importance of maintaining a secure computer system can be seen. If a jury are satisfied that the computer system has been professionally operated and maintained, they are more likely to believe that the computer print-out is accurate. It is vital that nothing should detract from the admissibility or weight to be attached to computer evidence. The ability of hackers to penetrate a computer system coupled with poor hardware and software monitoring and maintenance procedures are likely to destroy the admissibility of computer evidence or, at the very least, reduce its credibility.

A hacker or fraudster can make his subsequent prosecution much more difficult by altering or destroying information or programs stored in the computer system. The insertion of 'bugs' into the computer programs would be especially effective. The best way to prevent or nullify this is to keep back-up copies of the programs and data and preferably, several copies should be retained taken at different times, representing several generations of programs and data. In this way, a history is built up which can be used to support any claim that the system has been operating satisfactorily and any recent problems are the direct result of the criminal's actions. The retention of back-up copies spanning some years has many other benefits, legal and non-legal, and it should be a top priority in the operation of any computer system.

Section 23 of the Criminal Justice Act 1988 also provides for the admissibility of computer evidence in criminal proceedings applying where the statement in the document concerned has been made directly by the person concerned. An example might be where a person writes some notes concerning an assault he has witnessed, using a word processing system and that person cannot give direct evidence for any one of the following reasons:
a) The person has subsequently died or is unfit to give evidence because of

his bodily or mental condition, or

b) the person is no longer in the United Kingdom and it is not reasonably practicable for him to attend as a witness, or

c) the person cannot be found, after taking reasonable steps to find him. Section 23 is also subject to the provisos contained in section 69 of the Police and Criminal Evidence Act; that is, the document is accurate because there has been no improper use of the computer and the computer has been operating properly at all material times. The judge has a discretion to exclude evidence which is admissible by section 23.

Chapter 25
Computer crime – concluding remarks

SUGGESTIONS TO PREVENT OR MINIMIZE CRIMINAL ACTIVITIES

There are several things that the owner or operator of a computer system can do to prevent or minimize the possibility of criminal activities being successfully perpetrated against the computer system or the data or software stored therein. The main principle is to avoid complacency; it would be a very brave data processing manager who considers his system so secure that it is safe against criminals. To some extent, strong security can foster complacency and can even present the would-be criminal with an enjoyable challenge. However, the golden thread running through the suggestions below is that security is a most important means of protection and great care must be taken to develop a strong yet workable system of passwords and hierarchical access. Persons using the computer system should only be able to obtain access to those parts of the system which they will use. Different modes of access might be appropriate for different operators. For example, if the computer system contains a database, some users will only need to view and inspect the data, whilst others will be allowed to add to the data; yet others may be entitled to delete or edit the data or parts of the data. The scope of access granted to various people should reflect their responsibilities and be no more than is necessary for them to carry out their duties. Access will be by way of passwords and passwords which are easy to guess such as car registration numbers, spouses' names, etc. should be avoided as should the temptation of using easily remembered passwords. Passwords need to be changed frequently, and the use of a two password system, one password unique to each user and another for his level of access should be considered. A log of access to the computer system must be kept which notes user identification and times of ingress and egress, and these must be checked with users periodically. It must be made as difficult as possible for ordinary users to enter the computer's operating system.

With this general advice in mind, some more suggestions, related to specific criminal threats are described below.

Fraud and theft

The largest threat is from within; that is, from employees. Employees' attention needs to be drawn to the fact that security is taken seriously and incidents will be reported to the police. This must be reinforced by the operation of a system of spot checks and systems for double-checking (including manual systems) need to be maintained. These systems should be varied from time to time as variety is the criminal's greatest enemy and someone considering using the computer to commit a fraud will usually do so only after they have become cognizant of the systems in operation. Changes will frustrate attempts to do this. Spot checks should be carried out on accounts chosen at random and on any unusual transactions, for example, sudden movement in an account that has been dormant for some time.

As regards supplier/sub-contractor accounts and wages systems, it must be ensured that any new entries are genuine and that they have performed the work for which they are being paid. A data processing manager must learn to behave like an external auditor with his own computer systems and to use a high profile when it comes to checking that everything is as it should be.

Hacking

Obviously, security is very important here too. The location of passwords must be carefully considered; are they in a text file stored on the computer which can easily be inspected by a person working in the operating system? Some form of code for any passwords which must, of necessity, be stored on the computer system should be considered. If a computer system is being installed or expanded, the need for linking that system with a telecommunications system must be carefully considered. Is it essential to have remote access to the system? Would it be feasible to have computers at branch offices which are updated by being sent new copies of the data on disk or tape from time to time? Security needs to be made a high profile matter at branch offices.

Criminal damage (including time-bombs, viruses)

The danger here can come from hackers, employees, freelance programmers, sub-contractors, etc. Employees who have been dismissed or have been given notice of termination of their employment represent a significant threat of damage to a computer system for such a person may be out to avenge himself if he feels aggrieved. If an employee has given notice to leave his employment, or has been dismissed, that employee should be denied access to the computer system and should perhaps be given salary in lieu of notice. Passwords and security generally will need to be reviewed and changed depending on the employee's familiarity with the computer system. It should be borne in mind that the employee may have found out a considerable amount about the computer system during his employment; perhaps more than he needs to know for the purpose of performing his duties. It is worthwhile keeping a separate set of back-up copies of important programs and data in write-protected form. For example, when a new software package has been obtained the original disks need to be write-protected immediately and duplicates made which can be used as working copies.

Again, it needs to be made clear that security is taken seriously and that the computer system is constantly being monitored. A potential source of computer viruses is pirated software which is to be avoided at all costs as should software of doubtful pedigree. If a computer is attended to by a maintenance engineer, his diagnostic disks should be checked to ensure that they are write-protected for if not, he may have collected a virus on his rounds which could be passed on to any computer.

Intellectual property offences

So far as these offences are concerned, little can be done in terms of prevention apart from pursuing the pirates ruthlessly and using the full weight of the civil law as well as the criminal law. Copy-protection can be counter productive. Users should be educated about the important benefits of using genuine software, benefits such as support and the availability of updates. Care must be taken to prevent employees copying software and distributing it as this could breach the terms of the employer's licence agreement, allowing the licensor to revoke the licence and claim damages.

THE FUTURE

The Law Commission produced a Report in October 1989 on 'Computer Misuse' in which the creation of three new offences was recommended, directed at the problem of unauthorized acts in relation to computer systems, including hacking. These proposed offences are:

1. *Unauthorized access to a computer*. This covers computer hacking. It would be punishable with a maximum of three months' imprisonment or a fine of up to £1,000. The offence would be committed by a person who intended to gain access to a computer knowing that such access was unauthorized.
2. *Unauthorized access to a computer with intent to commit or facilitate the commission of a serious crime*. A 'serious crime' is one for which the maximum penalty is five years' imprisonment or more. This offence would cover a situation where a hacker accesses a computer system intending to erase data or intending to steal money. It would be triable either way and, if tried in the Crown Court, punishable with imprisonment of up to five years. This offence is a preliminary one and is similar but stronger than the law of attempts. There is no need for the serious crime to have been completed.
3. *Unauthorized modification of computer material*. This is, effectively, a way of strengthening and consolidating the law of criminal damage as it applies to computer programs and data. It would carry a maximum of five years' imprisonment and would be triable either way. One major

difference between this offence and criminal damage is that 'recklessness' is not sufficient for this proposed offence (as it is for criminal damage) and the offence would only be committed if the person involved intended to modify the data. It is, therefore, significantly narrower than criminal damage.

Originally, the Government planned to introduce legislation specifically to combat computer misuse in 1989/90 after a private member's Bill introduced by Emma Nicholson MP had been withdrawn. However, the anticipated computer misuse Bill was omitted from the Queen's Speech to Parliament in Autumn 1989. At the time of writing, a private member's Bill, introduced by Michael Colvin MP and based largely on the Law Commission's recommendations, is progressing through Parliament. The Bill, known as the 'Computer Misuse Bill', has Government support and may become law later in 1990. There remain a great many critics of the basic hacking offence (proposed offence 1, above) and it is arguable that simple hacking should not be criminalized, bearing in mind questions of civil liberties and the difficulty in enforcing such a law. Above all, computer security must be improved and this is a much more effective way to tackle the problems of computer crime than by legislation, even the proposed legislation.

SUMMARY

It has been shown that a wide variety of criminal offences can be committed using or involving computer technology. Other offences may also be carried out, e.g., murder or manslaughter can be achieved by interfering with a 'safety critical system' such as an air traffic control computer or a hospital computer monitoring the treatment of patients. Of course, some offences are not relevant to computer technology and it would be difficult to envisage a situation where rape could be carried out using a computer. However, given the ingenuity of the criminal mind, there are certain to be other forms of crime which will be attempted in the future.

The discussion in this Part has shown that the criminal law is able to cope with many forms of computer crime although there are a few weak points and grey areas. It is unlikely that a comprehensive computer crime statute will be enacted but there may be some minor additions to the law. Following the Law Commission Working Paper No. 110 on 'Computer Misuse', the subsequent Report and pressure from the computer industry, it is possible that legislation will be passed in mid to late 1990 clearly making computer hacking a criminal offence in its own right.

In most cases of computer crime, the question of evidence will be important in two respects: firstly, the obtaining of evidence and, secondly, its admissibility. On the first point, this will not usually present a problem as the victim will have most of the evidence on his own computer system unless the criminal has erased it all. Piracy is different in that the pirate himself may possess much of the evidence, although there are powers of search and seizure contained in the Copyright, Designs and Patents Act 1988 to cover this situation. As far as the admissibility of computer evidence in criminal proceedings is concerned, the statutory provisions are reasonably generous and contain important safeguards as regards evidence of a dubious quality.

Table 4 gives a summary of offences together with their maximum penalties and some comment concerning their scope.

Table 4 Summary of offences

Offence	Description	Maximum penalty	Comment
Fraud/theft related s.15 Theft Act 1968	Obtaining by deception	10 years	Difficulty with respect to machine being deceived (requires a human to be deceived).
s.1 Theft Act 1968	Theft	10 years	Will cover most cases involving computer 'fraud'.
s.17–20 Theft Act 1968	False accounting etc.	7 years	No particular difficulties with computer technology.
Cheating	Common law offence	unlimited	Only available for Inland Revenue and VAT frauds.
Hacking, criminal damage s.13 Theft Act 1968	Abstracting electricity	5 years	May be difficulty with respect to 'knowledge'.
s.1 Interception of Communications Act 1985	Interception of communcation during its transmission through a public telecommunications system	2 years	Suitable for computer 'eavesdropping'. If tried in MC, max. is a fine of £2,000.
s.43 Telecommunications Act 1984	The transmission of grossly offensive, indecent, obscene or menacing messages	Fine max. £400 summary trial only	Can only be tried in MC. Must be by public telecommunications system.
s.1 Criminal Damage Act	Destruction or damage to property belonging to another	10 years	May be intentional or reckless. Max. is life imprisonment if life is endangered. Consider damage to medium on which

Table 4 (cont)

			data is stored. If damage less than £4,000 then triable in MC only.
s.21 Theft Act 1968	Blackmail	14 years	Unwarranted demand with menaces. Triable in CC only.
Intellectual property related Copyright, Designs and Patents Act 1988	Secondary infringement generally making pirate copies for sale or 'dealing' with pirate copies		See Table 3 for penalties
s.1 Forgery and Counterfeiting Act 1981	Making a false instrument	10 years	Requires someone to believe it to be genuine.
s.1 Trade Descriptions Act 1968	Applying a false trade description, etc.	2 years	Trade description includes an indication of the manufacturer of the goods.
s.58 Trade Marks Act 1938	Applying a registered trade mark, etc. without permission	10 years	Amended by s.300 of the Copyright, Designs and Patents Act 1988.
s.25 Theft Act 1968	Going equipped to cheat	3 years	'Cheat' has the same meaning as 'obtaining by deception'.
Other Data Protection Act 1984	Holding personal data without being registered	Unlimited fine	

Note: CC – Crown Court, MC – Magistrates' Court.
Unless otherwise indicated, offences can be tried in either a Magistrates' Court or in the Crown Court and if tried in a Magistrates' Court, the maximum penalty available is 6 months' imprisonment and/or a fine not exceeding £2,000.

PART IV
Data protection

Computer technology has heightened fears about a society of the kind portrayed in Orwell's '1984', because of the power of computers in terms of information processing. There is a popular feeling that computers undermine human skills and that the growth of computer technology heralds the dawn of an austere and coldly logical society. Certainly, the power of computers can be misused and there needs to be a system of checks and balances to prevent abuse of this power. However, it is worth remembering that Hitler achieved all that he did without the use of a computer.

The common law has long provided remedies for the misuse of information, however it is stored. For example, the law of confidence protects confidential information and the law of defamation controls the publication of untrue information which may harm an individual and lower his standing amongst 'right thinking members of society'. These common law controls, however, are inadequate in the context of computer data which concerns individual persons, as for one thing, the aggrieved party must take action himself. A far better approach, as has been adopted by the Data Protection Act 1984, is to provide a system of registration, monitoring and control under the direction of a Registrar who has powers of enforcement and prosecution.

In this Part of the book, data protection law is examined and described together with a discussion of the practical consequences of the Data Protection Act 1984 and its implications.

Unless otherwise mentioned, all statutory references are to the Data Protection Act 1984.

Chapter 26
Outline of the Data Protection Act 1984

INTRODUCTION

There are many horror stories about people who have had information wrongly attributed to them and stored on computer to the effect that they are bad credit risks. In the past, such people have been unable to discover what information concerning them is stored on computer and have it corrected. Another problem has been the lack of control of organizations who pass on personal information to others, resulting in many people having been inundated with unsolicited mail. A more sinister aspect of computer stored information is a direct result of the powerful processing powers of computers and the ability to use computers to target certain groups of individuals. The dangers of permitting the use of sensitive information stored on computers to continue unchecked are manifold.

The Data Protection Act was enacted, appropriately in Orwellian terms, in 1984 to control the storage and use of information about individuals stored and processed by computer. Control of those who store and use such information using computers is provided for by a system of registration with penalties for failing to register and for acting beyond the scope of the registration. Additionally, the Act introduces a set of *Data Protection Principles* which must be followed by persons who store or process information using computers about living persons. Computer bureaux providing services to those who process such information are also controlled and must register under the Act. Individuals, about whom information is stored on computer, are given rights of access and a right to have inaccurate records corrected or deleted. They may also complain to the Data Protection Registrar (appointed under the Act) if they are unhappy about the way a person or organization is collecting or using information and, under certain circumstances, individuals have a right to compensation.

The Act is important on an international scale as it facilitates the import and export of computer data. Without this statutory control on the storage and processing of personal data, it would be difficult or impossible for organizations to transfer data to and from other countries which have laws protecting and controlling the use of data which concerns individual persons.

The history leading up to the Act is relatively long and, since 1961, there have been several Parliamentary Bills, Reports and White Papers concerning privacy and data protection. The Lindop Report (Report of the Committee on Data Protection, Cmnd 7341, H.M.S.O., December 1978) was a watershed in respect of moves towards legislation. In the late 1970s several countries introduced data protection laws, in particular, the United States of America, Sweden and West Germany. The final impetus was provided by the Council of Europe's Convention on Data Protection which was signed by the United Kingdom in 1981. The Convention included principles for data protection and proposed a common set of standards. In 1982, a White Paper was published, outlining the Government's intentions (Cmnd 8539) and following this a Bill was introduced in the House of Lords. However, this failed to become law because of the general election of 1983 and a new Bill was introduced after the election and eventually received the Royal Assent in July 1984. The Data Protection Act was implemented in easy stages, the last of which mainly concerned individuals' rights of access and came into effect on 11 November 1987. Thus, the whole Act is now in force.

OVERVIEW OF THE ACT

The purpose of the Data Protection Act 1984, according to the preamble, is to:

> regulate the use of automatically processed information relating to individuals and the provision of services in respect of such information.

Regulation is carried out by placing obligations on those who record and use personal data (known as data users) and computer bureaux providing services to data users. Rights are given to individuals who may have information about themselves stored on computer. The Act has teeth in the form of criminal penalties and also provides for civil remedies such as compensation. In fact the Act does not refer to computers but to automatic information processing equipment and it is not essential that the equipment is electronic, the Act will also apply to mechanical equipment which can be used to process information. For example, Hollerith's equipment for use in the United States census of 1890, which read information contained on punched cards, falls within the scope of the Act. The important thing is that automatic equipment, and the power associated with the automatic processing of information, is controlled regardless of the technology used.

The central focus of the Act is the establishment and maintenance of a register of data users who store, use or disclose information relating to individuals, and of computer bureaux involved directly or indirectly with such matters. The register contains details of these data users and the nature, source, use and disclosure of the information and, unless exempt, failure to register is a criminal offence. By 1989, in excess of 170,000 organizations and persons had registered under the Act. The Act contains eight Data Protection Principles (based upon the Council of Europe's Convention on Data Protection) all of which must be observed by data users although, as far as computer bureaux are concerned, only one is relevant; that is the taking of adequate security measures. The Data Protection Registrar can enforce the principles by way of enforcement notices, de-registration notices and transfer prohibition notices. The Registrar also produces guidelines (Second series, February 1989) which are written in a practical manner describing and explaining the provisions of the Act and compliance with it and how it affects data users, computer bureaux and individuals. Anyone who has control of a computer which is used with information relating to individuals would be well advised to ask the Data Protection Registrar for a copy of the guidelines. However, like the Highway Code, the guidelines do not carry the force of law, they are after all a simplification of the provisions of the Act and for a full understanding of the Act and its implications, recourse must be had to the Act itself.

Before looking further at the workings of the Act it is essential to look at section 1 as some important definitions are contained therein, and a grasp of these definitions is essential to an understanding of the Act's main provisions and their scope.

DEFINITIONS

The definitions given in section 1 of the Act are of fundamental importance to the interpretation of the Act, hence their position at the beginning of the Act. The word 'data' is commonly taken to refer to information which is processed by computer and this is the approach taken in the Act. However, popular use of the word is as a single collective noun as in 'the data is about to be processed' or 'this data has been produced by computer'. The Act, strictly correctly, uses the word as a plural as the following examples show:

the data are in the form . . . – Section 1(5)(c)

where the place to which the data are to be transferred . . . – Section 12(2)

The definitions are now discussed.

Data

information recorded in a form in which it can be processed by equipment operating automatically in response to instructions given for that purpose

This definition is very wide and will cover data stored in magnetic disk, punched tape, punched cards, bar codes, etc., as well as data stored in volatile computer memory. As mentioned earlier, the Act is not restricted to computers or electronic devices but applies to any automatic data processing equipment, even to a mechanical punch card reader. However, the guidelines produced by the Data Protection Registrar always refer to computers, presumably to make them more readily understood.

Personal data

> data consisting of information which relates to a living individual who can be identified from that information (or from that and other information in the possession of the data user), including any expression of opinion about the individual but not any indication of the intention of the data user in respect of that individual

Personal information is the real subject matter of the Act. The information must relate to a living person and, therefore, a database of dead authors or musicians, or comprising information about companies and organizations is not personal data. If the information is a mixture concerning individuals and companies then the Act will apply because some of the data are personal data. The individual must be identifiable from the information and the definition takes account of the situation where some information is stored on computer and other, complementary information is stored manually. For example, the computer information may contain a person's national insurance number but not his name. If the data user has a card index which cross-references the numbers with the identity of persons then the data are personal data notwithstanding that the computer data, taken alone, are insufficient to identify individuals. If this were not so it would be too easy to avoid the Data Protection Act, simply by keeping some information in paper files or on index cards. This would enable personal information to be located and processed quickly using the computer; it then being a relatively simple matter to retrieve the appropriate paper files.

An expression of opinion about an individual is included in the definition of personal data; for example, 'Joe Smith is an excellent salesman' or 'Mrs. Brown would appear to be a poor credit risk'. However, an indication of intention is not; for example, 'Mr. Smith will be promoted to sales manager on 1st September' or 'The company will offer Mrs. Brown a credit limit of £500'. Sometimes it may be difficult to draw a line between expressions of opinion and indications of intention as in the statement 'Because of Mr. Smith's performance, he is to be promoted in the near future'. There is a danger that data users might deliberately write their expressions of opinion in the form of indications of intention. If they do so, it will not be an easy matter to detect unless the Data Protection Registrar is alerted that this may have happened and is able to obtain a warrant from a circuit judge to enter the data user's premises for the purpose of inspecting the data.

Following these definitions of 'data' and 'personal data', section 1 identifies and defines the persons involved in the storage, use or processing of data beginning with the person to whom the data relate, i.e., the data subject.

Data subject

This is simply an individual who is the subject of personal data. He is the living individual referred to in the definition of 'personal data'.

Data user

A data user is a person who *holds* data. 'Person' in this context, unlike a data subject who must be a living person, includes legal persons such as limited companies, statutory authorities and other organizations. Of course, a living person can also be a data user. The identity of data users is very important as, subject to exceptions to be discussed later, they must register if they hold personal data. The word 'holds' has a special meaning, a person holds data if the following three requirements are present:

(a) the data (as defined above) form part of a collection of data processed or intended to be processed by or on behalf of that person . . . and
(b) that person (either alone or jointly or in common with other persons) controls the contents and use of the data comprised in the collection; and
(c) the data are in a form in which they have been or are intended to be processed as mentioned in paragraph (a) above or (though not for the time being in that form) in a form into which they have been converted after being so processed and with a view to being further so processed on a subsequent occasion.

These requirements are discussed and expanded below.

(a) What is a collection of data? Obviously if a computer database comprises nothing other than information about one person only, the data cannot form part of a collection. It would seem sensible that anything more would be considered a collection of data, such as a database containing information about two or more persons. Note that the data user does not have to process the data himself and he will still be considered to be a data user for the purposes of the Act if he engages or employs another to do this for him.

(b) Control would appear to relate to content and use rather than physical possession. A data user is one who decides what information is included in the data and when it is used. He does not have to be the only person who can make such decisions, as joint users (for example, partners in a small business) and users in common are included. An example of a user in common would be a person who along with others has access to a database and can update the information it contains without the express or implied agreement of the other users, such as where several persons subscribe to a credit database which they can individually amend or add to.

(c) The data may be stored on magnetic disk or punched cards and have been processed or are to be processed in that form in which case the person referred to in (a) and (b) above is a data user. Alternatively, the data may have already been processed and have been stored in a different form. For example, the data may have been on paper tape and have been processed and then stored on magnetic tape for long-term storage, the paper tape having been destroyed. If it is intended to process the data again in the future after retrieval from the magnetic tape then the person referred to in (a) and (b) above is still a data user. He will, however, no longer be a data user if he has processed the data, destroyed the original data and no longer has the data in a form from which they can be processed again in the future. This would occur, for example, if the data are stored on paper tape, processed producing a report printed out on paper and the paper tape then destroyed, because the data cannot be processed again from the paper print-out. Also, a person is not a data user if, regardless of the means of storage, he does not intend to process the data again. It could be argued, however, that where a print-out has been made and all other forms of the data have been destroyed, the data is still in a form from which it can be processed again if, for example, an optical character reader is used to scan the printed copy, enabling further processing to be carried out.

The definition of data user does not refer to personal data and a person is still a data user if he does not hold data about individuals but, in this case, the Act will not apply to him, unless he provides services to other data users who do hold personal data. A person who has a computer database of building materials and their current prices is a data user but he does not hold personal data. The Act applies only to those data users who hold personal data.

Computer bureaux

Computer bureaux are also regulated by the Act. A person, including legal persons such as companies, carries on a computer bureau if he provides others with services in respect of data, and he does so if *either* of the following are met:

(a) as agent for other persons he causes data [as defined above] held by them to be processed . . . or
(b) he allows other persons the use of equipment in his possession for the processing [of data as defined above] . . .

In both cases, reference must be made to the definition of data. In the first case, a computer bureau may act as an agent for a data user. For example, a data user may possess magnetic disks containing a database which he takes to a computer bureau which processes the data on the disks for him. In the second case, the data user himself operates the computer bureau's equipment. Because the definition of data refers to automatic processing equipment and not computers specifically, it is possible for a person without a computer who has mechanical equipment such as a punched card reader to be classed as a computer bureau. Therefore anyone providing services who has any kind of equipment which can process information automatically, in whatever form, should be aware of the implications of the Data Protection Act.

Processing

Continual reference is made in the Act to 'processing'. Most people engaged in the use of computers will identify processing with operations such as producing a payroll report or updating a database using a batch file. The Act defines 'processing' widely as follows:

in relation to data, [processing] means amending, augmenting, deleting or re-arranging the data or extracting the information constituting the data and, in the case of personal data, means performing any of those operations by reference to the data subject.

The Act is only concerned with automatic processing, but almost any operation on a database file done by computer will fall within this definition of processing. However, with respect to personal data, the processing must be done by reference to the data subject. If a company has a database comprising names of employees, their salaries and their position in the company, and the company decides to update the database after selective increases in salary have been agreed, then the processing is done by reference to the data subject. Each employee's record will be retrieved by reference to that employee and the salary altered by the appropriate amount. However, if the company simply wants to know how many employees they have of managerial status and uses the computer to produce a report showing how many managers they have, they are not processing the data by reference to the data subject. For the purposes of the report, the identity of individuals is irrelevant. According to the Data Protection Guidelines, processing by reference to the data subject will occur whenever the data user intends to locate and process information *because* it relates to an individual (Data Protection Guideline No.2 at p.14).

Many small businesses use computers solely for word processing and it would be inconvenient if they all had to register under the Data Protection Act. Word processing is excluded from the definition of processing, effectively exempting this activity from the Act's provisions. Section 1(8) of the Act states:

Subsection (7) above [giving the definition of processing] shall not be construed as applying to any operation performed *only* for the purpose of preparing the text of documents. [*emphasis added*]

This exception applies where the processing is done in relation to the preparation of documents only. If there is any other motive whatsoever, however subsidiary to the preparation of a document, then the exception does not apply. There is no problem if the computer is used as a simple word processor to produce letters and such like, even if the document is stored on a magnetic disk so that it may be retrieved and printed out again in the future or edited to produce a new document. Often, however, a list of names and addresses is stored in a separate computer file so that it may be merged with standard documents to produce 'individualized' letters. Such files may also contain names and positions of staff employed by the companies and persons in the main list. Is this within the scope of processing? If the operation involves some selectivity then, according to the Data Protection Guidelines (Guideline No.2 at pp.16–17), the Act will apply if the data are personal data because there is an additional purpose over and above the mere preparation of documents. For example, if a list of clients and contacts is stored in a file to be merged with letters using a word processing package and it is possible to instruct the computer to use only those with addresses in London then the Act will apply. The Act will also apply if the list is used or is intended to be used in its own right, for example, if the list is used for reference purposes enabling up to date information to be obtained. An example of this is where such a list is searched for a particular name so that his current telephone number can be found. It would appear that if a file containing personal data is maintained for use with standard letters ('mailshots'), it must be used in an all or nothing fashion and not used for any other purpose and certainly not as a database of useful information in its own right, otherwise an application for registration must be made.

If the list contains only the names and addresses of non-living legal persons, such as limited companies, the Act will not apply because the data are not personal data. An exemption from the main provisions of the Act in relation to 'mailing lists' is discussed later in this Part of the book.

Disclosing personal data

The disclosure of personal data, or information extracted from personal data, is regulated. If the identity of a data subject depends in part on information constituting the data and partly on other information in the possession of the data user, the data are not regarded as being disclosed, unless that other information is also disclosed or transferred. Disclosure does not have to be complete and partial disclosure, where a print-out is made available to a third party which only shows some of the information held by the data user, is sufficient if one or more individuals can be identified from it.

Taken together, the definitions outline the scope of the Act, especially as regards the types of computer data that are covered. Using the definitions above, it is possible to construct the flowchart in Figure 5 which can be used to determine whether the data held are such that the data user and/or computer bureaux as defined above must seek registration under the Act; this chart is subject to exemptions from the Act which will be considered in Chapter 27.

REGISTRATION

Unless exempt, all data users who hold personal data, and all computer bureaux providing services in respect of personal data, must register with the Data Protection Registrar. The application form (DPR1) and explanatory notes are available from Crown (Head) Post Offices and from the Data Protection Registrar; the fee for registration is currently £56 for a period of up to 3 years. Section 4 of the Act deals with registration and requires the Data Protection Registrar to maintain a register of data users and

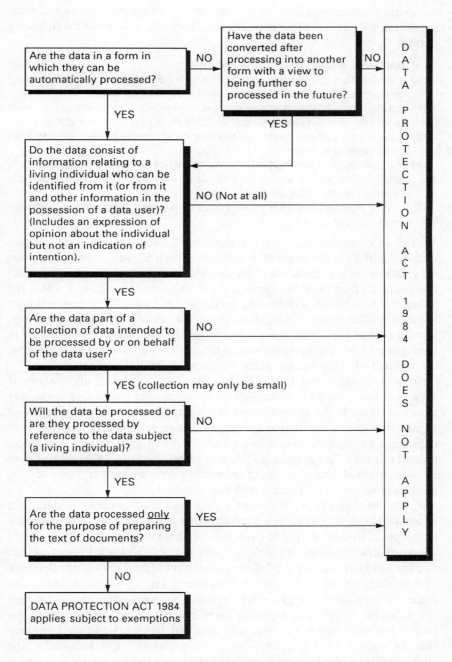

Figure 5   Whether data are within the scope of the Act

computer bureaux who hold or provide services in respect of personal data. By section 4(3), an entry in the register for a data user consists of the following details:

(a) the name and address of the data user;
(b) a description of the personal data to be held by him and of the purpose or purposes for which the data are to be held or used;
(c) a description of the source or sources from which he intends or may wish to obtain the data or information to be contained in the data;
(d) a description of any person or persons to whom he intends or may wish to disclose the data;
(e) the names or a description of any countries or territories outside the United Kingdom to which he intends or may wish directly or indirectly to transfer the data; and
(f) one or more addresses for the receipt of requests from data subjects for access to the data.

As far as computer bureaux are concerned, the entry is much simpler consisting of only the name and address of each bureau. Some data users may also be computer bureaux; for example, within a group of companies, one company may provide computer facilities to other companies within the group (each of which will be data users) whilst also holding personal data in respect of its own employees. If the applicant is a registered company, it must give its registered address as well as the number of the company in the register of companies, otherwise, if the applicant is carrying on a business, the address of the principal place of business should be given.

Some data users may find it convenient to make several applications if they have more than one collection of personal data (database), especially if one is likely to be altered, requiring an application for amendment of registration in respect of that collection. However, this may conflict with data subjects' right to access (see page 185 infra) and, as a consequence, individuals may find it more difficult to identify which collections of data include personal data concerning them and they may have to make several applications, which will result in additional cost.

Failure to register, in the case of a data user holding personal data, is a criminal offence which carries a maximum of a fine of £2,000 in a Magistrates' Court or an unlimited fine in the Crown Court (section 5(1)). The offence is one of strict liability and lack of knowledge of the Data Protection Act and the need to register is no defence, regardless of how reasonable that lack of knowledge may be in the circumstances. For computer bureaux the penalties for failing to register are the same but knowledge or recklessness are required. Therefore, a person carrying on an unregistered computer bureau providing services in respect of personal data will be guilty if he knew that he should have registered or if he ought to have known, in the circumstances. 'Recklessness' has special meanings so far as the law is concerned and is further discussed at page 184 infra, and in Chapter 22 in the section on criminal damage.

Registration commenced on 11 November 1985 and by 11 May 1986, failure to register became a criminal offence. Due to the enormous tasks of processing thousands of applications and of educating users of computers as to the workings of the Act and its exemptions, a fairly benign attitude was taken by the Data Protection Registrar towards those who were a little tardy in seeking registration, although it was not too long before the first prosecutions were commenced under the Act. For example, in December 1987, a motor agent who maintained detailed records of customers for marketing purposes was fined £500 for failing to register. Up to 31 May 1989, all prosecutions under the Act concerned failure to register and a total of eight concluded cases resulted in fines ranging from £100 to £1,000 (Fifth Report of the Data Protection Registrar, H.M.S.O., June 1989).

According to the Data Protection Guidelines (Guideline No.3), registration serves three main purposes, namely:

a) it enables individuals to discover, generally, who holds personal data, what the data may contain and for what they may be used. As a result of this basic information, an individual may make a subject access request to the data user concerned;

b) it enables data users to be open about their use of personal data and comply with the Data Protection Principles (many data users might be indifferent to this purpose but it is particularly important on an international scale);

c) it enables the Registrar to enforce the Data Protection Principles and other provisions of the Act.

The Data Protection Registrar may refuse an application if he considers that the details given are insufficient or he is satisfied, or he has insufficient information to decide, that the applicant is likely to break the Data Protection Principles (section 7(2)). A person making an application for registration, or alteration of an existing entry, who knowingly or recklessly furnishes the Data Protection Registrar with information which is false or misleading in a material respect commits an offence triable in the Magistrates' Courts only, carrying a maximum penalty of £2,000. If an application for registration is refused, the applicant may appeal to the Data Protection Tribunal. The Data Protection Guidelines should be consulted for further information about registration procedure, alteration, removal and renewal of entries on the register. A sample register entry is reproduced at the end of this Part of the book.

THE DATA PROTECTION PRINCIPLES AND ASSOCIATED CRIMINAL OFFENCES

Registered persons must not contravene the Data Protection Principles. If they do, the Registrar may serve an enforcement notice under section 10 of the Act requiring steps to be taken within a specified time so that the principles can be complied with. Normally, the Registrar will send a preliminary notice first, giving the data user 28 days to make representations as to why an enforcement notice should not be served. During this period, the data user may take action to remedy the contravention complained of, in which case it will be unnecessary to serve an enforcement notice. In the Data Protection Registrar's Fifth Report, it was stated that six preliminary notices had been served by 31 May 1989, four of which resulted in enforcement notices. Three of the latter concerned failures to stop unsolicited mail whilst the fourth, which is likely to lead to the first important case law on the Act, was served on a leading building society and is under appeal. It related to an alleged failure to give information in response to subject access requests.

Alternatively, the Registrar may serve a de-registration notice giving notice that all or part of a person's entries on the register will be removed or he may serve a transfer prohibition notice. Failure to comply with the Data Protection Principles may also result in criminal liability, so compliance with the principles is obviously important. The principles themselves are contained in Schedule 1 to the Act, together with explanatory notes to help with their interpretation.

The principles are largely based on the Council of Europe Convention on Data Protection. There are eight principles, all of which apply to data users. The last one also applies to computer bureaux. The principles are:

1. The information to be contained in personal data shall be obtained, and personal data shall be processed, fairly and lawfully.
2. Personal data shall be held only for one or more specified and lawful purposes.
3. Personal data held for any purpose or purposes shall not be used or disclosed in any manner incompatible with that purpose or those purposes.
4. Personal data held for any purpose or purposes shall be adequate, relevant and not excessive in relation to that purpose or those purposes.
5. Personal data shall be accurate and, where necessary, kept up to date.
6. Personal data held for any purpose or purposes shall not be kept for longer than is necessary for that purpose or those purposes.
7. An individual shall be entitled –
   a) at reasonable intervals and without undue delay or expense –
      i) to be informed by any data user whether he holds personal data of which that individual is the subject; and
      ii) to access to any such data held by the data user; and
   b) where appropriate, to have such data corrected or erased.
8. Appropriate security measures shall be taken against unauthorised access to, or alteration, disclosure or destruction of, personal data and against accidental loss or destruction of personal data.

These principles, which lie at the very root of data protection law, must be applied by data users (and computer bureaux with respect to principle No.8). A sensible approach is for a data user to develop a data protection policy which will govern the mechanism for compliance with the Act. None of the above principles needs unduly worry a data user and they are all quite reasonable. The last principle is concerned with security and has two threads to it; first, the security from unauthorized access, and second, in connection with back-up copies of databases containing personal data. The security aspect needs careful thought and the dangers of computer hackers gaining access to the computer system must be considered and guarded against. Similarly, the dangers of the data user's own employees or freelance workers destroying or passing on information relating to personal data to others must be considered. Security measures must be taken which are, in the light of current technology, adequate to provide a reasonable level of protection to the personal data. Password systems should be secure and changed frequently, back-up copies of personal data should be stored in locked fireproof cabinets and the degree of access to personal data should be kept to a minimum. If a hacker does gain access, the data user (or computer bureau) will nevertheless be regarded as complying with the eighth principle if he had taken reasonable and sensible security measures and takes further preventative action to guard against a reoccurrence.

CRIMINAL OFFENCES CONCERNING REGISTERED DATA USERS AND COMPUTER BUREAUX

Although important, the Data Protection Principles themselves do not directly define the criminal offences. Failure to comply with the principles may result in an enforcement, de-registration or transfer prohibition notice from the Registrar which is a serious matter in its own right. Most of the criminal offences are listed in section 5 of the Act and the penalties for non-registration have already been discussed. Breach of a principle does not, in itself, mean that an offence has been committed. However, an act or omission which breaches a principle will often also be an offence as the offences are, somewhat loosely, drawn from the principles. Apart from failure to register, the offences contained in section 5(2) are as follows and all relate to things done in contravention of the entry on the register as a data user or a data user who also carries on a computer bureau:

(a) holding personal data of any description other than that specified;
(b) holding or using personal data for a purpose other than the purpose or purposes described;
(c) obtaining (to be held by the data user) personal data or information to be contained in such data from a source other than as specified;
(d) disclosing personal data held by the data user to any person not described in the entry;
(e) transferring (directly or indirectly) personal data held by the data user to any country or territory outside the United Kingdom other than one named or described in the entry.

For the above offences to be committed, the contravention must be done knowingly or recklessly. These are not strict liability offences and they require *mens rea*, which is a legal term meaning literally a wicked or guilty mind, but, more accurately it means a criminal intention. A person behaves

183

'recklessly' if the risk of the relevant act or omission transpiring would be obvious to a reasonable man, whether or not that person thought about the possibility of the risk. It is, therefore, an objective test. The maximum penalties available are, in a Magistrates' Court, a fine of £2,000 or an unlimited fine in the Crown Court.

Not only are data users liable to prosecution but their servants and agents may also be liable to criminal prosecution for the offences under (b), (d) and (e) above, which relate to the purposes, disclosure and transfer of personal data. If a director or data processing manager working for a company registered as a data user knowingly or recklessly allow personal data to be disclosed to a third party who is not described in the register entry, then both the director (or data processing manager) and the company are liable to prosecution.

Senior officers of a company are also liable for any offence under the Act if the offence has been committed with the consent or connivance of, or is attributable to any neglect on the part of that officer (section 20). Senior officers are those such as directors, managers, company secretaries. This puts quite a heavy burden on such persons to make sure that the Act is complied with. If a company registered as a data user uses personal data, because of the deliberate actions of a senior manager, with the consent of a director of the company, for a purpose not mentioned in the register, the following prosecutions are possible:

a) the company can be prosecuted under section 5; it will be deemed to have committed the offence knowingly because the actions of the senior manager will be taken to be the actions of the company,

b) the manager can be prosecuted because he is a servant of the company and has committed the offence under section 5 knowingly,

c) the director can be prosecuted under section 20 because he has consented to the offence,

d) other senior officers may be liable because of neglect; for example, because they failed to take security measures and develop procedures to ensure that the Data Protection Principles were adhered to.

Section 15 of the Act makes the disclosure of personal data by a computer bureau (and its servants and agents) a criminal offence if it is done without the permission of the person for whom the computer bureau is providing services and is done knowingly or recklessly. Prosecutions for offences under the Data Protection Act can only be commenced by the Data Protection Registrar or with the consent of the Director of Public Prosecutions or, in Scotland, the Procurator Fiscal.

INDIVIDUALS' RIGHTS

The Data Protection Act introduces new rights for individuals about whom personal data is held by data users or in respect of services provided by computer bureaux. There is a right of access to personal data held by data users. Any individual can check to see if an organization has information about him stored on computer and can see a copy of that information on payment of a fee. However, these rights, known as the 'subject access provisions', depend on exemptions, as to which, *see* Chapter 27. If an individual finds that the data held about him are inaccurate, he has a right to have the data amended or erased and, if he has suffered damage as a result, an entitlement to compensation. An individual may also claim compensation for damage suffered if personal data about him have been lost or disclosed without authority. Finally, an individual may complain to the Data Protection Registrar if he thinks that the Data Protection Principles or any provisions of the Act have been or are being contravened. For the year ending 31 May 1989, a total of 1122 individuals complained to the Registrar. Approximately 35 per cent concerned consumer credit, 18 per cent were about subject access and 16 per cent related to direct mailing (*Fifth Report of the Data Protection Registrar*, H.M.S.O., June 1989).

Subject access

A fundamental tenet of the Data Protection Act is that individuals should be able to find out who holds information about them and to be able to see a copy of that information, and thus the secrecy associated with computer files stored by large impersonal organizations is removed, at least in theory. However, how does an individual find out who holds personal data concerning him? In many respects this is a major weakness of the Act and the best available source is the Data Protection Register which is kept at the Office of the Registrar at Wilmslow, Cheshire. The public can inspect the register by calling at the office, or certified copies of individual register entries can be obtained from the Registrar upon payment of a fee of £2. Larger public libraries keep copies of the index to the register. The register index is not very helpful and the information it contains is fairly sparse, comprising the name of the data user or computer bureaux and the registration number. Unless an individual knows that a particular organization is likely to hold personal data about him, such as his bank or employer, the register will not be of great assistance in tracking down all the other organizations which might have information about him stored on computer.

By section 21 of the Act, an individual is entitled to be informed by any data user whether that user holds data which includes personal data relating to the individual and to be supplied by the data user with a copy of the information constituting any such personal data. Where the information is expressed in terms which are not intelligible without explanation, such explanation must also accompany that information. Therefore, if some of the information is in code (for example, 'salary scale VI'), sufficient details of the code must be supplied by the data user so that the individual concerned can understand the information (for example, 'salary scale VI − £12,500 to £15,500').

An individual exercising his right to subject access must furnish the data

185

user with a written request containing sufficient details so that he can identify the individual and locate the information sought. Data users are entitled to charge a fee which must not exceed £10 and must comply with the request within forty days unless the individual has not provided sufficient information. In the latter case, the forty days runs from the date on which the data user receives such further information as he reasonably requires to identify the individual and locate the data. The information supplied by the data user should be as it was when the subject access request was made. However, if the information has been subsequently amended or some of it has been deleted, the data user may send a copy of the altered information, providing the alteration has not been made because of the subject access request. This is to prevent data users deleting information they do not want the data user to see, perhaps only to replace the information after fulfilling the request.

Complications arise when the personal data involved relate to another individual, such as a request to a bank from a person who has a joint bank account with his wife. The data user concerned does not have to divulge the whole of the information unless he is satisfied that the other person has consented to the disclosure. However, this does not allow the data user to decline to supply information and in the absence of consent of other individuals who can be identified from the information, the data user must still supply whatever information he can, blanking out references to these other individuals. For example, a data user may hold a computer file containing customer details. In addition to containing information relating to the customer, the file may also contain the names of salesmen who deal with the customers or names of third parties who recommended the data user to the customer. If a customer makes a subject access request, the data user must supply him with his details, but should edit the print-out so that the name of the salesman and the person who made the recommendation are omitted or cancelled out. The flowchart in Figure 6 illustrates the basic procedure for subject access.

Inaccurate data

Inaccuracy of personal data can affect an individual's employment prospects, his ability to obtain credit or even dash his hopes of romance. A data user could, for example, hold data which state that the data subject has a previous conviction or has failed to pay off a loan. A computer dating agency may have a computer record showing that a particular client does not like redheads when the opposite is true. What can the data subject, the individual adversely affected by such inaccuracies do to rectify the situation? He is entitled to have the inaccuracy corrected (or deleted) and may be able to claim compensation from the data user.

By section 22(4) of the Act, data are inaccurate if they are incorrect or misleading as to any matter of fact. An opinion about the data subject does not fall within this definition and the data must relate to some fact such as

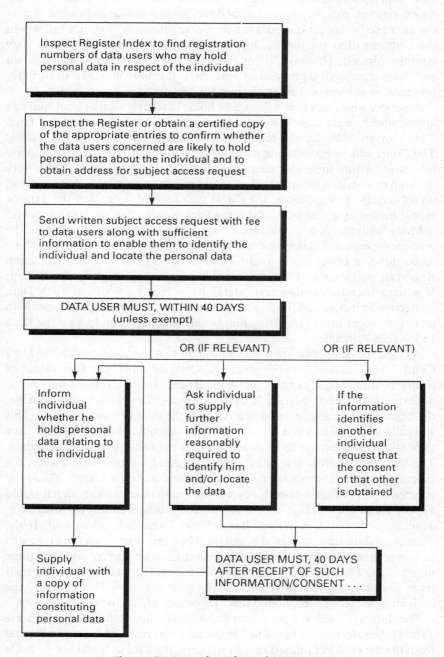

Figure 6 Procedure for subject access

past employment record, convictions for criminal offences, colour of eyes, marital status, etc. An expression of opinion such as one indicating that in the data user's view, 'Mr. Jones is a mediocre salesman' does not fall within the compensation provisions, however good a salesman Mr. Jones may consider himself. However, if Mr. Jones is not a salesman at all, the data are 'inaccurate'. An expression of opinion, if it is based on inaccurate data, however, is subject to the provisions for rectification or erasure.

A person who finds that a data user holds inaccurate data about him can apply, under section 24 of the Act, to either a County Court or the High Court for an order for the rectification or erasure of the inaccurate data. The Court will be bound to issue an order if it is satisfied that the data are inaccurate within the above meaning. However, if the inaccurate data were received or obtained from a third party or from the data subject himself then, under certain circumstances, the Court may instead order that the data be supplemented by a statement of the true facts such as the Court may approve.

Many individuals are reluctant to approach the Courts because of the possible expense and delay involved, but if an individual still wishes something to be done, a better tactic might be to complain to the Data Protection Registrar, particularly if the individual is prepared to forgo compensation. If a data user holds inaccurate data, he is in breach of the fifth Data Protection Principle and the Registrar may serve the offending data user with an enforcement order, requiring him to take steps to comply with the Data Protection Principles.

A claim for compensation must be brought to a County Court or the High Court. The choice between these Courts depends on the value of compensation sought as the County Court can award damages only up to a maximum of £5,000. Section 22 of the Act recognizes two forms of damage, the first being damage suffered as a result of the inaccuracy of the data. This will include such things as a loss caused to the individual because of his failure to obtain employment or to be awarded a contract because of inaccurate data. The loss may be economic or related to physical injury. Additionally, the claimant may be compensated for any distress he has suffered. Thus, the compensation available extends beyond pure economic loss although it would appear from the wording of section 22 that compensation for distress is available only if the individual has suffered some damage as well. If the inaccurate data have caused the individual to lose a contract which results in severe mental distress so that the individual is unable to work for three months, the compensation will be calculated on the basis of loss of profit from the contract *and* in respect of the time off work. However, if the individual suffers no economic loss, he cannot claim for distress.

The data user will not always be liable for compensation for inaccurate data. If the information contained in the data was received from or obtained from the data subject himself or a third party, the data user will not be liable if the data indicate the information was so acquired and the information has not been extracted except in a form including an indication to this effect. The same applies in the case of data acquired from the data subject or a third party where the data subject has notified the data user that he regards the data as inaccurate and an indication of this is added to the data or any information extracted from it. Furthermore, the data user has a defence if he can show that he has taken reasonable care in the circumstances to ensure the accuracy of the data at the material time, regardless of the source of the data. Therefore, a prudent data user will develop procedures for validating data he obtains and if he does this, he should have a defence to any claim for compensation. In particular, data should not be taken at face value and some reasonable attempt at verification should be made. If data are obtained from a third party (who perhaps supplies a database) or from the individual data subjects themselves, an indication of the source of the data should be included in the data and always printed with any information printed out or otherwise extracted from the data.

Loss or unauthorized disclosure of personal data

It will be unusual for the loss of personal data to cause damage to the individuals concerned and in many cases the individuals might be quite pleased to think that their records on a computer database have been destroyed or lost. In some cases, however, loss of personal data could be troublesome to an individual such as when the personal data are required to support an application for a job or a loan. Data users can protect themselves against the likelihood of a claim on the basis of loss of data simply by making sure that up to date back-up copies of personal data are kept in a secure place. The danger of a computer hacker penetrating a computer system and erasing personal data must also be considered and, if this happens, the data user (or a computer bureau) could find themselves liable for compensation to the data subjects involved.

Section 23 of the Data Protection Act allows data subjects who have suffered damage to claim compensation against data users and computer bureaux for the loss of personal data or for the destruction, without authority, of the personal data. The authority referred to is that of the data user or the computer bureau, as the case may be. It should be noted that a data user has every right deliberately to erase personal data, but in section 23 the Act is concerned with the accidental or negligent loss of data because of a lack of security measures or because of sloppy computing practices. Compensation is also available to affected data subjects for damage caused by the unauthorized disclosure of personal data, such as where a computer hacker or employee reads or distributes personal data which he has accessed without the permission of the data user or the computer bureau concerned. However, this does not apply if the disclosure, albeit unauthorized, is made to a person or organization listed on the Register as being a person to whom the data user intends or may wish to disclose the data. As with inaccurate data, a data user (or computer bureau) has a defence to a claim for compensation if he can show that he has taken reasonable care, in the circumstances, to avoid the loss, destruction, disclosure or access in question.

If personal data have been disclosed without authority in circumstances where a data subject is entitled to compensation, a Court may order the erasure of the data if it is satisfied that there is a substantial risk of further unauthorized disclosure of or access to that data (section 24(3)). However, where the disclosure has occurred from a computer bureau, the data user has an opportunity to be heard by the Court before such an order is made. For example, if the data are being processed by a computer bureau on behalf of a data user and the data are disclosed during this operation without the authority of the computer bureau, it would obviously be unfair on the data user if the erasure of the data were to be ordered. This provision allows the data user to respond, perhaps by confirming that he will use a different bureau in future which has better security arrangements, thus convincing the Court that further unauthorized disclosure is unlikely.

Chapter 27

Exemptions from and enforcement of the Data Protection Act 1984

EXEMPTIONS

The Data Protection Act contains several complicated exemptions from some or all of the provisions of the Act. In order to describe these exemptions, it is helpful to sub-divide them in terms of their scope as follows:
1. Exemptions from the whole of the Act (effectively).
2. Exemptions from the subject access provisions.
3. Exemptions relating to the disclosure of personal data.

1. Exemptions from the whole of the Act

These effectively give a person who holds and uses personal data exemption from the registration requirements and subject access provisions. However, they do not prevent the possibility that the exemption will be called into question at some time; for example, if a data subject who has been denied access to his personal data on the basis of an exemption applies to a Court for a determination of whether the exemption does indeed apply. These exemptions from the whole of the Act are based on:
a) national security (section 27),
b) payroll and accounts (section 32),
c) domestic and other limited purposes (section 33),
d) information required by law to be made available to the public (section 34).
These are considered below in more detail.

a) National security

This exemption applies if it is necessary for the purpose of safeguarding national security. Examples might include information about the armed forces or even spies. Any question as to the necessity for the exemption is to be resolved by a Cabinet Minister or the Attorney-General (Lord Advocate in Scotland) and a certificate signed by any such persons is conclusive evidence that the exemption is required. Even if the personal data are not exempt from registration, they may be exempt from the non-disclosure provisions if disclosure is for the purpose of safeguarding national security. The need for this exemption is plain but the certification arrangements mean that the Courts have, in effect, no control over the scope and application of this exemption.

b) Payroll and accounts

Personal data which fall within this exemption must satisfy both of two conditions, one concerned with the *purposes* for which the personal data are held, the other with the *disclosure* of the data. For the exemption to be available, at least one of the following purposes must apply with respect to the personal data:

a) *payroll* – calculating amounts payable (or deductions) by way of remuneration or pensions or making such payments,

b) *accounts* – keeping accounts or records of transactions for ensuring payments are made or for making financial or management forecasts in relation to the data user's business or other activity.

Additionally, for the exemption to apply, disclosure is limited to the situations listed below. The first list (i–v) applies only to data held for payroll purposes, the second list (a–b) applies to both payroll and accounts data. First, payroll data can be disclosed:

(i) to any person who pays the remuneration or pension; for example, a company may send payroll details to a bank which actually prepares and pays the salaries of the company's employees,

(ii) for the purpose of obtaining actuarial advice,

(iii) for the purpose of giving information about employees, etc. for use in medical research; for example, for determining occupational health risks,

(iv) if the data subject has requested or consented to the disclosure, generally or particularly,

(v) if the person making the disclosure has reasonable grounds for believing that (iv) above applies.

Personal data relating to either payroll or accounts can be disclosed:

a) for the purpose of audit or for giving information about the data user's financial affairs,

b) in circumstances covered by other exemptions from the non-disclosure provisions of the Act (the non-disclosure exemptions). This includes disclosure required by law, to obtain legal advice, to the data subject, to employees and agents of the data user, to prevent injury or damage to health, to safeguard national security and if failure to disclose would prejudice the prevention or detection of crime, the apprehension or prosecution of offenders or the assessment or collection of tax or duty.

If the data are used for any other purpose or are disclosed in circumstances other than those described above, the exemption will not apply except in cases where the data user can show that he had taken such care to prevent the disclosure as was reasonably required in all the circumstances. Prudent and careful use of the data is required to protect this exemption which, in practice, will be very useful to many business organizations.

c) Domestic and other limited purposes

There are three cases included in this exemption. The first applies to 'domestic' purposes; that is, where personal data are held by an individual and concerned only with the management of his personal, family or household affairs or for recreational purposes. The Act does not apply to a young boy who decides to keep a computer record of the dates of his relatives' birthdays and details of the gifts they gave him last Christmas. This exemption is necessary because it would be an unwelcome intrusion to expect private individuals using their computers for the sorts of purposes described above to have to register their use. Control of such activities would also be legally unenforceable in practice.

The second exemption applies to clubs; in particular, unincorporated members' clubs, such as a bridge club or the local Townswomen's Guild. However, the club must not be a company. There are two conditions to this exemption, the first is that all the members of the club have been asked if they object and they have not objected. The second condition is that the data are not disclosed except in very limited circumstances as in the non-disclosure exemptions described later. If a member of the club, having been asked, objects to information about him being held on computer by the club, the club has two options. The first option is for the club to hold that person's information in a paper file or on an index card instead. The second option is for the club to apply for registration under the Act, in which case it will be able to hold personal data relating to all its members, including the objector, on computer.

A third exemption under this category, i.e. domestic and other limited purposes, concerns 'mailing lists', that is, lists of names and addresses held for the purpose of distributing (or keeping a record of distribution of) articles or information to the data subjects. The list must contain only names and addresses or other information necessary for effecting the distribution. The data must not be used for any other purpose, and the data subjects must not object, after being asked, and the data must not be disclosed except under the non-disclosure exemptions.

d) Information required by law to be made available to the public

This exemption from the registration and subject access provisions applies if the data user only holds personal data which he is required by statute to make available to the public. This is when the data user is so required to publish the data or make it available for inspection, whether gratuitously or on payment of a fee, an example being the register of electors held and maintained by local authorities. Another example concerns registers of births, marriages and deaths and certificates of the same; the registers are available for inspection free of charge at the General Register Office, St. Catherine's House, London where copies of certificates can be obtained on payment of a fee.

2. Exemptions from the subject access provisions

Under certain circumstances, registered data users can refuse to allow a data subject to see a copy of his personal data. These circumstances relate to:
a) crime and taxation (section 28),
b) health and social work data (section 29),
c) data held for the regulation of financial services, etc. (section 30),
d) judicial appointments (section 31(1)),
e) legal professional privilege (section 31(2)),
f) statistical or research data (section 33(6)),
g) legal prohibition (section 34(2)),
h) situations where subject access is provided for under section 158 of the Consumer Credit Act 1974 (section 34(3)),
i) back-up data (section 34(4)),
j) if compliance would incriminate the data user (section 34(9)),
    The following exemption is temporary and can only serve to delay subject access:
k) examination marks (section 35).

a) Crime and taxation

This applies if the personal data are held for the purpose of the prevention or detection of crime, the apprehension or prosecution of offenders or the assessment or collection of any tax or duty. Further, the subject access, if it were to be granted, must be likely to prejudice any of the above matters. The exemption also applies to anyone discharging a statutory function who has obtained the data from a person who held the data for any of the above purposes. An example might be personal data held by the police which has been given to the Crown Prosecution Service which is considering whether to prosecute the individual concerned. However, if compliance with the subject access request would not prejudice any of the purposes mentioned, the exemption does not apply.

b) Health and social work data

The Act empowers the Secretary of State to make orders concerning exemptions from subject access. The following orders have been made: Data Protection (Subject Access Modification) (Health) Order 1987, S.I. 1987 No. 1903 and Data Protection (Subject Access Modification) (Social Work) Order 1987, S.I. 1987 No. 1904. They apply to personal data relating to the physical or mental health of a data subject (health data) or held in connection with social services functions (social data). With respect to health data, the exemption from subject access applies if the data are held by:
a) a health professional, for example, persons such as medical or dental practitioners responsible for the clinical care of the data subject, or
b) any other person (so long as the information constituting the data was

first recorded by a health professional); this will include bodies such as insurance companies holding details of a medical examination made for the purpose of arranging life assurance for a data subject.

The data user can withhold data if giving access to the data subject would be likely to:

a) cause serious harm to the physical or mental health of the data subject, or
b) lead the data subject to identify another person (other than the health professional involved in the care of the data subject) who has not consented to the disclosure of his or her identity.

The Department of Health has made it clear that this exemption should be relied on only in exceptional circumstances. An example might be where a doctor has diagnosed a fatal illness and considers that it would be in the data subject's best interests for him not to discover this.

The social work exemption applies to bodies such as local authorities, the probation service, local education authorities, etc. The body concerned can withhold data if access would be likely to prejudice the carrying out of social work by:

a) causing serious harm to the physical or mental health or emotional condition of the data subject or any other person, or
b) leading the data subject or any other person who is likely to obtain access to the data to identify another individual (other than someone involved professionally in social work) who has not consented to the disclosure of his or her identity.

Again, it is clear that this exemption will be relied upon only in exceptional circumstances. As far as health data and social data are concerned, it is important that such records should be frank and explicit and without these exemptions, the content might be restrained.

c) Data held for the regulation of financial services, etc.

As with the health and social work exemptions above, this required an order from the Secretary of State and such an order was made in 1987: Data Protection (Regulation of Financial Services etc.) (Subject Access Exemption) Order 1987, S.I. 1987 No. 1905. It applies to personal data held for the purposes of discharging particular functions in cases where subject access would be likely to prejudice the proper discharge of those functions. The functions concerned are designed to protect the public from dishonesty, incompetence or malpractice resulting in financial loss by persons in the fields of banking, insurance, investments and the like.

d) Judicial appointments

Personal data consisting of information received from a third party which is relevant to the making of judicial appointments and held by government departments is exempt from the subject access provisions. For example, the Lord Chancellor's Department has a computer database of leading Queen's

Counsel who may be considered for appointment as judges, and this database may contain information such as whether they are freemasons or whether present judges consider that these individuals are worthy of appointment to the bench. This database must, of course, be registered but requests by persons included in the database can rightfully be refused. As with health and social work data, it is important that such records can be frank and forthright.

e) Legal professional privilege

There is a duty of confidentiality implied by law owed by a lawyer to his client. The lawyer is not permitted to disclose any information about his client's affairs without permission. The need for this extremely high duty of confidentiality is obvious and the lawyer may have been told by his client of matters concerning other individuals, such as information about a person the client intends to sue. If another person wants to find out what a lawyer has been told by his client, the lawyer can claim legal professional privilege and can refuse to divulge any information. The Data Protection Act recognizes the importance of legal privilege and exempts from the subject access provisions to personal data which consist of information in respect of which a lawyer could claim legal professional privilege. For example, if a client accused of a crime tells his solicitor that a certain Mr. Smith had plotted with him and the solicitor enters this information on a computer database, Mr. Smith can be denied access to that data even though it is personal data of which Mr. Smith is the data subject.

f) Statistical or research data

Personal data which are held for the purposes of either preparing statistics or carrying out research are exempt from the subject access provisions on condition that they are not used or disclosed for any other purpose and the resulting statistics or results are not made available in a form which identifies any of the data subjects. However, disclosure can be made in certain circumstances such as to the data subject or at his request or with his consent, to a computer bureau so that it can carry out its functions, or if the person making the disclosure reasonably believes any of the above are applicable.

g) Legal prohibition

The Secretary of State has made an order exempting personal data from the subject access provisions if the disclosure of the information is prohibited or restricted by statute and the Secretary considers that this ought to prevail over the subject access provisions in the interests of the data subject or any other individual; see the Data Protection (Miscellaneous Subject Access Exemptions) Order 1987, S.I. 1987 No. 1906. The Order applies to information contained in adoption records and with respect to the special educational needs of children.

h) Situations where subject access is provided for under section 158 of the Consumer Credit Act 1974

The problem of incorrect information held by credit agencies has worried people for many years. The difficulty in having corrections made and the dangers of mistakenly being labelled as a bad risk were foremost concerns. The Consumer Credit Act 1974, inter alia, attempted to remedy this situation and by section 158, an individual is entitled to obtain a copy of a file relating to him which is kept by a credit reference agency. This right to access is wider than the equivalent right under the Data Protection Act because the latter only applies to data in a form in which they can be processed by automatic processing equipment whereas the right of access under the Consumer Credit Act covers all forms of storage, including paper files, index cards, etc. There is, therefore, no need for subject access under the Data Protection Act as regards credit reference agencies and hence the exception.

i) Back-up data

This exemption appears to be superfluous as it does not affect the subject access right to the original data. If an organization has a database of personal data on the hard disk of a computer and also has a back-up copy of the database on floppy disks, a data subject can obtain access to his personal data stored on the hard disk but not to that on the back-up floppy disks. However, this exemption might be important if the back-up copy of the database has not been updated for some time and is out of date. In any case, the exemption only applies to data to be used purely as a back-up, to replace other data that have been lost, damaged or destroyed. It will not apply to archive copies of data which are retained by the data user so that, for example, they may be consulted at some future time.

j) If compliance would incriminate the data user

A long-standing principle of English law is that a person is excused giving such evidence as would incriminate him. An extension of this is an accused person's right to silence. A data user can refuse a subject access request (or a notice or order under the subject access provisions) if compliance with the request would expose him to criminal proceedings for an offence *other than an offence under the Data Protection Act*. However, if the data user discloses data in response to a subject access request or is ordered to disclose the data, it can still be used as evidence in a civil trial; for example, for compensation.

k) Examination marks

This is not a true exemption and only allows a data user who holds examination marks to delay disclosure to the data subject. The information must be held for the purpose of determining the results of an academic, professional or other examination or enabling such determination or in consequence of the determination of any such results. In the case of an undergraduate, such information might include the marks he obtained in each subject by examination (including assessed coursework) and the details of the degree classification to be awarded to the student.

Normally, a data user must comply with a subject request within forty days but, in respect of examination marks, the data user does not have to respond until either the end of five months after the request or forty days after the day the results are announced (published or made available to candidates) whichever is the earlier. If the request is complied with more than forty days after it was made, the response by the data user must include all the information held at the time of the request *and* subsequently. The following dates provide an example of the workings of these provisions:

1. Student sits examination   4 June 1990
2. Marks entered on a computer   29 June 1990
3. Student makes subject access request   3 July 1990
4. Results published   24 July 1990

Normally, the request must be complied with within forty days from the request at the latest; that is, within forty days of 3 July, which gives 12 August as being the latest date for compliance. However, in the case of examination marks, the request must be complied with by the earlier of five months after the request (3 December 1990) or forty days after publication (2 September 1990). Therefore, the data user must supply the data by 2 September. But, unlike other subject access requests which may take account of amendments, in this case, the information supplied must include that held on 3 July (the request date) *and* must also include any subsequent amendments up to the date of reply. Consequently, a data user holding examination marks must be careful to make sure that he retains copies of the data prior to any amendments or deletions so that he can provide all this information. For example, if the student's degree classification is changed, perhaps from a lower second honours degree to an upper second honours degree after mistakes have been found in the marking, the response must show this fact indicating the marks before and after correction. This requirement could prove very embarrassing for the data user.

3. Exemptions relating to the disclosure of personal data

These are known as the non-disclosure exemptions. When applying for registration (or amendment or renewal of registration), a data user must specify to whom he intends or may wish to disclose the personal data he holds. Subject to the exemption provisions, disclosure to any other person or organization is a criminal offence. Similarly, computer bureaux must not disclose personal data without the authority of the data user. However, the Act makes provision for disclosure in other circumstances (whether or not an entry to that effect is on the register). Those circumstances are, when the disclosure:

a) is for the purpose of safeguarding national security (section 27),
b) relates to crime and taxation (section 28),
c) is for legal purposes (section 34(5)),
d) is to the data subject or with his consent (section 34(6)),
e) is to the agent or servant of the data user or computer bureau concerned (section 34(6)),
f) relates to an emergency (section 34(8)).

a) Safeguarding national security

In some cases, as seen earlier, if certified by a Minister of the Crown, personal data are exempt from the registration and subject access provisions if the exemption is required for the purpose of safeguarding national security. If this exemption does not apply, personal data may still be exempt from the non-disclosure provisions. A data user may hold personal data which may be of assistance to a government department which is trying to investigate a spy ring or a terrorist organization and, in such a case, the data user is allowed to disclose the personal data to that department; a good example of safeguarding the national security. If a Minister of the Crown certifies that the data are or have been disclosed for this purpose, this is conclusive evidence of the fact.

b) Crime and taxation

As with the subject access exemption, personal data held for the prevention and detection of crime, the apprehension or prosecution of offenders or the assessment or collection of any tax or duty are exempt from the non-disclosure provisions as long as non-disclosure would be likely to prejudice the prevention and detection of crime, etc. This exemption might apply to situations where the data user discloses personal data to the police or Inland Revenue and the data user can rely on the exemption as long as he has reasonable grounds for believing that failure to disclose would be likely to prejudice one of the matters mentioned above.

c) For legal purposes

Personal data may be disclosed if required by statute or any rule of law, by order of a court, for the purpose of obtaining legal advice or in legal proceedings where the data user (or computer bureau) is a party or witness. This exemption will apply to disclosures made to the Inland Revenue by an employer which are required by Act of Parliament.

d) To the data subject or with his consent

Normally, a data user must comply with a subject access request but this exemption from non-disclosure is wider than the subject access provisions. It allows disclosure to:
 (i) the data subject or a person acting on his behalf,
 (ii) to anyone else if the data subject (or anyone acting on his behalf) has requested or consented to the disclosure.
Also covered are cases where the data user (or computer bureau) has reasonable grounds for believing that either of the above applies. For example, a data subject may have engaged a solicitor to act on his behalf in some matter and the solicitor may request disclosure. The data user may grant the request (he is not forced to) if he knows the solicitor is acting for the data subject or he has reasonable grounds for believing this is so. The data user must obviously check the credentials of a person making such a request otherwise he cannot claim to have reasonable grounds for believing that the exemption applies. If he does not check, the exemption will not apply and the data user may also be in breach of the eighth data protection principle; that is, taking appropriate security measures to guard against unauthorized disclosure of personal data.

e) To agents or servants

It is obviously essential that both data users and computer bureaux are permitted to disclose personal data to their employees or others acting on their behalf. This exemption only applies, however, if the disclosure is for the purpose of enabling employees, agents and the like to perform their functions *as such*. An employer cannot disclose personal data to an employee so that he can, for example, carry out private research which is not connected to the employee's duties.

f) Emergency disclosure

The final non-disclosure exemption applies when the personal data are urgently required to prevent injury or other damage to the health of any person or persons; for example, if the personal data contain details of an injured person's blood group. Two points to note are that the disclosure must be required as a matter of urgency and that it only applies to personal injury or health and not to damage to property or financial loss. If, in fact, the exemption does not apply, a person making the disclosure is excused if he had reasonable grounds for believing that the data were required urgently in such circumstances.

ENFORCEMENT OF THE ACT

By section 36 of the Data Protection Act, the Registrar has a duty to promote observance of the Data Protection Principles, compliance with which he can enforce by means of notices. The Registrar may also prosecute persons he considers to have committed offences under the Act, except in Scotland where prosecutions are brought by the Procurator Fiscal. Additionally, the Registrar is given powers of entry and inspection, on application to a circuit judge, if he suspects a criminal offence has been committed or there has been a breach of the Data Protection Principles.

The Data Protection Registrar can serve the following notices:

- enforcement notice (section 10)
- de-registration notice (section 11)
- transfer prohibition notice (section 12)

In practice, the Registrar will normally try to resolve a problem with the data user or computer bureau concerned before serving an official notice, giving the data user or computer bureau an opportunity to make representations as to why the notice should not be served. Thus, the Registrar may serve a preliminary notice prior to serving a notice under the Act. There are no provisions for preliminary notices under the Act but this development has been agreed between the Data Protection Registrar and the Council of Tribunals. The decision to serve any of the notices is at the Registrar's discretion but failure to comply with an enforcement or transfer prohibition notice is a criminal offence.

Enforcement notices

If the Registrar is satisfied that a data user is in breach of one or more of the Data Protection Principles (or a computer bureau is in breach of the eighth principle), he may serve an enforcement notice. Situations where an enforcement notice might be appropriate are where a data user holds inaccurate data or uses the data for a purpose other than one stated in the Register (unless within the scope of the exemptions) or a computer bureau is operating unsatisfactory security measures.

An enforcement notice will contain:

a) a statement of the principle or principles which the Registrar is satisfied have been or are being contravened,

b) the Registrar's reasons for believing a breach of the principles has occurred or is occurring,

c) the steps to be taken in order to comply with the notice,

d) the time limit for taking those steps, and

e) a statement regarding the right of appeal to the Data Protection Tribunal.

The time limit will usually be at least 28 days, giving sufficient time for appeal. If the data user or computer bureau intends to appeal, the steps specified need not be taken whilst the appeal is pending. If there are special circumstances and the Registrar considers that the steps required by the notice should be taken as a matter of urgency, he may include a statement to that effect in the notice. In such cases, the steps must be taken within 7 days regardless of whether the data user or computer bureau wishes to appeal. In deciding whether to serve an enforcement notice, the Registrar must consider if the breach of the Data Protection Principles has caused or is likely to cause damage or distress to any person.

De-registration notices

The consequences of de-registration can be harsh. The data user or computer bureau concerned will no longer be able to hold data or provide services in respect of personal data, without committing a criminal offence. De-registration notices are served under the same circumstances as for enforcement notices but, in the case of de-registration notices, the Registrar must be satisfied that an enforcement notice will not adequately secure compliance with the Data Protection Principles. A de-registration notice will contain:

a) a statement of the principle or principles which the Registrar is satisfied have been or are being contravened,

b) the Registrar's reasons for believing a breach of the principles has occurred or is occurring,

c) the Registrar's reasons for believing that an enforcement notice will not adequately secure compliance with the Data Protection Principles,

d) the details which the Registrar intends to remove from the Register (the Registrar may decide to de-register the whole or part of an entry on the Register),

e) the time that de-registration will take effect, and

f) a statement regarding the right of appeal to the Data Protection Tribunal.

Normally, 28 days will be allowed before removal of an entry (or part of an entry) by the Registrar, giving the recipient of the notice time to appeal and, if he does appeal, the removal will be delayed until completion of the appeal procedure. However, if the Registrar considers that, because of special circumstances, the particulars to be removed from the Register should be so removed as a matter of urgency, he may include a statement to that effect and remove the entry (or part of the entry) at the end of 7 days, regardless of any pending appeal. As with an enforcement notice, the Registrar must consider whether the breach of the Data Protection Principles involved has caused or is likely to cause damage or distress to any person. Up to 31 May 1989, no de-registration notices had been served.

Transfer prohibition notice

This notice concerns the control of the transfer of personal data to countries outside the United Kingdom. The notice may prohibit transfer absolutely or until certain specified steps are taken. The Registrar's powers depend on whether the destination country (that is, the country to which the data are to be transferred) is bound by the European Convention on Data Protection. If the destination country is not bound by the Convention, the Registrar may serve a notice if he is satisfied that the transfer is likely to contravene or lead to a contravention of the Data Protection Principles.

If the destination country is bound by the Convention, the Registrar may prohibit transfer which is likely to contravene, or lead to a contravention of, the Data Protection Principles in either of the following cases:

a) the data user intends to give instructions for the further transfer of the data to another country not bound by the Convention (that is, the data user intends to use a Convention country as a stepping-stone to the final destination), or

b) the data are sensitive (for example, relate to racial origin of data subjects or their political opinions) and, with respect to such types of data, the Secretary of State has altered or added to the Data Protection Principles.

A transfer prohibition notice will contain:

a) a statement of the principle or principles which the Registrar is satisfied are likely to be contravened,

b) the Registrar's reasons for reaching that conclusion,

c) whether the notice is absolute or, if not, what steps must be taken before transfer can proceed,

d) the time the notice is to take effect,

e) a statement regarding the right of appeal to the Data Protection Tribunal.

Normally, the notice will not take effect for at least 28 days and if the data user appeals against the notice during that period, the notice will not take effect, if ever, until the completion of the appeal process. If the Registrar considers that, because of special circumstances, the notice should come into effect urgently, he may order that the notice will come into effect in 7 days. The Registrar, when deciding whether to serve a transfer prohibition notice, must consider if the notice is required to prevent damage or distress to any person. Additionally, the Registrar must have regard to the general desirability of facilitating the free transfer of data between the United Kingdom and other states and territories. Thus, the Registrar has to strive to seek a balance between the interests of individuals and the need for the free flow of data across international boundaries. No transfer prohibition notices had been served up to 31 May 1989.

All forms of notice will be served on individuals by hand or by post at the individual's last known address. In the case of an organization the notice will be served by hand or by post to the principal office, addressed to the 'proper officer', being the company secretary or other person charged with the conduct of the organization's general affairs and the principal office is, in the case of a registered company, its registered office.

Powers of entry and inspection

These powers are contained in Schedule 4 to the Act and can be exercised by the Data Protection Registrar after obtaining a warrant from a circuit judge who will grant the warrant if he is satisfied that an offence under the Act has been or is being committed or that any of the Data Protection Principles are being contravened by a registered data user or computer bureau. The judge must be satisfied that the Registrar has reasonable grounds for his suspicions and that:

a) the Registrar has given the occupier of the premises in question seven days notice in writing demanding access,
b) the access was demanded at a reasonable time and was unreasonably refused, and
c) the occupier has been notified of the Registrar's intended application for a warrant and, therefore, has had the opportunity to be heard by the judge concerned.

However, if the above procedure would defeat the object of the entry; for example, if it would be likely that the data user would erase or alter personal data, thus destroying the evidence, the judge may issue a warrant as a matter of urgency. Because of the likelihood of an errant data user destroying or removing evidence, it is more likely that warrants will be issued as a matter of urgency, although the Registrar would have to convince the judge issuing the warrant that, given the opportunity, the data user (or computer bureau) would try to defeat the purpose of the entry and inspection.

A warrant will permit the Registrar (or someone acting on his behalf) to use such force as is reasonably necessary to enter and search the premises within 7 days; to inspect, examine and operate any test respecting any automatic data processing equipment on the premises and to inspect and seize any documents or other materials (presumably including items such as magnetic disks and tapes) which may be evidence of an offence or a breach of the principles. A person who deliberately obstructs a person executing a warrant commits a criminal offence. Similarly, failure without reasonable excuse to give the person executing the warrant such assistance as may reasonably be required is also a criminal offence. Warrants are not available in the case of personal data which are exempt from Part II of the Act; the registration requirements.

Appeals

The Data Protection Act sets up an appeals system and, by section 13, an aggrieved data user or computer bureau can appeal against:

a) a refusal by the Registrar of an application for registration or alteration of registered particulars; or
b) any notice which has been served by the Registrar.

Appeals go to the Data Protection Tribunal and there is a further right of appeal against the Tribunal's decisions to the High Court. At the time of writing, no appeals have been heard by the Tribunal, although the first one is pending.

The composition of the Tribunal is laid down in section 3 of the Act and it will consist of a legally qualified chairman or deputy chairman together with an equal number of persons representing the interests of data users and data subjects alike. The Tribunal can consider questions of law and fact; an example of a question of law is whether an exemption applies to a particular use of data and an example of a question of fact is whether a data user *knowingly* disclosed personal data. The Tribunal can allow or refuse the appeal or substitute its own decision or notice if it considers that either:

a) the refusal or notice appealed against is unlawful, or

b) if the appeal relates to the Registrar's exercise of discretion, that he should have exercised it differently.

Any person obstructing the proceedings before the Tribunal can be dealt with in the High Court for contempt of court. The specific procedures for the Tribunal are laid down in the Data Protection Tribunal Rules 1985, S.I. 1985 No. 1568.

Chapter 28
Summary

The Act attempts to reconcile individuals' interests with the need to recognize the importance of computer technology as far as keeping and processing records is concerned.

The storage and use of sensitive information relating to individuals is controlled by registration and the interests of data users is recognized by a substantial list of total and partial exemptions from the Act's provisions. Whether the Act achieves the balance in a fair and equitable manner is a matter of some discussion, and organizations such as the National Council for Civil Liberties (NCCL) consider that the law does not go far enough in protecting individuals' privacy (*see* Cornwell, R. & Staunton, M., *Data Protection: Putting the Record Straight*, NCCL, 1985). In particular, the NCCL would like manual records to be included within the ambit of the Act, it considers that the scope of some of the exemptions is too broad (particularly with respect to national security, crime and taxation) and that the Registrar's powers and role should be increased.

After consultations with data users and data subjects, the Registrar reviewed the operation of the Data Protection Act and made suggestions for changes to the law. The results of the consultations and the Registrar's views are contained in Part B of the *Fifth Report of the Data Protection Registrar* (H.M.S.O., June 1989). A few of the main recommendations in this comprehensive report are listed below:

a) the registration system should be maintained, but on a restricted basis including organizations of certain types or holding personal data of a sensitive nature. This will result in a reduction of the register to about one-third of its present size;

b) the Registrar should have more powers of inspection and enhanced supervision and enforcement powers to counter-balance the effects of a restricted registration system;

c) data users should supply more information in response to subject access requests to counter-balance the fact that less information will be contained in the register. The problem of subject access where a data user has multiple entries on the register would disappear in the proposed new registration system as each registered data user would only have one entry;

d) the exemptions would be modified and simplified, some being repealed (for example, payroll and accounts, mailing lists) because they would no longer be required under the proposed changes to the registration system;

e) it should be a criminal offence to compel a person to exercise his subject access rights to gain information which would not otherwise be obtainable; this is to prevent employers requiring prospective employees to use their subject access rights to confirm, for example, that the individual does not have any criminal convictions;

f) the exclusion of intentions from the definition of personal data should be repealed.

There are several other recommendations made in the Report, but it is unlikely that there will be any major legislative changes to data protection law in the near future. The fact that the Act has not, at the time of writing, generated any significant case law is testimony to the quality of draftsmanship and the general acceptance of the Act's spirit amongst data users and data subjects alike.

Apart from the Act, there exist other legal remedies for persons aggrieved at information concerning them held on a computer or otherwise. For example, the law of confidence can be used to prevent disclosure of confidential information by way of a court injunction; the law of defamation may be available if the information is incorrect and is likely to injure a person's reputation. Other areas of law which might be applicable depending on the circumstances are the law of copyright, contract and tort.

Figure 7 is an example of an entry in the Data Protection Register and has been reproduced by kind permission of the Data Protection Registrar.

```
**********************************************************************************
DATA PROTECTION ACT 1984          REGISTER OF DATA USERS AND COMPUTER BUREAUX
REGISTRATION NUMBER D0055192          START OF REGISTER ENTRY          DATE COPY PRINTED 13 APR 1987
**********************************************************************************

REGISTERED 21 FEB 1986    LAST AMENDED          EXPIRES  20 FEB 1989    TYPE OF ENTRY DATA USER ONLY

NAME    XYZ TRADING COMPANY

ADDRESS    COLUMN HOUSE
           23 HIGH ST
           MARKET DRAYTON
           SHROPSHIRE

           G10 0RN

COMPANY REGISTRATION NUMBER  1409861

OTHER NAMES     ALLPORT CONFECTIONERY

ORGANISATION SUB-DIVISION     NORTHERN SALES DIVISION

ADDRESSES FOR THE RECEIPT OF REQUESTS FROM DATA SUBJECTS FOR ACCESS TO THE DATA
          94 GROSVENOR PARK RD
          WALTHAMSTOW
          LONDON

          NE1 7RN

THIS REGISTER ENTRY CONTAINS PARTICULARS OF PERSONAL DATA HELD FOR 1 PURPOSE(S)

**********************************************************************************
* NOTE ON THE INTERPRETATION OF THE FOLLOWING SECTIONS                          *
*                                                                              *
* 1  UNDER PURPOSE, IF A LIST OF TYPICAL ACTIVITIES WHICH MIGHT BE CARRIED OUT APPEARS, IT IS ILLUSTRATIVE ONLY  IT *
*    SHOULD NOT BE TAKEN THAT THE DATA USER IS ACTUALLY PERFORMING EVERY ACTIVITY *
* 2  SIMILARLY, IT SHOULD NOT BE TAKEN THAT DATA IN EVERY CLASS LISTED ARE HELD ON EVERY DATA SUBJECT, NOR THAT ALL *
*    ITEMS OF DATA HELD ARE OBTAINED FROM, DISCLOSED TO OR TRANSFERRED TO EVERY CATEGORY LISTED *
**********************************************************************************

PURPOSE

PURPOSE FOR WHICH DATA ARE TO BE HELD OR USED
P006 Public Relations and External Affairs
The Promotion of mutual understanding between the data and the user representatives
of the public, public authorities or other organisations
Typical activities are the identification of individuals or organisations for representation or lobbying on matters of
concern to the user, the maintenance of associated records, analysis for management purposes and statutory returns
```

1

```
DESCRIPTION OF PERSONAL DATA TO BE HELD
  TYPES OF INDIVIDUAL ( DATA SUBJECTS ) ABOUT WHOM DATA ARE TO BE HELD

    S007 Current. Past. Potential Account holders
    S014 Current. Past. Agents, other intermediaries
    S024 Current. Past. Potential Correspondents and enquirers


CLASSES OF PERSONAL DATA TO BE HELD

    C001 Personal identifiers
    C054 Professional expertise
    C055 Membership of committees

SOURCE OR SOURCES FROM WHICH THE DATA USER INTENDS OR WISH TO OBTAIN THE DATA OR THE INFORMATION TO BE CONTAINED
IN THE DATA. AND PERSON OR PERSONS TO WHOM THE DATA USER INTENDS OR MAY WISH TO DISCLOSE THE DATA (DISCLOSURES)

  INDIVIDUALS OR ORGANISATIONS DIRECTLY ASSOCIATED WITH THE DATA SUBJECTS

  D101 The data subjects themselves                                 Source Disclosure
  D106 Colleagues. business associates                              Source Disclosure


  INDIVIDUALS OR ORGANISATIONS DIRECTLY ASSOCIATED WITH THE DATA USER.

  D207 Persons making an enquiry or complaint                              Disclosure


  INDIVIDUALS OR ORGANISATIONS ( GENERAL DESCRIPTION ).

  D376 Survey or research organisations. workers                   Source Disclosure
  D381 Traders in personal data                                    Source Disclosure

  ADVERTISING MEDIA

COUNTRIES OR TERRITORIES OUTSIDE THE U.K  TO WHICH THE DATA USER INTENDS OR MAY WISH TO TRANSFER THE DATA

  T999 Worldwide
  PUBLICITY.PROMOTIONS + ADVERTISING

*************************************************************************************
                                                      END OF REGISTER ENTRY
*************************************************************************************
REGISTRATION NUMBER: D0056192
*************************************************************************************

                                        2
```

Figure 7 Sample entry on the Data Protection Register
(Reproduced by kind permission of the Data Protection Registrar)

209

Selected Bibliography

General

Arnold, C. (ed.), *Yearbook of Law, Computers and Technology*, Butterworths, (1986,7,8,9).

Bellord, N., *Computers for Lawyers*, Sinclair-Browne, 1983.

Mawrey, R.B. & Salmon, K.J., *Computers and the Law*, BSP Professional Books, 1988.

Tapper, C., *Computer Law*, 4th edn., Longman, 1990.

Wolk, S.R. & Luddy, W.J., *Legal Aspects of Computer Use*, Prentice-Hall, 1986.

Computers and intellectual property

Cornish, W.R., *Intellectual Property: Patents, Copyright, Trade Marks and Allied Rights*, 2nd edn., Sweet & Maxwell, 1989.

Dworkin, G. & Taylor, R.D., *Copyright, Designs and Patents Act 1988*, Blackstone, 1989.

Niblett, B., *Legal Protection of Computer Software*, Oyez, 1980.

Computer contracts

Morgan, R. & Steadman, G., *Computer Contracts*, 3rd edn., Longman, 1987.

Pearson, H.E., *Computer Contracts: An International Guide to Agreements and Software Protection*, Financial Training Publications, 1984.

Remer, D., *Legal Care for your Software*, 2nd edn., Gower, 1984.

Rennie, M.T. Michelle, *Computer Contracts Handbook*, Sweet & Maxwell, 1985.

Rennie, M.T. Michelle, *Further Computer Contracts*, Sweet & Maxwell, 1988.

Computers and crime

Audit Commission, *Survey of Computer Fraud and Abuse*, H.M.S.O., 1987.

Law Commission, *Computer Misuse* (Working Paper No. 110), H.M.S.O., 1988.

Law Commission, *Criminal Law: Computer Misuse* (Law Com. No. 186), Cmnd 819, H.M.S.O., 1989.

Data protection

Charlton, S. & Gaskill, S., *Encyclopedia of Data Protection*, Sweet & Maxwell, 1988.

Cornwell, R. & Staunton, M., *Data Protection: Putting the Record Straight*, National Council for Civil Liberties, 1985.

Data Protection Registrar, *Fifth Report of the Data Protection Registrar*, H.M.S.O., June 1989.

Data Protection Registrar, *Guidelines* (a series of eight guidelines concerning rights and obligations under the Data Protection Act 1984), 2nd series, February 1989. Available free of charge from the Office of the Data Protection Registrar, Springfield House, Water Lane, Wilmslow, Cheshire, SK9 5AX.

Evans, A., *Data Protection Policies and Practice*, Institute of Personnel Management, 1987.

Gulleford, K., *Data Protection in Practice*, Butterworths, 1986.

Niblett, B., *Data Protection Act 1984*, Oyez, 1984.

Report of the Committee on Data Protection, 'The Lindop Report' Cmnd 7341, H.M.S.O., December 1978.

Savage, N. & Edwards, C., *Guide to the Data Protection Act*, Blackstone, 2nd edn., 1988.

Index